Prophets with Honor

PROPHETS
WITH HONOR

Great Dissents and Great Dissenters
in the Supreme Court

ALAN BARTH

VINTAGE BOOKS
A DIVISION OF RANDOM HOUSE, NEW YORK

VINTAGE BOOKS EDITION, MARCH 1975

Copyright © 1974 by Alan Barth
All rights reserved under International
and Pan-American Copyright Conventions.
Published in the United States by Random House, Inc.,
New York, and simultaneously in Canada
by Random House of Canada Limited, Toronto.
Originally published by Alfred A. Knopf, Inc., in 1974.

Library of Congress Cataloging in Publication Data

Barth, Alan.
 Prophets with honor.

 Includes bibliographical references.
 1. Civil rights—United States.   2. Dissenting
opinions—United States.   I. Title.
[KF4749.B33   1975]   342'.73'085   74–20993
ISBN 0–394–71571–3

Manufactured in the United States of America

To the Memory of

Hugo L. Black and Felix Frankfurter,

Olympians of the Law

CONTENTS

ACKNOWLEDGMENTS

In the writing of this book, I have had invaluable help from friends—some of it consisting of suggestions and criticism, some in the form of sympathetic interest. Without attempting to slough off on any of them the slightest responsibility for my own shortcomings, I want very much to express publicly my feeling of indebtedness to them. Long ago, when the idea for this book first formed in my mind, Malcolm Cowley gave me generous encouragement. Judge Stanley A. Weigel, Joseph L. Rauh, John P. MacKenzie, Eugene Katz, Edwin D. Wolf, and Andrew C. Barth read parts of the manuscript as it progressed and gave me the benefit of candid criticism. Lawrence Speiser let me talk about the project endlessly and contributed much stimulating comment.

It is a particular pleasure to acknowledge the encouragement and help I have received throughout the gestation of this book from my publishers. Anthony M. Schulte heartened me immeasurably by his continuing and patient interest and by imaginative suggestions regarding the book's development; Dan Okrent, my editor, gave me the most searching and understanding kind of criticism. I am immensely grateful to both of them.

In doing the research requisite for the book, I was accorded the privilege of working at the Supreme Court library, a paradise for my purposes. Everyone on the staff there showed me the utmost kindness and consideration.

My wife's help in typing, reading, and talking about the book runs beyond the reach of public acknowledgment. Happily, she understands my gratitude.

A.B.

APOLOGIA

Although legal writing is generally thought to make arid reading, I have always, for my own part, found fascination in the opinions of appellate courts, and especially in those that come from the Supreme Court of the United States. Not always by any means, yet not infrequently, these opinions deal in a disciplined, orderly, rational way with issues of the highest moment, embodying decisions which vitally affect the whole American community. They deal often, moreover, not only with great abstract principles of law and polity, but with the lives and fortunes of ordinary individuals, so that they are filled sometimes with the real stuff of drama. The questions that come to the Supreme Court for decision involve the weighing of difficult and often subtle considerations; and they involve in many instances not the easy choice between right and wrong, but the hard choice of emphasis between contending rights and social interests.

I have a clear feeling that these judicial judgments are too little read by laymen. If they seem forbidding, they are nevertheless immensely rewarding. They afford a fresh way of looking at contemporary affairs and especially at the emerging patterns of social development. And they also afford, for those who enjoy this sort of exercise, exhilarating clashes between men of learning and intellect in regard to significant competing values.

Opinions written for the Supreme Court—that is, for a majority of the justices at a given time—are supposed to define as clearly and concisely as possible the meaning and application of the law in the context of a particular case. Dissenting—as also concurring—opinions, on the other hand, are meant to convey the individual views of the justices who write them, and so, on occasion, they convey also some of the passion with which those views are charged. Freed from the constraints entailed in trying to express the sense of a majority, they embody, at times, passages of great force, eloquence, and ardor. Now and then they rise to the level of literature, offering some of the most pungent polemical writing ever produced in America.

When I first thought about this book, I meant it to be simply an anthology of dissents selected for their literary quality and their significance as turning points in American jurisprudence. I quickly discovered, however, that I wanted to tell much more than I had expected about the cases themselves—about the human beings involved and about the social and political climate of the time in which the cases were decided. And there was also much more than I had anticipated that I wanted to offer to readers in the way of generalization about how the Court makes up, and occasionally changes, its collective mind. What has come out of my reading and reflection and writing, therefore, is the discussion of half a dozen great legal issues in which seminal dissenting opinions, essentially prophetic in their nature, played a role in producing major adaptations of the Constitution to the facts of life in contemporary America.

The full texts of these dissenting opinions—plus one brilliant and immensely influential concurring opinion by Justice Louis D. Brandeis, which is, in content, more a dissent than a concurrence—are presented in an appendix for those who may wish to refer to them. In addition, I have quoted extensively from these opinions in discussing them. I have also presented the corresponding opinions of the Court in considerable detail, seeking to let the justices set forth their own arguments in their own terms and to provide an adequate basis upon which readers may reach their own conclusions as to the merits of the controversies.

The cases that I have chosen all concern the invocation of individual rights or liberties guaranteed by the Constitution.

I might as well acknowledge candidly at the outset that, in part at least, this is because these are the cases that most arouse my personal interest and excitement. They raise troubling questions: whether the obvious public interest in effective law enforcement should be allowed to justify police intrusion on private communications by means of electronic eavesdropping devices; whether due process of law requires that an indigent defendant in a criminal prosecution be afforded the assistance of counsel at public expense; whether freedom of speech forbids the public to punish expressions of opinion that are deemed dangerous to the public safety; and so on, through the whole gamut of conflicts between minorities and majorities, between private rights and public purposes.

But beyond my own enthusiasm for such questions, there is justification for my choice, perhaps, in the fact that civil liberty has afforded a main focus for the Court's attention in recent decades, and has constituted also the principal area in which the Court has reversed long-established constitutional doctrines. This has happened, as I try to show, because of past inattention to this area and because the country's growth and the attendant changes in its living conditions and social values have required the Court to develop new safeguards for individuality and personal freedom.

Finally, it may fairly be urged in defense of my selection that the protection of individuality—of heterodox opinion or eccentric conduct—is a fundamental purpose of the American Constitution. It is a constitution designed not only to "promote the general Welfare," but equally to "secure the Blessings of Liberty to ourselves and our Posterity." Freedom—the opportunity to achieve and express the individual's fullest potentialities—is the genius of America.

In any case, these civil-liberties issues have given rise to some stirring and superb judicial opinions, some of them for the Court, more of them in criticism of it and in opposition to its prevailing view. Dissents give judges an opportunity to look beyond the circumstances of a particular case and discuss its larger implications in terms of general principles and its impact on the future. This is why I think of them, at their best, as prophetic. The opinions presented here seem to me to be, in themselves, of surpassing interest. If readers who are not lawyers are led to find them so, to find enjoyment in the reading of them, this book will have accomplished its essential aim.

Prophets with Honor

I

THE USES OF DISSENT

Judicial dissent—the subject of this book—is, at its best, a form of prophecy in the Biblical sense of that term. It reflects, at least on occasion, not only a protest against what the dissenter deems error or injustice, but an Isaiahlike warning of unhappy consequences. Like a seer, the dissenter sometimes peers into the future. He will be accounted wise or foolish as the unfolding of events proves him right or wrong.

"A dissent in a court of last resort," Charles Evans Hughes wrote in 1928, "is an appeal to the brooding spirit of the law, to the intelligence of a future day, when a later decision may possibly correct the error into which the dissenting judge believes the court to have been betrayed."[1]

Obviously, a dissent of this sort is not an attempt to win over one's colleagues. It deals with a die already cast, an issue already determined. The most that the dissenter can hope to do, so far as the present is concerned, is to persuade contemporaries off the court that his associates were mistaken, to

[1] Charles Evans Hughes, *The Supreme Court of the United States* (New York: Columbia University Press), 1928, p. 68.

mobilize public opinion against them, as it were—a dubious satisfaction since the Court is not supposed, in any case, to be responsive to popular pressure. A judicial dissent, then, is basically a plea to posterity.

Dissents are written in courts of appeals because judges become aroused, because they are irritated or indignant and want the world to know that they do not share in a judgment that seems to them fraught with folly. "Dissenting opinions," Chief Justice Hughes remarked in the context just quoted, "enable a judge to express his individuality. He is not under the compulsion of speaking for the Court and thus of securing the concurrence of a majority. In dissenting, he is a free lance."[2] This is an extremely significant factor in shaping the character and quality of dissents, since justices of the Supreme Court are, sometimes, frustrated firebrands not averse to an occasional display of temperament and personality. A dissenting opinion momentarily lets them off the judicial leash. It affords an outlet for individuality, independence, idiosyncrasy—a divergence from accepted, official, or conventional wisdom.

When a justice writes an opinion for the Court, his business is to state as clearly and compellingly as possible the grounds and the rationale of the Court's decision in order to give the judges of inferior courts, and the bar in general, a definitive understanding of the law's reach and import. The more simply he can do this, the better for those who must interpret the law for litigants and clients. The more simply he can do it, moreover, the more widely can he win the concurrence of his colleagues. Rhetorical flourishes, emotional outbursts may be gratifying to a writer and yet repelling to a colleague—especially a colleague who is asked to subscribe to what is written as an expression of his own views. Majority opinions, therefore, tend to be bare-boned versions of a consensus, prosaically defining and expounding the law.

Justice Robert H. Jackson, in an interview, said much the

[2] *Ibid.*, p. 68.

same thing as Chief Justice Hughes. "It's more fun," he put it, "to write a dissenting opinion or a concurring opinion than to write a majority opinion, because you can just go off and express your own view without regard to anybody else. When you're writing for the Court, you try to bring your view within the limits of the views of all those who are supporting you. That oftentimes requires that you temper down your opinion to suit someone who isn't quite as convinced as you are or has somewhat different grounds. That oftentimes presents great difficulty. . . ."[3]

The trouble with a dissenting opinion, of course, is that it casts a certain shadow on the majority opinion, which is, after all, at least for the time being, the authoritative view of the issue that the Court has considered. A dissent makes it plain that one or more jurists, as eminent as those who constitute a majority of the Court, think the matter has been wrongly decided. But this is unavoidable in a Supreme Court. Only difficult and troubling questions come before it. In the Court's earlier days, there were some who thought that every justice ought to state his own view of every case in an individual opinion, setting forth his own reasons for his decision. But this not only imposed an impossible burden on the Court; it operated also to promote confusion. Hughes made another observation about dissents that deserves to be remembered:

There are some who think it desirable that dissents should not be disclosed as they detract from the force of the judgment. Undoubtedly, they do. When unanimity can be obtained without sacrifice of conviction, it strongly commends the decision to public confidence. But unanimity which is merely formal, which is recorded at the expense of strong, conflicting views, is not desirable in a court of last resort, whatever may be the effect on public opinion at the time. This is so because what must ultimately sus-

---

[3] Taped interview prepared for the Oral History Project of Columbia University and quoted by Philip B. Kurland in his account of Robert Jackson in *Justices of the United States Supreme Court,* 4 vols. (New York: Chelsea House, 1969), IV, pp. 2563–2564.

tain the court in public confidence is the character and inde-
pendence of the judges. They are not there simply to decide cases,
but to decide them as they think they should be decided, and while
it may be regrettable that they cannot always agree, it is better
that their independence should be maintained and recognized than
that unanimity should be secured through its sacrifice. This does not
mean that a judge should be swift to dissent, or that he should
dissent for the sake of self-exploitation or because of a lack of that
capacity for cooperation which is of the essence of any group
action, whether judicial or otherwise. Independence does not mean
cantankerousness, and a judge may be a strong judge without
being an impossible person. Nothing is more distressing on any
bench than the exhibition of a captious, impatient, querulous
spirit. . . .[4]

Although dissenting opinions are generally prompted by
strong feelings and often connote a condemnation of the judgment of colleagues, there is a tradition in the Court that they
ought to be stated in terms that indicate respect, and even
deference, for the majority holding a different view. "I should
now, as is my custom, when I have the misfortune to differ
from this court," said Chief Justice John Marshall in an early
dissent, "acquiesce silently in its opinion, did I not believe that
the judgment of the Circuit Court of Virginia gave general
surprise to the profession and was generally condemned."[5]

Justice Oliver Wendell Holmes—"The Great Dissenter"—
usually introduced with deceptive mildness and self-depreca-
tion dissenting opinions which he went on to press with biting
vigor. In the very first of his dissents on the Supreme Court,
he began by saying that he believed it "useless and undesira-
ble, as a rule, to express dissent." A year later he commenced
his powerful disagreement with the majority in the famous
Lochner case by observing that "I regret sincerely that I am
unable to agree with the judgment in this case and that I think
it my duty to express my dissent."[6]

---

[4] Hughes, *op. cit.*, pp. 67–8.
[5] Bank v. Dandridge, 12 Wheaton 90, quoted by Hughes.
[6] Lochner v. New York, 198 U.S. 45 (1905).

Although the dissents discussed in this book are all drawn from the Supreme Court of the United States, dissenting opinions delivered in the top state courts and in the federal courts of appeals have often had great significance and influence. Disagreement regarding a constitutional question in an appellate court may prompt the U.S. Supreme Court to accept the contested case for review; and a forceful dissenting opinion by a respected appellate court judge may operate powerfully to win the confidence of a Supreme Court majority.

It would be romantic to suppose that dissenting opinions always, or even very often, embody great wisdom or refute error on the part of the majority. All too frequently, a dissent expresses no more than an aberrant view arising out of an individual justice's prejudices—or out of what Hughes called "cantankerousness." The record is full of instances in which dissenters voiced extravagant forebodings that served only to call the validity of prophecy into question. One tends today, for example, to react with more amusement than anxiety to the sense of doom expressed by Justice McReynolds (with the support of Justices Van Devanter, Sutherland, and Butler) over a Court decision that upheld a New York law empowering a milk control board to fix minimum and maximum retail prices. McReynolds expressed their disagreement with the majority by asserting with simple majesty that "to adopt such a view, of course, would put an end to liberty under the Constitution. . . ."

In 1957, the Court came to the conclusion that a defendant had a right to inspect and use for impeachment purposes reports made to the Federal Bureau of Investigation by prosecution witnesses regarding matters about which such witnesses had testified at his trial. To Justice Tom C. Clark, ordinarily rather bland and self-restrained, this seemed to herald something like the end of the solar system. He said in his dissenting opinion:

This fashions a new rule of evidence which is foreign to our federal jurisprudence. The rule has always been to the contrary. . . .

The rule announced today has no support in any of our cases. Every
federal judge and every lawyer of federal experience knows that it
is not the present rule. Even the defense attorneys did not have the
temerity to ask for such a sweeping decision. . . .

Unless the Congress changes the rule announced by the Court
today, those intelligence agencies of our Government engaged in
law enforcement may as well close up shop, for the Court has
opened their files to the criminal and thus afforded him a Roman
holiday for rummaging through confidential information as well as
vital national secrets. . . .[7]

There are many such predictions of disaster in the reports
of the Supreme Court. There are many instances of petulance,
querulousness, and irascibility in the innumerable dissents that
have been expressed in regard to judicial rulings long since
accepted by the country as wise and reasonable and fair. But
to acknowledge that there has frequently been folly in dissents
is not to deny that occasionally the future has been illuminated
by their discernment and understanding. Dissent has played
a seminal role in the functioning of the Supreme Court. Sometimes it has served to stir the sensibilities and prod the conscience of the country, eventually leading the Court—which
is, in a true sense, the custodian of the country's conscience—
"to correct the error into which the dissenting judge believes
the court to have been betrayed."

It is with such dissents that this book will endeavor to deal.
One test of the quality of a dissenting opinion, obviously, is
the subsequent acceptance of it as the majority view. All of
the dissents to be discussed here have, in point of fact, met
that test; all of them in time came to be recognized as right
and to be adopted by Court majorities. It seems fair to say of
them that they were, in a true sense of the term, prophetic,
foreseeing changes in the American political and economic
environment and seeking adaptations to those changes that
were in accord with advancing standards of decency, fairness,
and the general welfare.

[7] Jencks v. United States, 353 U.S. 657, 680–82 (1957).

The Supreme Court, empowered as it has been to invalidate acts of the legislative and executive branches of state and national governments, has at once mirrored and at the same time powerfully shaped the character of the American Union. Although it has, in considerable measure, been insulated from political influences by the life tenure of its members and by the aura of Olympian detachment surrounding it, the Court is not impervious to social developments. It has responded, in recent years, to changing popular attitudes regarding the rights of blacks and of women, regarding the role of religion, regarding the activities of wage earners and labor unions, and regarding the representation of sex in art and entertainment. At the same time, it has helped to form those attitudes. The process by which the Court changes its mind tells a good deal about how it works and how it responds over a period of time to the tides of public opinion and the pressures of national need, to public readiness for the acceptance of change.

It was a realistic awareness of this process that led Justice Hugo Black, at the conclusion of an anguished dissent in a case testing the limits of free speech, to say:

> *Public opinion being what it now is, few will protest the conviction of these Communist petitioners. There is hope, however, that in calmer times, when present pressures, passions, and fears subside, this or some later Court will restore the First Amendment liberties to the high preferred place where they belong in a free society.*[8]

If it can be said that the dissenting opinions presented in the following chapters are informed by any coherent, unifying philosophy, it is to be discerned in a tolerant, compassionate, libertarian view of life and a preference for diversity over uniformity as the best way of furthering the general welfare. It is to be discerned, too, in a view of the Constitution not as a strait jacket, but as a foundation for societal development, the real meaning of which is to be gleaned not in a mere static,

---

[8] Dennis v. United States, 341 U.S. 494 (1951).

prosaic translation of its terms, but in a creative interpretation of its great aims and its great bulwarks against the tyranny of democratic majorities.

Of the six dissenting opinions recounted and hailed in the following chapters as "prophetic," all but one—although they were expressed over a span of half a century—achieved vindication under the Supreme Court presided over by Chief Justice Earl Warren. Here is evidence enough, in itself, to suggest that the Warren Court, as asserted so often by its admirers and its detractors alike, wrought a revolution in American constitutional law. If so, it was a revolution long overdue. It amounted mainly, moreover, to a belated majority recognition of rights and values asserted, prematurely perhaps, by dissenting judges endowed with exceptional vision and sensitivity.

In his book on the Supreme Court, Chief Justice Hughes gave a number of instances of dissenting opinions that in time became the law. It is interesting to note that none of them had anything to do with civil liberty—that is, with the protection of individual rights as opposed to the power of the state. One of his cases involved the validity of municipal bonds; another dealt with the authority of a state to exclude a foreign insurance company from doing business within its borders; still another concerned restriction in licenses under patents. Although all of these were significant, no doubt, in giving content to still undefined clauses of the Constitution, they tended to concern corporate, business, and governmental, rather than individual, interests. The dissents presented here all argue for a recognition or enlargement of individual or minority rights.

Courts deal with the necessities of their time. In the early years of the Republic, the Court presided over by Chief Justice John Marshall occupied itself, naturally, with the great task of defining the powers granted by the Constitution to the newly formed government of the United States. "This government," the great chief justice wrote, "is acknowledged by all to be one of enumerated powers. The principle, that it can exercise only the powers granted to it, would seem too apparent to have required to be enforced by all those arguments which its enlightened friends, while it was depending before the people, found it necessary to urge. That principle is now universally admitted. But the question respecting the extent of the powers actually granted, is perpetually arising, and will probably continue to arise, as long as our system shall exist."[9]

Sailing as it was compelled to do without charts to guide it, without precedent voyages of discovery, the Marshall Court strove to steer the Constitution between rocks and whirlpools—between the demands of states jealous of a sovereignty they had only tentatively surrendered and the needs of a Union destined to become a great nation. It had no time for persons. It was engaged in the creation of a People.

The Court on which Roger Taney sat as chief justice was preoccupied, inescapably, with the problems of slavery and sectionalism and with the terrible strife threatening the existence of the Union. It attempted, with tragic consequences, to do more than a court can do in the American polity. After the Civil War, Courts, under a succession of chief justices, were engrossed for the better part of a century with economic problems, with the impact of the Industrial Revolution, with the growth of commerce, and with the role of government as a regulator of the economy.

The Warren Court faced an altogether different challenge. It was called upon not to forge a revolution, but to adjust to a revolution that had taken place in the life of the country, to adapt eighteenth-century institutions to twentieth-century circumstances. Calling the Warren Court "a Court of relevant justice," Arthur Goldberg, for a brief period one of its members, said: "It was one of the great virtues of the Warren

---

[9] John Marshall, in McCulloch v. Maryland, 4 Wheaton's Reports 400 (1819).

Court that it brought to constitutional adjudication a common-sense willingness to deal with the hard and often unpleasant facts of contemporary life."[10] If the Court under John Marshall can be credited with fabricating the essential framework of the American political structure, the Court under Earl Warren must be credited with bringing that structure into some measure of consonance with its own time.

The country has grown prodigiously in its two hundred years—in population, in power, in its influence upon the world. A society once overwhelmingly rural in residence and agricultural in occupation has become predominantly urban and industrial, a shift occasioning a gigantic social upheaval with attendant alterations in social values. Technological development with all its impact on mobility and on the nature of work, the interrelatedness brought about by progress in communications techniques, the relative crowdedness of contemporary life, and other changes in the environment have had imponderable effects upon public feeling and upon judicial thought.

The sixteen-year period, 1953 to 1969, during which Earl Warren sat as chief justice of the United States, was a period of unprecedented change, dramatic alike in its pace and in its scope. When the executive and legislative branches of the government seemed sunk in inertia, preoccupied with remote wars and other foreign relations, the judicial branch assumed a kind of leadership in bringing American institutions into some degree of accord with American ideals, professions, and the pressing requirements of a technologically advanced, economically integrated, and vastly enlarged urban society.

A lot of old accounts came due during that time. It was the Court that recalled the promise of American life for blacks and set the stage for a redress of ancient wrongs and grievances. It was the Court that recognized the threat to religious liberty involved in the growing intrusion of religious observances into the practices of public schools and other public institutions.

[10] Arthur Goldberg, *Equal Justice: The Warren Era of the Supreme Court* (Evanston, Ill.: Northwestern University Press, 1971), p. 31.

It was the Court that reminded those policemen and prosecutors who were brazenly cutting constitutional corners in their zeal to catch and convict criminals that due process of law is an indispensable aspect of justice; it infused new meaning into the concept of due process, making it an effective guarantor of procedural fairness in both state and federal law enforcement. When the country's representative bodies seemed powerless to throw off their bondage to rural rule, it was the Court that reasserted the basic tenet of democracy, that citizens are entitled to an equal voice in the political process. The Court's strong egalitarian strain brought closer to realization than ever before in American history the basic premise of the Declaration of Independence, that "all men are created equal" and that "they are endowed by their Creator with certain unalienable rights." If this amounted to excessive "activism" on the Court's part, it nevertheless served imperative public purposes. It is hardly too much to say that the Warren Court revitalized democracy in America.

The Supreme Court does not easily acknowledge error or overturn its own past judgments. *Stare decisis*,[11] the authority of the past, has always and necessarily been a vital principle in the Court's conduct. Without it, lawyers would have no way of telling their clients with any assurance that activities they wanted to undertake were within the law, or that they could count on the courts for enforcement of contracts to which they were parties. If they were not able to depend on settled principles of law, judges of lower courts would find it difficult indeed to rule regarding the complex statutory and constitutional issues brought before them; and rulings might often be entirely different in different jurisdictions. The importance of established and reliable precedents led Justice Brandeis on one occasion to remark that "In most matters it is

---

[11] *Black's Law Dictionary*, 4th ed., defines *stare decisis* as "to abide by, or adhere to, decided cases."

more important that the applicable rule of law be settled than that it be settled right."

But on constitutional, as distinguished from common-law, questions, the Supreme Court has been more flexible, recognizing that the Constitution is an evolving charter. "In cases involving the Federal Constitution," Justice Brandeis went on to say, "where correction through legislative action is practically impossible, this Court has often overruled its earlier decisions. The Court bows to the lessons of experience and the force of better reasoning."

The Court is, besides, and above all else, an institution—with all that the term implies regarding roots and a respect for tradition. It is no mere *ad hoc* committee, passing judgment on issues in the light alone of contemporary interest and policy. It is a continuing body, linked to the past and to the future, in the deliberations of which predecessors are colleagues whose voices are never to be stilled. This conception of the Court was expressed by Justice Edward White in an opinion in which he was joined by the elder Justice John M. Harlan, himself among the great dissenters:

The fundamental conception of a judicial body is that of one hedged about by precedents which are binding on the court without regard to the personality of its members. Break down this belief in judicial continuity, and let it be felt that on great constitutional questions this court is to depart from the settled conclusions of its predecessors, and to determine them all according to the mere opinion of those who temporarily fill its bench, and our Constitution will, in my judgment, be bereft of value and become a most dangerous instrument to the rights and liberties of the people.[12]

Behind this respect for precedent lies an awareness that judges have an attachment to the law with roots that go far deeper than their personal preferences and prejudices. "Judges," said Justice Benjamin Cardozo in the second of his

---

[12] Pollock v. Farmers' Loan and Trust Co., 157 U.S. 429, 652 (1895), dissenting opinion.

brilliant lectures on *The Nature of the Judicial Process,* "are not commissioned to make and unmake rules at pleasure in accordance with changing views of expediency or wisdom." And Justice Felix Frankfurter, a profound student of the Court's enduring values and traditions, stated the standard for judicial decision in these words:

Because the Court is without power to shape measures for dealing with the problems of society but has merely the power of negation over measures shaped by others, the indispensable judicial requisite is intellectual humility, and such humility presupposes complete disinterestedness. And so, in the end, it is right that the Court should be indifferent to public temper and popular wishes. Mr. Dooley's "th' Supreme Coort follows th' iliction returns" expressed the wit of cynicism, not the demand of principle. A court which yields to the popular will thereby licenses itself to practice despotism, for there can be no assurance that it will not on another occasion indulge its own will. Courts can fulfill their responsibility in a democratic society only to the extent that they succeed in shaping their judgments by rational standards, and rational standards are both impersonal and communicable.[13]

What it comes down to, then, is a recognition that precedent is a valuable stabilizer, not lightly to be overridden, yet not slavishly to be obeyed. Justices of the Supreme Court are rarely Titans; they are mortal men, endowed usually with more than ordinary intellectual powers and with exceptional richness of learning and experience, but nevertheless subject like other mortal men to vagaries and failures of understanding. And so, from time to time, the Court confesses error and corrects itself, overturning its own past judgment, not capriciously on the basis of changing personal preferences, but rationally, in the light of logic and experience.

The factors that enter into such reversals are, of course, complex and difficult to isolate in particular cases. Perhaps

---

[13] American Federation of Labor v. American Sash and Door Co., 335 U.S. 538 (1949).

the simplest of them is a change of mind by an individual justice. This does not occur very frequently, of course; when it does occur, it affords a rather reassuring sense that justices are, after all, but human. In a case involving the use of a concealed microphone to obtain damaging admissions from a suspected narcotics peddler, Justice William O. Douglas recalled and recanted his action in a comparable case fourteen years earlier when he had joined the Court in upholding a somewhat similar sort of eavesdropping. "Since that time," he wrote, "various aspects of the problem have appeared again and again in the cases coming before us. I now more fully appreciate the vice of the practices spawned by *Olmstead* and *Goldman*. Reflection on them has brought new insight to me. I now feel that I was wrong in the *Goldman* case."[14]

The candor of this acknowledgment was matched by a recantation that Justice Robert H. Jackson wrote into a concurring opinion in 1950. "I concur in the judgment and opinion of the Court," he declared. "But since it is contrary to an opinion which, as Attorney General, I rendered in 1940, I owe some word of explanation. I am entitled to say of that opinion what any discriminating reader must think of it—that it was as foggy as the statute the Attorney General was asked to interpret. . . . The opinion did not at all consider aspects of our diplomatic history, which I now think, and should think I would then have thought, ought to be considered in applying any conscription Act to aliens. . . . Precedent, however, is not lacking for ways by which a judge may recede from a prior opinion that has proven untenable and perhaps misled others. . . . Baron Bramwell extricated himself from a somewhat similar embarrassment by saying, 'The matter does not appear to me now as it appears to have appeared to me then.' And Mr. Justice Story, accounting for his contradiction of his own former opinion, quite properly put the matter: 'My own error, however, can furnish no ground for its being adopted by this

---

[14] On Lee v. United States, 343 U.S. 747 (1952).

Court. . . .' If there are other ways of gracefully and good naturedly surrendering former views to a better considered position, I invoke them all."[15]

A second, and quite obvious, factor that enters into judicial reversals arises from changes in the personnel of the Court. "Over time," Professor Alexander M. Bickel has remarked, "the Supreme Court speaks for and with the dominant political alliance. The appointment power, which is political, ensures as much."[16]

Generally speaking, presidents hope to see their own political philosophy reflected in the men they nominate to seats on the Supreme Court. The hope is often disappointed, of course. Nevertheless, few things that a president does more indelibly leave upon the future the imprint of his personality. In an editorial comment, January 14, 1939, on the confirmation of Felix Frankfurter's nomination to the Court, *The Nation* made this point with exceptional felicity:

The good that Presidents do is often interred with their Administrations. It is their choice of Supreme Court justices that lives after them. The noisy battles of Roosevelt I still echo in the phrases he added to the language, but nothing else he did has had so much effect on our national development as the appointment of Justice Holmes. Wilson's Clayton Act and his Federal Trade Commission, of which so much was expected, stand as monuments to futility. But the Calvinistic stubbornness and righteous belligerency that crammed the nomination of Justice Brandeis down the throat of an unwilling Senate have continued to bear fruit in our constitutional law. We believe that in the perspective of history the appointment of Felix Frankfurter to the Supreme Court will not seem the least of Franklin Roosevelt's accomplishments. . . .

There is an irony in the final paragraph of *The Nation's* editorial: "Mr. Roosevelt gave the court new vitality with the

---

[15] McGrath v. Kristensen, 340 U.S. 162 (1950).
[16] Alexander M. Bickel, *The Supreme Court and the Idea of Progress* (New York: Harper & Row, 1970), p. 88.

appointment of Black; he gives it new and rich talents for
conciliation, adjustment, and statesmanship in Frankfurter. . . ."
In a very short time, it seems likely, the editors of *The Nation*
experienced keen disappointment in the performance of Justice
Frankfurter; be that as it may, it soon became apparent that he
and Justice Black, both chosen by the same president, marched
to the music of very different drums. Strong personalities such
as these are bound to go their own ways when they take their
places on the Court. That is the virtue of life tenure. During
the more than two decades of their service together on the
Supreme Court, Frankfurter and Black unremittingly carried
on one of the most fascinating intellectual controversies in the
history of the law. The clash of judicial philosophies between
men of the highest intellect and integrity found expression in a
long succession of cases, some of them recounted in this book.
Such differences of view have not only a great counterbalanc-
ing value; they have great value, too, in stimulating the minds
of adversaries to their best abilities.

The uncertainty of presidential influence upon the Court
through individual nominations seems evident enough when
one recalls that Woodrow Wilson named to it not only Louis
Brandeis but James C. McReynolds, who became the very
exemplar of reaction; and the colorless, ineffectual Charles
Whittaker as well as Earl Warren was chosen by President
Eisenhower. Yet presidents undoubtedly affect the tenor of
the Court. If the ideas of Franklin D. Roosevelt's New Deal
were frustrated for a time by the Supreme Court appointments
of his predecessors, they were rather unmistakably perpetuated
beyond his own tenure in office by his own appointees. And
doubtless the very different mark of Richard Nixon will be
upon the Court for a number of years to come.

The impact of personnel changes in the Court is difficult to
trace anyway, in part because the attitude of judges to particular problems is not always consistent and is frequently unpre-
dictable, in part because a lapse of many years usually occurs
between a decision and the reversal of it. In only one of the

instances recounted in this book—the Court's turnabout within
three years in the two flag-salute cases—can the changes in the
composition of the Court be clearly identified as a decisive
influence.

Advances in knowledge also play a part in the changing of
judicial minds. New concepts of manners and morals, new
insights into human nature may considerably affect a judge's
view as to what is constitutionally permissible and what is not.
Yesterday's obscenity, for instance, may become today's con-
ventionality. All men learn a little from living, and even judges
may mature upon the bench. Sociology and psychiatry have
made some contributions to human understanding. There
could be worse mottoes for emblazonment upon the porticoes
of courthouses than Richard Overton's quiet observation, "For
no man knoweth but in part, and what we know we receive
it by degrees, now a little and then a little. He that knows the
most was once as ignorant as he that knows the least. Nay, is
it not frequent among us, that the thing that we judged heresy
we now believe is orthodox?"[17]

"The life of the law," Justice Holmes wrote, "has not been
logic; it has been experience. The felt necessities of the time,
the prevalent moral and political theories, intuitions of public
policy, avowed or unconscious, even the prejudices which
judges share with their fellow-men, have had a good deal more
to do than the syllogism in determining the rules by which
men should be governed."[18] Experience has had a good deal to
do also—more, probably, than any other factor—with impelling
the Supreme Court on occasion to change its mind. Experience
has led the Court from time to time to realize that doctrines
and principles of law, adopted in good conscience and upon
the basis of what seemed compelling reason, simply do not fit
the realities of life—in short, simply do not work.

[17] Quoted by H. N. Brailsford, "The Arraignment of Mr. Persecution," in
The Levellers and the English Revolution (London: The Cresset Press, 1961),
pp. 55–56.
[18] Oliver Wendell Holmes, Lecture I, "Early Forms of Liability," in *The
Common Law* (Boston: Little, Brown & Company, 1881), p. 5.

The impact of experience has been manifest in pretty nearly every one of the cases presented in this book. The Court's fidelity to *stare decisis* led it to try to live as long as it could with decisions made in the past. Justices strove in every imaginable way to rationalize and retain doctrines laid down by their predecessors. And only implacable necessity persuaded them to break with the past. Succeeding chapters will show how the Court shifted and strained, for instance, to remodel and adapt the "separate but equal" rule, adopted in 1896, to the circumstances of the twentieth century. In the field of public education, the Court focused its attention upon the inequality rather than upon the separation, holding in case after case that the educational opportunities offered to black students were inferior to those available to whites—until at last it recognized that the inequality was inherent in the separation and inseparable from it. The elder John Marshall Harlan had presciently pointed this out in 1896; but it took the Court half a century and more to come round to an acceptance of it.

Similarly, the Court tried for twenty years to hold to a view of due process adopted in 1942, allowing states to prosecute indigent defendants in criminal trials without giving them the assistance of counsel. Before very long after the rule was adopted, it began to be clear that defendants lacking lawyers were heavily handicapped; and for a decade the Court overturned every conviction brought before it and obtained in this way, clinging to the rule yet always citing "special circumstances" which made the application of it seem insupportable. At last, in 1963, the Court acknowledged what had become virtually self-evident—that the majority had been wrong and the dissenters right in 1942; and so it reversed itself, bringing its principle into conformity with its practice. What the record reveals is that the Court reverses itself—with rare exceptions—only after a succession of cases shows a doctrine to be untenable in the light of current conditions.

The process of self-correction has been repeated again and again when experience overrode a logic demonstrably outworn.

There could hardly be a healthier symptom of vitality in a judicial body. Dissenters are, in a sense, men who speak "before their time," that is to say, men who foresee the future before events make it manifest to their contemporaries. Perhaps, then, one may fairly call them prophets.

II

"OUR CONSTITUTION
IS COLOR BLIND"

———————

Plessy v. *Ferguson*, John Marshall Harlan dissenting[*]

Whether or not the Supreme Court may fairly be said to follow
the election returns, it undoubtedly follows the country's folk-
ways. The prejudices of a people find reflection in their laws
and in their administration of justice. In no area of American
life has this been more apparent than in the status and the
opportunity accorded to black citizens. Blacks have moved
from slavery to an emancipation that was no more than another
form of servitude, and from there to a recognition at last, if
not yet an actual realization, of their claim to civil and political
equality. And at each stage of this development, the Supreme
Court of the United States has given to the prevailing pattern
of race relations the stamp of its judicial approval. As Dr. Kenneth B. Clark has remarked, "Judicial decisions tend to reflect moral, social, and political realities of the society at a
particular point in time."[1] Yet they reflect also the hopes and

———

[*] 163 U.S. 537 (1896).

[1] Kenneth B. Clark, "The Social Scientists, the Brown Decision, and Con-
temporary Confusion," in *Argument: The Complete Oral Argument Before the
Supreme Court in Brown v. Board of Education of Topeka, 1952–55*, ed.
Leon Friedman (New York: Chelsea House, 1969), p. xxxi.

promises—and the stirrings of conscience—of the society.

The institution of human slavery can probably be reckoned the most blighting tragedy in American history. No institution could seem more at odds with the spirit of the United States Constitution, a document essentially libertarian, idealistic, and grounded in respect for human dignity. Nevertheless, in 1857 the Supreme Court concluded that blacks whose ancestors were imported into this country, and sold as slaves, were not members "of the political community formed and brought into existence by the Constitution" and that "they are not included and were not intended to be included under the word 'citizen' in the Constitution and can, therefore, claim none of the rights and privileges which that instrument provides for and secures to citizens of the United States."[2]

Dred Scott ranks, no doubt, as the most maleficent judgment in the Supreme Court's history. It served only to sharpen the slavery issue, to end northern hope of any rational solution respecting it, and to hasten the day of southern secession and civil war. In the course of the terrible conflict that tore and tortured the American community in the 1860s, President Lincoln issued the Emancipation Proclamation, freeing the slaves throughout the area where insurrection prevailed. Soon after the war, the Thirteenth Amendment, abolishing slavery anywhere under the American flag, was added to the U.S. Constitution. And not long afterward, the Fourteenth and Fifteenth Amendments were adopted for the plain purpose of assuring citizenship to black Americans and putting them on a basis of parity with white Americans so far as political and civil rights were concerned.

Each of these amendments contained language expressly empowering Congress to adopt legislation designed to enforce it. Congress used this power to enact a series of civil-rights statutes assuring the freedmen equality of treatment in virtually every aspect of life—from voting to acceptance and service in

[2] Dred Scott v. Sanford, 19 Howard 393 (1857).

restaurants, inns, railways, and every sort of public accommodation. They aimed at lifting the black man, all at once, from
the depths and degradation of slavery to the heights of independence and responsibility—even to the unaccustomed authority of public office. The adjustment was at once too abrupt
and too sweeping to be within the capacity of either blacks or
whites.

The Confederacy was conquered, but by no means converted. Southerners were not about to abandon their deeply
ingrained view of the black as an inferior being. Prof. Carl B.
Swisher, a biographer of Chief Justice Taney and a distinguished authority on constitutional development, observed that
"In spite of a degree of acquiescence in the results of the
war . . . the enactment of the so-called 'black codes' by southern
states made it clear that the freedmen were to be dealt with as
a separate class and that from the beginning they were to be
denied civil privileges enjoyed by white people."[3]

The result of Reconstruction, in short, was reaction. It produced among white southerners—perhaps an inevitable consequence of enforced reform—a sense of injured innocence, of
persecution, and of implacable enmity. The South found consolidation in these emotions and was led, through them, to a
resistance to almost every form of modernization and progress
that could be said to have northern origins. And so the South
denied itself any share in the nation's phenomenal economic
growth. It remained imprisoned in its own bitterness; and, far
from being reconstructed, the southern mind clung fanatically
to its primary social principle: that the black was an inferior,
subordinate creature in relation to whom the white man—any
white man—must be considered a master.

The chief casualty of Reconstruction's failure was, of course,
the freedman, the black, who was supposed to be its chief
beneficiary. He became, instead, a helpless pawn in a fierce

[3] Carl B. Swisher, *American Constitutional Development* (Boston: Houghton
Mifflin Co., 1943), p. 313.

struggle for national political advantage. In the end, the northern radicals who wanted to make the South over in their own image gave up on the project and abandoned the black to the mercies of the white southerners whom they had goaded him to defy. In 1877, the troops that afforded the indispensable foundation for Reconstruction were withdrawn from the states of the Confederacy. This was done in conformity with a somewhat cynical, or at least highly opportunistic, compromise to settle the disputed Hayes-Tilden election of 1876. Democrats acquiesced in the acceptance of Rutherford B. Hayes, a Republican, as president, although their own candidate, Samuel J. Tilden, had won a popular majority in the national balloting—and perhaps an electoral majority as well—in return for an agreement by Hayes that the military occupation of the South would be brought to an end. When the troops withdrew, the carpetbaggers quickly scurried after them. And the South was left to deal with its problems on its own terms.

Those terms were undoubtedly made harsher by the impoverishment and humiliation the white majority of the South had endured. The more or less benevolent paternalism toward blacks that had characterized the patrician planter class of the ante-bellum South gave way more and more to a redneck element, the tenant farmers and sharecroppers, and the downtrodden millworkers who became increasingly numerous as the South sought industrialization as a solution for its economic plight.

What developed in the South—and what was to be fastened upon it for a century—was a caste system in which the black became the American untouchable. As John Dollard pointed out in his brilliant dissection of "Southerntown," caste "replaced slavery as a means of maintaining the essence of the old status order in the south."[4] The new status order gave the wretched, disinherited, desperate white southern peasantry a sense that

[4] John Dollard, *Caste and Class in a Southern Town* (New Haven: Yale University Press, 1937), p. 62.

they were not at the very bottom of the social and economic ladder, that they were superior at least to the blacks. And so they reinforced this sense of superiority by an impassioned racism, grounded in their fear and hatred, sanctioned by religion, enforced by indescribable violence and cruelty, and institutionalized by rigid rules of segregation.

It was in the 1880s and 1890s—the period of the Ku Klux Klan, mob violence, and lynching, all aimed at keeping the black man "in his place"—and in the early years of the 1900s that Jim Crow became a fixed way of life in the region. The origin of the term *Jim Crow* is uncertain; but there is no uncertainty at all as to its meaning and its purpose. Jim Crow laws constituted a systematic code for keeping the black bound and helpless, for humiliating and subjugating him, and for segregating him rigidly from all contact and communication with white people. "That code," observed C. Vann Woodward, "lent the sanction of law to a racial ostracism that extended to churches and schools, to housing and jobs, to eating and drinking. Whether by law or by custom, that ostracism eventually extended to virtually all forms of public transportation, to sports and recreations, to hospitals, orphanages, prisons, and asylums, and ultimately to funeral homes, morgues, and cemeteries."[5]

Perhaps the most odious aspect of the Jim Crow code was its pointless meanness and cruelty—as though the status and security of the white majority depended on grinding the black man's face in the dirt, upon systematically injuring and degrading him. Some of the instances of state segregation statutes catalogued by Woodward challenge credence. North Carolina and Virginia, for example, found it wise to pass laws that forbade all fraternal organizations that permitted members of different races to address each other as "brother." Alabama saw fit to adopt a law prohibiting white female nurses from attending black male patients. A New Orleans ordinance segregated white and colored prostitutes in separate districts. A Birming-

[5] C. Vann Woodward, *The Strange Career of Jim Crow* (New York: Oxford University Press, 1955), p. 8.

ham ordinance made it unlawful for a black person and a white person to play together or in company with each other at dominoes or checkers. Oklahoma banned any companionship between the races while boating or fishing. Thus did the dominant race demonstrate its "superiority."

In all of this, the Supreme Court of the United States played a lamentable role. It ratified the country's complacency. Gunnar Myrdal, in his great work on the American racial problem, first published in 1944, rendered a judgment on the Court which seems altogether just: "It is generally held that the Supreme Court acted in agreement with and actually expressed what was then the general sentiment even in the North. The North had gotten tired of the Negro problem and, anyhow, saw no immediate alternative other than to let the white southerners have their own way with the Negroes. But it must not be forgotten that the decisions of the Court had themselves a substantial share in the responsibility for the solidification of Northern apathy."[6]

The definitive judicial ratification of Jim Crow—the end of all effort, at least for a long time to come, to give vitality to the Fourteenth Amendment as a guarantor of equality to black people—came with the Supreme Court's decision in the landmark case known as *Plessy* v. *Ferguson.* Justice John Marshall Harlan's great dissenting opinion in that case is the central subject of this chapter. But the strength of the current carrying the Court toward capitulation became clear as early as 1883 in a decision involving what were called the "Civil Rights cases." These cases arose under the Civil Rights Act of March 1, 1875, which provided, in part, that all persons "shall be entitled to the full and equal enjoyment of the accommodations, advantages, facilities, and privileges of inns, public conveyances on land and water, theaters and other places of public amusement. . . ." In an ingenious opinion by Justice Bradley, the Court came to the conclusion that the Thirteenth, Fourteenth,

[6] Gunnar Myrdal, *An American Dilemma* (New York: Harper & Row, 1944), p. 516.

and Fifteenth Amendments were intended to do no more than protect former slaves against discrimination by official state action and conferred no power upon Congress to prohibit discrimination by individuals or business corporations engaged in normal commercial undertakings. "It would be running the slavery argument into the ground," the Court declared, "to make it apply to every act of discrimination which a person may see fit to make as to the guests he will entertain, or as to the people he will take into his coach or cab or car, or admit to his concert or theatre, or deal with in other matters of intercourse or business."[7]

To this straitened view of the equal protection clause of the Fourteenth Amendment, only a single dissent was recorded in the Supreme Court. It, too, came from John Marshall Harlan. He wrote:

> *The opinion in these cases proceeds, it seems to me, upon grounds entirely too narrow and artificial. I cannot resist the conclusion that the substance and spirit of the recent amendments of the Constitution have been sacrificed by a subtle and ingenious verbal criticism. . . . Constitutional provisions, adopted in the interest of liberty, and for the purpose of securing, through national legislation, if need be, rights inhering in a state of freedom, and belonging to American citizenship, have been so construed as to defeat the ends the people desired to accomplish, which they attempted to accomplish, and which they supposed they had accomplished by changes in their fundamental law. . . .*

Later in his dissent Justice Harlan dealt with the majority contention that the forms of discrimination forbidden by the Civil Rights Act of 1875 involved only social relations:

> *I agree that government has nothing to do with social, as distinguished from technically legal rights of individuals. No government ever has brought, or ever can bring, its people into social intercourse against their wishes. Whether one person will permit*

[7] Civil Rights Cases, 109 U.S. 3 (1883).

or maintain social relations with another is a matter with which government has no concern. I agree that if one citizen chooses not to hold social intercourse with another, he is not and cannot be made amenable to the law for his conduct in that regard; for even upon grounds of race, no legal right of a citizen is violated by the refusal of others to maintain merely social relations with him. What I affirm is that no State, nor the officers of any State, nor any corporation or individual wielding power under State authority for the public benefit or the public convenience can, consistently either with the freedom established by the fundamental law, or with that equality of civil rights which now belongs to every citizen, discriminate against freemen or citizens, in those rights, because of their race, or because they once labored under the disabilities of slavery imposed upon them as a race. The rights which Congress, by the act of 1875, endeavored to secure and protect are legal, not social rights. The right, for instance, of a colored citizen to use the accommodations of a public highway, upon the same terms as are permitted to white citizens, is no more a social right than his right, under the law, to use the public streets of a town, or a turnpike road, or a public market, or a post office, or his right to sit in a public building with others, of whatever race, for the purpose of hearing the political questions of the day discussed. . . .

Although this powerful dissent sparked a brief boom in the North for Harlan for the presidency, it evoked no general outcry in the country at the Court's relegation of the black to, at best, second-class citizenship. The country, North and South alike, had exhausted its capacity for moral indignation over the race problem. It was busy getting rich and comfortable through the exploitation of a continent. The Supreme Court, unanimous except for Harlan's astringent realism, was quite prepared to go along with the popular inclination to forget about the freedmen.

So, the southern states, having won from the Supreme Court the assertion that Congress could not compel them, through federal legislation, to deal generously, or even fairly, with their black citizens, began at a steadily accelerating pace to move, through their own legislatures, to a system of enforced

segregation and of contrived, purposeful humiliation that, in
Professor Woodward's words, "put the authority of the state
or city in the voice of the street-car conductor, the railway
brakeman, the bus driver, the theater usher, and also into the
voice of the hoodlum of the public parks and playgrounds.
They [the Jim Crow laws] gave free rein and the majesty of
the law to mass aggressions that might otherwise have been
curbed, blunted, or deflected."[8]

Among the Jim Crow laws was a Louisiana statute that,
according to its title, was enacted in order "to promote the
comfort of passengers on railway trains." It provided that "all
railway companies carrying passengers in their coaches in this
State, shall provide equal but separate accommodations for the
white, and colored races, by providing two or more passenger
coaches for each passenger train, or by dividing the passenger
coaches by a partition so as to secure separate accommodation" and that "No person or persons shall be admitted to
occupy seats in coaches, other than the ones assigned to them
on account of the race they belong to."

This provision was clearly intended to promote the illusion
of comfort and superiority for white passengers; the equally
clear—and intended—effect on blacks was, of course, to promote the illusion of their inferiority. Separation of classes of
citizens is sometimes justified, of course, when the separation
affords benefits to both and is mutually acceptable—as, for
instance, separation of the sexes in the use of public lavatories.
But the patent purpose of the Louisiana statute was to gratify
one class by degrading another.

A group of Louisiana blacks formed a Citizens Committee to
Test the Constitutionality of the Separate Car Law and retained a white northerner named Albion Winegar Tourgée to
serve as their counsel. There is a titillating, if acerbic, account

[8] Woodward, *op. cit.*, p. 93.

of Tourgée's life in the *Dictionary of American Biography*,[9] which begins by characterizing him succinctly as "carpet-bagger, author." It tells little about his career as a lawyer save that during Reconstruction he became a superior court judge in Kentucky, and that "as a judge, Tourgée was a bitter political partisan. . . ." He was also a prolific writer, contributing numerous articles to newspapers and magazines, serving as editor or publisher of a succession of journalistic ventures that ended uniformly in failure, and producing half a dozen novels about Reconstruction. "All of his novels," in the opinion of his *DAB* "biographer"—who does not appear to have been an unreserved idolator—"are conventionally romantic, show little originality, and lack literary finish. His political articles, reflecting the author, are dogmatic and egotistical."[10] The sketch makes no mention whatever of his connection with the landmark Supreme Court case known as *Plessy* v. *Ferguson*.

With the collaboration of another lawyer named James C. Walker, Tourgée went about preparing a lawyerlike test of the Louisiana law, casting as the protagonist in the piece of theater they were projecting a man named Homer Adolph Plessy, an octoroon—that is to say, of his eight great-grandparents, seven had been white and only one black.

Homer Plessy had proceeded to buy a first-class ticket on the East Louisiana Railway, theoretically entitling him to travel in a first-class coach from New Orleans to Covington, Louisiana, entirely within the state. But when, on June 7, 1892, he seated himself in orderly fashion in a first-class car reserved for white passengers, the conductor promptly asked him to move to a car marked "Colored." Plessy demurred, was arrested, and, through his lawyers, brought suit against the railroad.

Plessy's complaint was heard by a judge named John Ferguson, and it was thus that the celebrated case took its title. Two issues were raised in the complaint: the first, that a railroad

[9] *Dictionary of American Biography* (New York: Scribner's, 1936), XVIII, p. 603.
[10] *Ibid.*

conductor had no qualifications for determining what race a
passenger belonged to, was virtually incidental to the primary
issue—namely, that state action requiring segregation by race
violated the equal protection clause of the Fourteenth Amendment. That clause provided that "no state shall . . . deny to any
person within its jurisdiction the equal protection of the laws."
Judge Ferguson ruled against Plessy on both counts; and the
Supreme Court of Louisiana unanimously upheld him. In 1896,
the Supreme Court of the United States reviewed the case and
almost unanimously sustained the courts below it. Again, as in
the Civil Rights cases, there was a lone dissent by Justice John
Marshall Harlan, perhaps the most eloquent and prophetic
dissent in the whole history of the United States Supreme
Court.

Tourgée's brief and argument before that Court deserves attention. He made a plea that compensated in passion for what
it may have lacked in legal logic:

*Suppose a member of this court, nay suppose every member of it,
by some mysterious dispensation of providence, should wake to-
morrow with a black skin and curly hair—the two most obvious
and controlling indications of race—and in traveling through that
portion of the country where the "Jim Crow Car" abounds, should
be ordered into it by the conductor. It is easy to imagine what
would be the result, the indignation, the protests, the assertion of
pure Caucasian ancestry. But the conductor, the autocrat of Caste,
armed with the power of the state conferred by this statute, will
listen neither to denial or protest. "In you go or out you go," is his
ultimatum.*

*What humiliation, what rage would then fill the judicial mind!
How would the resources of language not be taxed in objurgation![11]*

And regarding the determination of Plessy's race, Tourgée
had this to say:

The crime, then, for which he became liable to imprisonment so

[11] Brief before the U.S. Supreme Court for plaintiff in error.

*far as the court can ascertain, was that a person of seven-eighths
Caucasian blood insisted in sitting peacefully and quietly in a car
the State of Louisiana had commanded the company to set aside
exclusively for the white race. Where on earth should he have gone?
Will the court hold that a single drop of African blood is sufficient
to color a whole ocean of Caucasian whiteness?*[12]

Tourgée's most notable contribution to the case came, however, in his peroration to the Court. "Justice," he said, "is
pictured as blind, and her daughter, the law, ought at least to
be color-blind." Perhaps this felicitous phrase made an enduring impression on the mind of John Marshall Harlan: what
appears to be a reflection of it found expression in the most
memorable line of Justice Harlan's dissent—"Our Constitution
is color-blind. . . ."

But Tourgée's appeal to the sensibilities and the conscience
of the justices had little impact upon men whose attitudes
accurately mirrored the overwhelming apathy and complacency
of the country regarding the race problem. The opinion of the
Court, written by Justice Henry Billings Brown, rivaled the
Dred Scott decision for callousness. It began by going back to
the murky distinction between social and legal rights utilized
by the Court in the Civil Rights cases. "The object of the
Fourteenth Amendment," Justice Brown declared, "was un
doubtedly to enforce the absolute equality of the two races
before the law, but in the nature of things it could not have
been intended to abolish distinctions based upon color, or to
enforce social, as distinguished from political equality, or a
commingling of the two races upon terms unsatisfactory to
either." He then went on to an assertion that, for sheer smug-
ness, can hardly have been surpassed anywhere in the pages of
judicial prose:

*We consider the underlying fallacy of the plaintiff's argument to
consist in the assumption that the enforced separation of the two*

[12] *Ibid.*

races stamps the colored race with a badge of inferiority. If this be so, it is not by reason of anything found in the act, but solely because the colored race chooses to put that construction upon it. . . . Legislation is powerless to eradicate racial instincts or to abolish distinctions based upon physical differences, and the attempt to do so can only result in accentuating the difficulties of the present situation. If the civil and political rights of both races be equal, one cannot be inferior to the other civilly or politically. If one race be inferior to the other socially, the Constitution of the United States cannot put them upon the same plane. . . .

Justice Harlan's dissent from this gloss upon reality was a roar of outrage.[13] It was, at the same time, a powerfully organized and closely reasoned refutation of the Court's opinion. And, finally, it afforded a prophetic insight into the corrosive consequences of segregation and discrimination. It would take more than half a century for the country and the Court to come round to a recognition of Justice Harlan's realism and moral indignation—and even longer to undo the dreadful consequences that he foresaw of its blindness and torpor.

The truest function of dissent in a court of last resort was served by the emotional as well as intellectual content of this extraordinary opinion. It began with a reminder of the fundamental proposition set forth in the Declaration of Independence —the proposition that "all men are created equal." He wrote:

. . . in view of the Constitution, in the eye of the law, there is in this country no superior, dominant, ruling class of citizens. There is no caste here. Our Constitution is color-blind, and neither knows nor tolerates classes among citizens. In respect of civil rights, all citizens are equal before the law. The humblest is the peer of the most powerful. The law regards man as man, and takes no account of his surroundings or of his color when his civil rights as guaranteed by the supreme law of the land are involved.

Harlan peered, then, into the future, foreseeing the dread effects of caste and class distinction given legal sanction:

[13] The complete text of this dissent can be found in the appendix.

In my opinion, the judgment this day rendered will, in time, prove to be quite as pernicious as the decision made by this tribunal in the Dred Scott Case. . . . *The present decision, it may well be apprehended, will not only stimulate aggressions, more or less brutal and irritating, upon the admitted rights of colored citizens, but will encourage the belief that it is possible, by means of state enactments, to defeat the beneficent purposes which the people of the United States had in view when they adopted the recent amendments of the Constitution. . . . Sixty millions of whites are in no danger from the presence here of eight millions of blacks. The destinies of the two races in this country are indissolubly linked together, and the interests of both require that the common government of all shall not permit the seeds of race hate to be planted under the sanction of law. What can more certainly arouse race hate, what more certainly create and perpetuate a feeling of distrust between these races, than state enactments which in fact proceed on the ground that colored citizens are so inferior and degraded that they cannot be allowed to sit in public coaches occupied by white citizens? That, as all will admit, is the real meaning of such legislation as was enacted in Louisiana. . . .*

Once more Harlan turned his indignation to that red herring contention of the majority—that what was at stake here was not a civil right, but an attempt to legislate social equality:

. . . That argument, if it can be properly regarded as one, is scarcely worthy of consideration; for social equality no more exists between the two races when traveling in a passenger coach or a public highway than when members of the same races sit by each other in a street car or in the jury box, or stand or sit with each other in a political assembly, or when they use in common the streets of a city or town, or when they are in the same room for the purpose of having their names placed on the registry of voters, or when they approach the ballot-box in order to exercise the high privilege of voting. . . .

If evils will result from the commingling of the two races upon public highways established for the benefit of all, they will be infinitely less than those that will surely come from state legislation regulating the enjoyment of civil rights upon the basis of race. We

boast of the freedom enjoyed by our people above all other peo-
ples. But it is difficult to reconcile that boast with a state of the law
which, practically, puts the brand of servitude and degradation
upon a large class of our fellow-citizens, our equals before the law.
The thin disguise of "equal" accommodations for passengers in
railroad coaches will not mislead anyone, or atone for the wrong
this day done.

John Marshall Harlan, the man who wrote this moving thrust
against the time's overbearing current of popular and judicial
opinion, was a patrician product of the ante-bellum South. Born
to a distinguished and affluent family in Kentucky in 1833,
educated in that state at Centre College and at the Law School
of Transylvania University (then called the Harvard of the
West), there was very little in his background to suggest that
he would become, in time, the Supreme Court's lone dissenter
against the "separate but equal" doctrine, the Court's sole champion of the Reconstruction amendments to the Constitution.

The Harlans were not plantation owners and did not grow
cotton. They kept about a dozen "house" slaves to do the
manual and household work, which enabled them to live in
fashionable ease, treating their slaves with kindness and consideration and indeed in several instances giving freedom to
blacks who had served them well and faithfully. What they did,
however, they did out of a sense of *noblesse oblige*; they had no
misgivings about slavery as an institution. They regarded slaves
as property, no more to be taken away from their lawful owners
than any other chattel.

A decade after the end of the Civil War, when the Judiciary
Committee of the Senate was considering the nomination of
John Harlan to the Supreme Court, a Union Army general
wrote to the committee asserting that Harlan had told him
during the war that "he had no more conscientious scruples in
buying and selling a Negro than he had in buying and selling
a horse, that the right of property in a Negro was identical with
that of the property in a horse, and that the liberation of slaves

by our general government was a direct violation of the Constitution of the United States."[14]

In 1854, when he was a mere twenty-one years of age, Harlan entered politics in Kentucky, choosing rather inexplicably as his avenue of entrance the then-burgeoning Know-Nothing Society—that rabidly nativist, xenophobic, and anti-Catholic collection of underground and secret organizations that took as its motto, "Put none but Americans on guard." In the 1850s the society, calling itself the American party, exercised a powerful influence on politics nationally. With Know-Nothing support, Harlan was elected city attorney of Frankfort, Kentucky, in 1854, campaigned for the organization's Kentucky candidates in 1855, and for its unsuccessful presidential nominee, Millard Fillmore, in the national election of 1856. Running for Congress under the banner of the Whig party in 1858, Harlan wholeheartedly supported the *Dred Scott* decision—he was then twenty-five years old—and lost the election by only 50 votes.[15] In the same year, he won election to a county judgeship.

Although Harlan felt strongly that slaves were a form of property and could not constitutionally be freed save by their owners, he believed also, and with great fervor, that the American Union was indissoluble and that secession could not be countenanced. When the Civil War came at last, Harlan, then twenty-eight years old, formed a regiment of Kentucky volunteers, was commissioned their colonel, and led them into the Union Army, where they served under the command of General George Thomas. He told his men frankly, however, that he would lead them over to the Confederate side if Lincoln and

[14] Quoted by Alan Westin, "John Marshall Harlan and the Constitutional Rights of Negroes: The Transformation of a Southerner," *Yale Law Journal* 66, no. 637 (April, 1957). The account here of Harlan's career draws heavily on Professor Westin's illuminating article, on Frank B. Latham's brief biography of the justice, *The Great Harlan* (New York: Cowles Book Co., 1970), and on Professor Louis Filler's biographical sketch in *The Justices of the United States Supreme Court, 1789–1969: Their Lives and Major Opinions*, 4 vols., eds. Leon Friedman and Fred L. Israel (New York: Chelsea House and London: R. H. Bowkes, 1969), Vol. II, p. 1281.

[15] Latham, *op. cit.*, pp. 15–17.

the Radical Republicans in Washington tried to abolish slavery.[16]

Although he did not carry out this threat, Harlan resigned his commission in 1863 for family reasons, returned to Kentucky, and ran successfully for the attorney generalship of that state, vehemently attacking the president both for his Emancipation Proclamation and for his suspension of the writ of *habeas corpus*. After the war, Harlan campaigned against ratification of the Thirteenth and Fourteenth Amendments.

Despite the transformation that took place in the mind and heart of this patrician southerner in his mature years, there can be no blinking the fact that he was, and remained all his life, a racist in the true meaning of that term, a man who never lost a strong sense of white superiority. The distinction between legal equality and social equality was real for him, however differently from his colleagues he conceived it. Even in his forthright—and futile—1871 campaign for the governorship of Kentucky, he disclaimed any support for "social equality" for blacks. "No law," he said, "ever can or will regulate such relations. Social equality can never exist between the two races in Kentucky." And it is interesting that he illustrated his concept of social equality at that time by saying that in the public schools it was obviously "right and proper" to keep "whites and blacks separate."[17] This distinction stayed strongly in his mind; it was expressed in his dissent in the Civil Rights cases, already quoted in this chapter, and was also reflected in his *Plessy* dissent. "The white race," he remarked in the course of the latter opinion, "deems itself to be the dominant race in this country. And so it is, in prestige, in achievements, in education, in wealth and in power. So, I doubt not, it will continue to be for all time, if it remains true to its great heritage and holds fast to the principles of constitutional liberty."

At the same time, he was a man of the highest Christian values, a man of genuine humanity, a man, to use his own

16 *Ibid.*, p. 24.
17 Quoted by Westin, *op. cit.*, p. 663.

standard, who believed deeply in "the principles of constitutional liberty." Having fought against the adoption of the Thirteenth, Fourteenth, and Fifteenth Amendments, he understood perfectly well that they were intended to put black men on a parity with white men in every respect in which government touched their lives; and he was not a man to pretend that they meant something different. When these amendments became a part of the Constitution, they achieved a kind of sanctity in Harlan's mind; and when he took an oath as an associate justice of the Supreme Court to uphold the Constitution, he took an oath to uphold all the parts of it. There was very little casuistry in John Harlan.

Moreover, he began to feel quite naturally in the 1870s a powerful revulsion against the violence and cruelty to which blacks were subjected by the various white vigilante groups determined to subjugate and humiliate them. The sadistic quality of these terror tactics was altogether abhorrent to him. If he regarded blacks as socially inferior to Caucasians, as less richly endowed by nature, he felt all the more strongly that this imposed upon the dominant race obligations of kindness and responsibility. In addition, he recognized increasingly that order could be restored to the states that had constituted the Confederacy only through observance and respect for the law. The relations between the races had been changed as the result of a terrible national conflict. The issue had been decided; and it was better now to abide by the decision than vainly to resist it.

When his beliefs changed, he changed his political label. It was as a Republican that he campaigned in 1871 for the governorship of Kentucky. Jeered at and sometimes reviled by his political enemies as a turncoat and traitor to the South, Harlan, candidly acknowledging his change of mind, declared simply: "Let it be said that I am right rather than consistent."

Harlan lost the gubernatorial race, but two of his statements in the course of the campaign merit recollection. One of them related to the terrorization of blacks. "For myself," he said, "I

say that I have no terms to make with that band of murderers
and assassins, denominated Ku Klux Klan; nor shall I have any
terms to make with them if I shall become the Chief Magistrate
of the Commonwealth; nor has the Government of the United
States any terms to make with them. . . ."[18] And in a campaign
speech delivered at Livermore, Kentucky, on July 26, 1871, he
spelled out the philosophy in regard to race that was to govern
his thoughts and his conduct for the remainder of his life:

*It is true, fellow citizens, that almost the entire people of Ken-
tucky, at one period in their history, were opposed to freedom,
citizenship and suffrage of the colored race. It is true that I was at
one time in my life opposed to conferring these privileges upon
them, but I have lived long enough to feel and declare, as I do this
night, that the most perfect despotism that ever existed on this
earth was the institution of African slavery. It was an enemy to
free speech; it was an enemy to good government; it was an enemy
to a free press.*

*The time was, and not long ago in Kentucky, when any declara-
tion, such as I now make, against the institution of slavery, would
have imperiled my life in many portions of the State. With slavery,
it was death or tribute. It knew no compromise, it tolerated no
middle course. I rejoice that it is gone; I rejoice that the Sun of
American Liberty does not this day shine upon a single human slave
upon this continent; I rejoice that these human beings are now in
possession of freedom, and that that freedom is secured to them in
the fundamental law of the land, beyond the control of any state.*

*It seemed wise to the majority of the people of this nation, not
only to secure them their freedom in this way, but also to secure
them the right of citizenship, and the rights of suffrage; and I am
now thoroughly persuaded that the only mode by which the nation
could liberate itself from the conflicts and passions engendered by
the war in connection with the institution of African slavery was to
pass these Constitutional Amendments, and to place it beyond the
power of any State to interfere with or diminish the results of the
war now embodied in these amendments. They are irrevocable
results of the War; and because the Republicans of the State of*

[18] Quoted by Westin, p. 661.

Kentucky now acquiesce in those amendments, or now declare them to be legitimate and proper, it is not just or candid to charge them with inconsistency.[19]

Harlan was a champion of freedom in every form, of freedom of speech and of the press in particular. His mind was solid rather than subtle, and indomitably independent. It may be that, more genuinely even than Justice Holmes, John Harlan deserved to be called "the Great Dissenter." Holmes, who sat on the Court with him for many years, gave him a kind of grudging and supercilious admiration, referring to him as "the last of the tobacco-spitting judges." And in a letter to his friend, Sir Frederick Pollock, Holmes wrote regarding Harlan: "that sage, although a man of real power, did not shine either in analysis or generalization, and I never troubled myself much when he shied. I used to say that he had a powerful vise the jaws of which couldn't be got nearer than two inches to each other."[20]

In a loving and lovely little book, *Mr. Justice Holmes*, Francis Biddle, once the justice's law clerk and later attorney general of the United States, offers a fragmentary anecdote that tells a good deal about both of these eminent men:

Holmes never could understand Harlan, who seemed to him to be discoursing continually about the rights of the people, a dema-gogue rather than a thinker. His opinions were interminably long and he never caught the ultimate. . . . Harlan seemed hard and humorless. But one day, the day that Holmes was seventy, there was a little nosegay of violets before him on the bench; and he dis-covered it was from Harlan, and was moved, and it stirred him to find a hidden spring of tenderness in the older man, who after all had fought the battle according to his lights. . . . [21]

[19] Quoted by Westin, pp. 659–60.
[20] *Holmes-Pollock Letters*, ed. Mark DeWolf Howe, 2 vols. (Cambridge, Mass.: Belknap Press), II, pp. 7–8.
[21] Francis Biddle, *Mr. Justice Holmes* (New York: Charles Scribner's Sons, 1946), p. 111.

The essentially simplistic quality of Harlan's mind is illustrated, perhaps, by a statement he made to a newspaper reporter in Washington in 1906. "I believe," he said, "that the Bible is the inspired Word of God. Nothing which it commands can be safely or properly disregarded—nothing that it condemns can be justified. No civilization is worth preserving which is not based on the doctrines or teachings of the Bible."[22]

"Separate but equal" was an untenable doctrine. Nevertheless, the Court, mindful of the principle of *stare decisis*, clung to it doggedly for the next half-century, although in the years during and after Franklin D. Roosevelt's New Deal, with increasing constraint and awkwardness.

How largely segregation resulted in handicaps for blacks was made apparent enough in the 1947 report of the President's Committee on Civil Rights, *To Secure These Rights*. To consider but a single aspect of segregation—health care, for example—the report observes: "Many hospitals will not admit Negro patients. The United States Public Health Service estimates on the basis of a preliminary survey that only approximately 15,000 hospital beds out of a total of one and one-half million beds are presently available to Negroes. . . . The ratio of Negro physicians to the total Negro population was about one to 3377, while that of the total number of physicians to the general population of the country was one to 750."[23] The training of the black doctors was, moreover, markedly inferior, since most medical schools, like most hospitals, declined to admit black students or residents. It is hardly surprising in the light of such discrimination that the life expectancy of blacks was ten years less than that of whites, and the maternal death rate of blacks was more than double that of whites.

---

[22] Quoted by Westin, p. 639.
[23] *To Secure These Rights*, Report of the President's Committee on Civil Rights (Washington, D.C.: U.S. Government Printing Office, 1947), p. 73.

Along with this kind of disadvantage went, of course, exclusion from almost every sort of cultural exposure—in the North almost as rigidly as in the South. Theater, ballet, concerts (at least of the more formal sort) were out of bounds for blacks. The upper levels of scholarship, scientific research, business enterprise, and, indeed, all the professions were generally closed to them. Intellectual distinction, except in extraordinary instances, was "proved" to be unattainable for blacks by putting it hopelessly beyond their reach. The separate-but-equal gloss not only put a stamp of inferiority on blacks, it *made* them inferior. The gulf between the segregated black and white worlds—between poverty and wealth, between stultification and opportunity, between despair and hope—presented an unbridgeable abyss between the races as long as segregation was the rule. Segregation, of itself, made equality utterly impossible.

The New Deal brought the beginning of what C. Vann Woodward has aptly called "the new Reconstruction"—a regeneration of concern for the condition of black Americans. A lot of factors entered into that regeneration: changes in the character of the national economy; a wartime manpower shortage that gave blacks a chance at jobs in factories and gave whites a chance at the experience of working alongside them; the consolidation of blacks in cities as influential voting blocs; American aspirations for leadership in the world of nations and embarrassment at the gap between racial practices and pretensions.

Perhaps the most important single influence was the mass migration that took place in the middle of the twentieth century from country to city within the confines of the United States—a migration comparable to the westward movement of people from Europe to America and then across the continent from the Atlantic to the Pacific in the decades before and after the century began. Just as multitudes of men and women moved then in search of freedom and economic opportunity, so Americans moved from rural to urban residence for much the same purposes.[24]

The black man, who was a major element in this mass migration, unfortunately had no equipment for adjusting to the change. Industrial employment required more literacy and education than cotton picking—much more than most blacks had been granted. Unwanted and unwelcomed, they were caged in the decaying inner cities from which the European migrants of earlier decades had managed to liberate themselves. Also often uneducated and unskilled, the Europeans were, nevertheless, a part of the dominant white society; and they brought with them pride, ambition, rich traditions, a sense of identity. There were few settlement houses or night schools or cultural communities to help the migrant blacks; there was only a determination to keep them at the bottom, to restrict them to the least desirable jobs, to hire them last, to fire them first, to segregate and exclude them. The melting-pot tradition had no application to blacks.

It was in the light of these converging factors that the Supreme Court wrestled during the middle years of the twentieth century with fresh challenges to the injustices of segregation and Jim Crow repression. In case after case, it became more and more difficult to square the separate-but-equal doctrine of the *Plessy* decision with basic constitutional principles of equality and fairness. In some situations the Court managed to squirm out of its strait jacket—as, for instance, when it declared unconstitutional a Virginia law requiring segregation on buses; the Court did not overturn *Plessy* v. *Ferguson*, but simply found the law an improper burden on interstate commerce.[25]

---

[24] According to the Statistical Abstract of the United States, urban population rose between the 1940 census and the 1960 census from 74 million to 125 million; rural population dropped from 57 million to 54 million. In 1940, about 9 million persons were employed on farms, as compared with 43 million in trade and industry; by 1960, the number of farm workers had dropped to 4 million, while the nonagricultural workers had increased to 64 million.

[25] Morgan v. Virginia, 328 U.S. 373 (1946).

The process of adjustment in regard to education began at the graduate level and worked its way down to the grade schools. In 1938, the Court balked at a pretense by state authorities that they were satisfying the separate-but-equal standard when they offered to pay the tuition of a black law student at a law school of equal standing in another state. The Court did not strike down the standard; it merely insisted that the facilities afforded black students be genuinely equal as well as separate. "The white resident is afforded legal education within the State," the Court's opinion observed tartly; "the Negro resident having the same qualifications is refused it there and must go outside the State to obtain it. That is a denial of the equality of legal right to the enjoyment of the privilege which the State has set up, and the provision for the payment of tuition fees in another State does not remove the discrimination."[26] Chief Justice Hughes wrote the opinion of the Court; only Justices McReynolds and Butler dissented.

Some years later the Court dealt with a case that pretty well reduced segregation in education to its essential absurdity— and certainly to its essential meanness. The state of Oklahoma observed the separate-but-equal standard by admitting a black student to graduate instruction in its state university, but it seated him in a section of the classroom bounded by a rail on which there was a sign reading, "reserved for Colored"; it required him to sit at a designated desk in the library, and it forbade him to eat in the university cafeteria while other students were using it. In this instance, a unanimous Court, speaking through Chief Justice Vinson, was more than tart; it went close to declaring separation inescapably incompatible with equality. These restrictions, it said,

signify that the State, in administering the facilities it affords for professional and graduate study, sets McLaurin apart from the other students. The result is that appellant is handicapped in his pursuit of effective graduate instruction. Such restrictions impair

[26] Missouri ex rel. Gaines v. Canada, 305 U.S. 337 (1938).

and inhibit his ability to study, to engage in discussions and ex-change views with other students and, in general, to learn his profession. . . .[27]

In a rather similar case decided on the same day—and again unanimously through an opinion by Chief Justice Vinson—the Court virtually asserted that separate educational facilities are inherently and necessarily unequal. Referring to a separate law school set up by the state of Texas for black students, the Court noted:

> *What is more important, the University of Texas Law School possesses to a far greater degree those qualities which are incapable of objective measurement but which make for greatness in a law school. Such qualities, to name but a few, include reputation of the faculty, experience of the administration, position and influence of the alumni, standing in the community, traditions and prestige. . . .*[28]

The pertinacity with which the Court kept intimating, al-though not directly declaring, that segregated schools are in-herently discriminatory produced frenzied efforts in the South to bring the black school systems up to some sort of parity with the white school systems. These were futile efforts, of course, seeking as they did to overcome half a century of neglect and of gross, intentional discrimination. There was no way to do that quickly; indeed, there was no way to do it at all except by desegregation.

The Court itself at last squarely faced and acknowledged this stubborn fact of life when it heard and decided the grade-school and high-school segregation cases, known collectively as *Brown* v. *Board of Education*,[29] in the years 1952 to 1955. The decision in these cases expressly overturned the separate-but-equal doctrine of the *Plessy* decision, at least as far as public education is concerned.

---

[27] McLaurin v. Oklahoma State Regents, 339 U.S. 637 (1950).
[28] Sweatt v. Painter, 339 U.S. 629 (1950).
[29] 347 U.S. 483 (1954).

The school-segregation cases were prepared with extraordinary care by the black plaintiffs and their distinguished lawyers, and were heard with exceptional deliberation by a Supreme Court sensitive to the magnitude and the social implications of the issue before it. One factor in the great controversy that must certainly be accorded major significance was the federal government's action in the final days of the Truman administration in filing a brief as a friend of the Court attacking the constitutionality of school segregation.

Defending segregation and the conduct of the southern states that maintained it in their school systems was a battery of state attorneys general and other lawyers headed by the aging John W. Davis, who in 1924 had been the Democratic presidential candidate, and in 1952 was recognized as perhaps the most formidable courtroom advocate of his day. The main thrust of Davis's powerfully organized argument was that the southern states, relying on a long line of Supreme Court decisions that held separate-but-equal facilities to be constitutionally permissible, had developed their public education in good faith on a segregated pattern. Davis said to the Court in his peroration:

Let me say this for the State of South Carolina. It does not come here, as Thad Stevens would have wished, in sackcloth and ashes. It believes that its legislation is not offensive to the Constitution of the United States. It is confident of its good faith and intention to produce equality for all its children of whatever race or color. It is convinced that the happiness, the progress and the welfare of these children is best promoted in segregated schools, and it thinks it a thousand pities that by this controversy there should be urged the return to an experiment which gives no more promise of success today than when it was written into their Constitution during what I call the Tragic Era.

I am reminded—and I hope it won't be treated as a reflection on anybody—of Aesop's fable of the dog and the meat: The dog, with a fine piece of meat in his mouth, crossed a bridge and saw the shadow in the stream and plunged for it and lost both substance and shadow.

Here is equal education, not promised, not prophesied, but present. Shall it be thrown away on some fancied question of racial prestige?

It is not my part to offer advice to the appellants and their supporters or sympathizers, and certainly not to the learned counsel. No doubt they think what they propose is best, and I do not challenge their sincerity in any particular period but I entreat them to remember the age-old motto that the best is often the enemy of the good.[30]

It must have been a seductive argument, coupled as it was with the reminder that legislators have a right to rely on settled judicial issues—have a right to believe that the Constitution means what the Supreme Court in the past has said it means.

Paul E. Wilson, assistant attorney general of Kansas, stated the proposition flatly and forcefully:

It is our position that the principle announced in the Plessy *case and the specific rule announced in the* Gong Lum *case*[31] *are absolutely controlling here.*

We think it is sheer sophistry to attempt to distinguish those cases from the case that is here presented, and we think the question before this Court is simply this: Is the Plessy *case and the* Gong Lum *case and the "separate but equal" doctrine still the law of this land?*

We think if you decide in favor of these appellants, the Court will necessarily overrule the doctrines expressed in those cases and, at the same time, will say that the legislatures of the seventeen or twenty-one states, that the Congress of the United States, that dozens of appellate courts have been wrong for a period of more than seventy-five years, when they believed and manifested a belief that facilities equal though separate were within the meaning of the Fourteenth Amendment.

Justice Harold Burton responded to this with a question

[30] *Argument . . . , op. cit.,* p. 217.
[31] In *Gong Lum* v. *Rice,* 275 U.S. 78 (1927), the Supreme Court held that a child of Chinese parentage could be excluded from a white school and required to go to a black school under a state segregation law.

that showed something of how deeply the argument troubled him and delineated something, too, of the limits of strict constructionism.

Don't you recognize it as possible that within seventy-five years the social and economic conditions and the personal relations of the nation may have changed so that what may have been a valid interpretation of them seventy-five years ago would not be a valid interpretation of them constitutionally today?[32]

A strong pull in the direction of overturning the separate-but-equal doctrine was presented by Thurgood Marshall, the chief counsel for the black school children, and later, himself, to become an associate justice of the Supreme Court. "Is it fair to assume," Justice Stanley Reed asked him from the bench, "that the legislation involving South Carolina, as these cases do, was passed for the purpose of avoiding racial friction?" And Mr. Marshall answered, in part, as follows:

I think, considering the legislatures, that we have to bear in mind that I know of no Negro legislator in any of these states, and I do not know whether they consider the Negro's side or not. It is just a fact. But I assume that there are people who will say that it was and is necessary, and my answer to that is, even if the concession is made that it was necessary in 1895, it is not necessary now because people have grown up and understand each other.

They are fighting together and living together. For example, today they are working together in other places. As a result of the ruling of this Court, they are going together on the higher level. Just how far it goes—I think when we predict what might happen, I know in the South where I spent most of my time, you will see white and colored kids going down the road together to school. They separate and go to different schools, and they come out and play together. I do not see why there would necessarily be any trouble if they went to school together.[33]

[32] *Argument . . . , op. cit.*, p. 32.
[33] *Ibid.*, pp. 66–67.

Later in the argument, James E. Nabrit, another of the lawyers for the plaintiffs, this time dealing with the special problem of segregated schools in the District of Columbia, summed
up the contention for a recognition of change, for adaptation
to new circumstances. Mr. Nabrit said in his peroration:

> It would appear to me that in 1952, the Negro should not be
> viewed as anybody's burden. He is a citizen. He is performing his
> duties in peace and in war, and today, on the bloody hills of Korea,
> he is serving in an unsegregated war.
>
> All we ask of this Court is that it say that under the Constitution
> he is entitled to live and send his children to school in the District of
> Columbia unsegregated, with the children of his war comrades.
> That is simple. The Constitution gives him that right. . . .
>
> We submit that in this case, in the heart of the nation's capital,
> in the capital of democracy, in the capital of the free world, there
> is no place for a segregated school system. This country cannot
> afford it, and the Constitution does not permit it, and the statutes of
> Congress do not authorize it.[34]

The argument for adaptation to changed circumstances in a
changed political climate prevailed. Indeed, it was principally
on this basis that the Court bottomed its decision. Noting that
public education and compulsory school attendance were rar-
ities until the twentieth century, Chief Justice Earl Warren
wrote for the Court:

> In approaching this problem we cannot turn the clock back to
> 1868 when the Amendment was adopted, or even to 1896 when
> Plessy v. Ferguson was written. We must consider public education
> in the light of its full development and its present place in Ameri-
> can life throughout the Nation. Only in this way can it be deter-
> mined if segregation in public schools deprives these plaintiffs of
> the equal protection of the laws.
>
> Today, education is perhaps the most important function of
> state and local governments. Compulsory school attendance laws
> and the great expenditures for education both demonstrate our

[34] *Ibid.*, p. 142.

recognition of the importance of education to our democratic society. It is required in the performance of our most basic public responsibilities, even service in the armed forces. It is the very foundation of good citizenship. Today it is a principal instrument in awakening the child to cultural values, in preparing him for later professional training, and in helping him to adjust normally to his environment. In these days, it is doubtful that any child may reasonably be expected to succeed in life if he is denied the opportunity of an education. Such an opportunity, where the state has undertaken to provide it, is a right which must be made available to all on equal terms.

We come then to the question presented: Does segregation of children in public schools solely on the basis of race, even though the physical facilities and other "tangible" factors may be equal, deprive the children of the minority group of equal educational opportunities? We believe that it does. . . .

Whatever may have been the extent of psychological knowledge at the time of Plessy v. Ferguson, *this finding is amply supported by modern authority.*[35] *Any language in* Plessy v. Ferguson *contrary to this finding is rejected.*

We conclude that in the field of public education the doctrine of "separate but equal" has no place. Separate educational facilities are inherently unequal.

The Supreme Court was unanimous in this decision. Its unanimity—a powerful influence in winning public acceptance of so dramatic a change in a national culture pattern—came about in considerable measure through the tact, patience, and astute judicial leadership of Chief Justice Earl Warren, who had assumed his office just in time to hear argument in this landmark case. That unanimity was maintained in the Court through a succession of subsequent cases regarding the use of parks, recreational facilities, and other facilities made avail-

---

[35] At this point in its opinion, the Court in a footnote cited half a dozen scholarly studies by well-known psychologists and sociologists respecting the baleful influence of segregation on children. Critics of the decision have remonstrated that the Court ought not to have taken judicial notice of such nonlegal works of scholarship—as though they believed that judges, to be judicious, ought to keep themselves ignorant of the facts of life.

able to the public under state sponsorship. The separate-but-equal fallacy was discarded—forever, one may hope.

What part did John Marshall Harlan's fierce and eloquent dissent in *Plessy* play in persuading the Supreme Court fifty-eight years later to recognize the evils he foresaw and reject a formulation of the law on which lawyers and judges had confidently relied for so many years? It is interesting, although probably of very little significance, that in his rather terse opinion for the Court in *Brown* v. *Board of Education* Chief Justice Warren made no reference to Harlan's *Plessy* dissent—an opinion, it must be remembered, that concerned public transportation, not public schools. The bases on which Harlan rested his objections to the *Plessy* rule were quite different, moreover, from Warren's premises in overturning that rule. Warren's principal argument was that changes in American life—the contemporary importance of public education, compulsory school attendance, new understanding of the psychological impact of forced segregation—made racially segregated schooling in 1954 inherently unequal and therefore a denial of the equal protection of the laws, whatever it may have been in Homer Plessy's day. He contended simply that, in the slow process of political evolution, the time had come for the abandonment of racial segregation.

All the same, John Marshall Harlan had played a vital role in that process. He stated the fundamental truth that racial segregation violated the essential spirit and aim of the Fourteenth Amendment, that it inevitably injured and humiliated the minority race, and that it inexorably bred hatred and disunity within the country. Harlan foresaw those evils before they became generally apparent. He spoke as a seer, before his time—before the time was ripe for the acceptance of what he saw.

It can hardly be said that the vision and fire of Harlan's dissenting opinion turned the Court around, as though in 1954 that dissent was suddenly read with understanding for the first time. Yet it can hardly be said, either, that his vision and fire were altogether without effect upon succeeding judges. Every time members of the Supreme Court were called upon to decide a case entailing racial segregation, they were obliged to reread the fatuous words of Justice Brown and to be reminded by Justice Harlan's stinging refutation that the decision was juridically—and ethically—wrong. Harlan's dissent had become a part of the law's literature and, as happens with most prophecy, its rightness was recognized long before its warning was heeded. That impact is the utimate justification of dissent in a court of last resort.

III

"THE RIGHT MOST VALUED
BY CIVILIZED MEN"

Olmstead v. *United States*, Louis D. Brandeis dissenting*

For half a century, and probably more, the telephone has been an indispensable means of communication in this country. By the 1920s it was in general use throughout the United States, although it is said that Herbert Hoover was the first American president to keep such an instrument on his desk; preceding presidents had gone to an adjoining room in the White House to make their telephone calls. If the telephone of the 1920s was still a fairly primitive instrument by contemporary standards, the techniques for tapping it were then relatively primitive, too; and users of the telephone generally believed that, except on rural party lines, they could carry on conversations in confidence. No business enterprise of any magnitude could be conducted without the telephone, and social intercourse was deeply dependent on it. For legitimate and illegitimate undertakings alike, it was an absolute necessity. Thus, for example, in Seattle, Washington, in 1924, it was effectively employed in a service industry that met the demands of a great

* 277 U.S. 438 (1928).

number of otherwise law-abiding consumers but that, nevertheless, undoubtedly transgressed an act of Congress, adopted in 1920, forbidding the transportation or sale of alcoholic beverages anywhere in the United States.

An enterprising, energetic individual named Ralph Olmstead headed a complex, highly integrated organization engaged in the business of bootlegging in the Puget Sound area of the state of Washington. His was by no means a shoestring operation. Begun with an investment of $10,000 of his own and $1,000 from each of ten associates, it had grown to embrace a small fleet of seagoing vessels and speedboats to bring liquor in from British Columbia, a ranch or farm outside Seattle where large quantities of the stock in trade were stored in an underground cache, trucks and automobiles for local delivery, and several garages that served as storage depots. Numerous office workers, sales personnel, scouts, transfer men, telephone operators, dispatchers, three bookkeepers, and a lawyer were required to handle the daily sale of more than 200 cases in the Seattle area. It was considered a poor month in which the organization's volume fell below $200,000. When, at last, Prohibition agents rounded up all those involved and persuaded a grand jury to indict them for conspiring to violate the Volstead Act, they named in the indictment no fewer than ninety-one persons. They were tried in three groups, and the trials took five weeks, during the whole of which the jury was sequestered. Some of those named in the conspiracy were never apprehended; some were acquitted; in the end twenty-one individuals were convicted on two counts of conspiracy. They were given fines and jail sentences.

The principal office of the Olmstead business was located in Room 1025 of the Henry Building in Seattle. Under the direction of William M. Whitney, the federal agent in charge at Seattle, Treasury agents rented Room 925 directly beneath the bootleggers' headquarters. Richard L. Fryant, another Prohibition agent and a former telephone-company lineman, installed a tap on a telephone listed as Elliott 6785 and located in the room above. Subsequently, other telephones belonging to the bootleggers were tapped in their homes as well as in their offices.

For a period of about five months, the Prohibition agents listened indiscriminately and omnivorously to all that was said on the syndicate telephones. They had no recording devices to take down what they overheard. So, instead, they relied on Agent Whitney's wife, who was a stenographer and who took down some of the conversations in shorthand; they tended to be tediously similar. Sometimes the agents themselves listened, taking notes as they did so, and told the substance of what they remembered to Mrs. Whitney, who wrote down an account of it. By these means, the eavesdroppers compiled a volume of 775 pages that they took into court with them and used to refresh their recollections when the Olmstead crowd was placed on trial. They identified the speakers whose words they quoted by an asserted recognition of their voices on the telephone: the Prohibition men and the bootleggers knew each other pretty well.

This is a form of testimony reasonably open to objection. Identification by ear is even more liable to be mistaken than identification by eye. Notes taken by one person and transcribed by another may embrace inaccuracies, not to mention fabrications. At the trial, the defense fought furiously to keep testimony based on the 775-page book from being presented to the jury. Witnesses were charged with offering testimony that was not genuinely independent. The voice identifications were denounced as unreliable. All of the material was challenged by defense attorneys as "incompetent, irrelevant and immaterial."

Defense objections to this testimony had, moreover, a still more formidable foundation. A Washington state law made it a misdemeanor to tap a telephone. The defense contended that all the prosecution evidence based upon wiretapping must be excluded from the trial because it was obtained by lawless action on the part of the government's agents. Finally, and fundamentally, the defense asserted that the testimony based on wire tapping was inadmissible because it was derived from an unreasonable search of a sort expressly forbidden by the Fourth Amendment to the United States Constitution. The Fourth Amendment provides that "The right of the people to be secure in their persons, houses, papers, and effects, against unreasonable searches and seizures, shall not be violated."

The trial judge rejected all these objections, however, and the testimony of the Prohibition agents, refreshed constantly from the big volume, droned on and on, day after day, disclosing beyond any possibility of doubt that a thriving and extensive traffic in liquor had been going on, almost openly. The bootleggers had hardly troubled to disguise their activities and seemed more amused than annoyed by the efforts of the Prohibition agents to catch them. There were numerous intimations in the tapped conversations that they felt thoroughly safeguarded by arrangements with local police authorities. Prohibition Agent Earl Corwin, for example, testified that he listened to the following exchange:

> *McLean asked how things were going, and Olmstead said, "Fine, I have been wrapping and delivering like hell all day today." McLean said, "You will be unlucky at that some day." Olmstead replied, "No, I won't. The City won't, and the Federals can't." McLean said, "They will slip up on you." And Olmstead used some very obscene language and said they were too slow to catch cold.*

Relations between the bootleggers and the federal agents were, on the whole, rather open and good-tempered. The bootleggers knew they were under constant surveillance but apparently felt sure that the officers would be unable to do anything about them. Earl Corwin testified at another point in the trial about the raiding of a garage where the agents knew that the syndicate stored liquor for delivery:

> *We made a search of the garage and Green and Olmstead said, "You are certainly not going to take us down for this?" And I replied,*

"We do not know yet." He said, "You ought to wait until you find us with some whiskey. If you had waited half an hour longer, you probably would have." I said, "We may wait for it to get here." He said, "No, we always have our scouts on the outside, and the load is headed off by now and you might as well go home. What do you say to all of us going downtown to breakfast together? Everything is off for the morning." A few minutes later I asked Kern what he was doing there, and he said he came to get his car repaired. Olmstead said, "Yes, we all brought our cars to have them repaired." They were all standing lined up in a row. After making a thorough search of the garage, Mr. Whitney and I left and I took up a position about half a block from the garage. Immediately after I left, all of them drove out and went away.

Raids such as this netted only the small fry of the Olmstead syndicate and provided proof of no more than minor culpability in what the government men knew to be a major conspiracy. Undoubtedly, knowledge of the syndicate's operations gleaned through wire tapping was of immense help to the agents in implicating the principal conspirators and in convincing a jury by the evidence of their own admissions that they were conscious participants in a gross, intentional violation of the law.

It is impossible, nevertheless, to ignore the fact that these were admissions that the defendants did not mean to make— or, at least, did not mean to make for the benefit of the court —and thus there is substance to the defense argument that they amounted not only to searches of a sort forbidden by the Fourth Amendment, but also to a compulsory self-incrimination forbidden by the Fifth Amendment.

The testimony at the Olmstead trial reveals, moreover, another troubling—and ineradicable—characteristic of wire tapping: its dragnet quality. It engorges not only what law-enforcement officers may be seeking, but a great deal of wholly irrelevant information of no public significance. Some testimony given at the trial, over vehement defense objection, by

G. W. Behner, a government witness, affords an illustration of the point.

> *On November 29, 1924, at 4:55 P.M., over Kenwood 1050, I heard Bill Smith. The conversation was between Bill Smith and a woman who gave her name as Hazel. There was a lot of general conversation regarding a meeting. She asked Smith where he was and he said he was just up the hill from the place and she asked him if he could come down to supper, and Smith replied that he could not come, that he had to work, that he had to clean everything out. Then there was some general conversation about a meeting between the two that night and the woman suggested meeting downtown and Bill Smith said that she knew that he could not run around Ruth downtown.*

The pertinence of this testimony to a prosecution for conspiracy to violate the Volstead Act is not readily discernible. And what "Ruth" may have thought about it when she heard it, the record does not disclose.

The trial judge's determination that the information gleaned by wire tapping was admissible in the prosecution of Olmstead and his associates won agreement from two of the three judges who reviewed the case for the Ninth Circuit Court of Appeals. They upheld the convictions.

Chief Judge Frank H. Rudkin dissented, however—and in language that showed the intensity of his feeling. He quoted an earlier decision of the Supreme Court, holding that "no law of Congress can place in the hands of officials connected with the postal service any authority to invade the secrecy of letters and such sealed packages in the mail; and all regulations adopted as to mail matter of this kind must be in subordination to the great principle embodied in the fourth amendment of the Constitution." Judge Rudkin himself then went on to say:

And, it is the contents of the letter, not the mere paper that is thus protected. What is the distinction between a message sent by letter and a message sent by telegraph or by telephone? True, the one is visible, the other invisible; the one is tangible, the other intangible; the one is sealed and the other unsealed, but these are distinctions without a difference. A person using the telegraph or telephone is not broadcasting to the world. His conversation is sealed from the public as completely as the nature of the instrumentalities employed will permit, and no federal officer or federal agent has a right to take his message from the wires in order that it may be used against him. Such a situation would be deplorable and intolerable to say the least. Must the millions of people who use the telephone every day for lawful purposes have their messages interrupted and intercepted in this way? Must their personal, private and confidential communications to family, friends and business associates pass through any such scrutiny on the part of agents, in whose selection they have no choice, and for the faithful performance of whose duties they have no security? Agents, whose very names and official stations are in many instances concealed and kept from them? If ills such as these must be borne, our forefathers signally failed in their desire to ordain and establish a Government to secure the blessings of liberty to themselves and their posterity.

The *Olmstead* case did not come to the Supreme Court of the United States until 1928. The Court agreed to hear it under the distinct limitation that the hearing should be confined to the single question of whether the use of evidence of private telephone conversations between the defendants and others, intercepted by means of wire tapping, amounted to a violation of the Fourth and Fifth Amendments. In its opinion and in some of the dissents, however, the Court went beyond this limitation and dealt with the other principal issue raised by the defense—whether evidence obtained through violation of a state law is admissible in a federal court. Chief Justice William Howard Taft, former president of the United States and a symbol of establishmentarianism, wrote a long, detailed, and powerfully reasoned opinion of the Court:

There is no room in the present case for applying the Fifth Amendment unless the Fourth Amendment was first violated. There was no evidence of compulsion to induce the defendants to talk over their many telephones. They were continually and voluntarily trans-acting business without knowledge of the interception. Our con-sideration must be confined to the Fourth Amendment. . . . The Amendment itself shows that the search is to be of material things —the person, the house, his papers or his effects. The description of the warrant necessary to make the proceedings lawful, is that it must specify the places to be searched and the persons or things to be seized. . . .

The Amendment does not forbid what was done here. There was no searching. There was no seizure. The evidence was secured by the use of the sense of hearing and that only. There was no entry of the houses or offices of the defendants. . . .

By the invention of the telephone fifty years ago and its applica-tion for the purpose of extending communications, one can talk with another at a far distant place. The language of the Amendment cannot be extended and expanded to include telephone wires reach-ing to the whole world from the defendant's house or office. The intervening wires are not part of his house or office any more than are the highways along which they are stretched. . . .

Congress may, of course, protect the secrecy of telephone mes-sages by making them, when intercepted, inadmissible in evidence in federal criminal trials, by direct legislation, and thus depart from the common law of evidence. But the courts may not adopt such a policy by attributing an enlarged and unusual meaning to the Fourth Amendment. The reasonable view is that one who installs in his house a telephone instrument with connecting wires intends to project his voice to those quite outside, and that the wires beyond his house and messages while passing over them are not within the protection of the Fourth Amendment. Here, those who intercepted the projected voices were not in the house of either party to the conversation.

So much for the Fourth Amendment. From here, the chief justice went on to consider the contention that the wiretap evidence "was inadmissible because the mode of obtaining it was unethical and a misdemeanor under the law of Washington." He dealt with this no less magisterially:

The common law rule is that the admissibility of evidence is not affected by the illegality of the means by which it was obtained. . . .

Nor can we, without the sanction of congressional enactment, subscribe to the suggestion that the courts have a discretion to exclude evidence, the admission of which is not unconstitutional, because unethically secured. This would be at variance with the common law doctrine generally supported by authority. There is no case that sustains, nor any recognized text book that gives color to such a view. Our general experience shows that much evidence has always been received although not obtained by conformity to the highest ethics. The history of criminal trials shows numerous cases of prosecutions of oath-bound conspiracies for murder, robbery, and other crimes, where officers of the law have disguised themselves and joined the organizations, taken the oaths and given themselves every appearance of active members engaged in the promotion of crime, for the purpose of securing evidence. Evidence secured by such means has always been received.

A standard which would forbid the reception of evidence if obtained by other than nice ethical conduct by government officials would make society suffer and give criminals greater immunity than has been known heretofore. In the absence of controlling legislation by Congress, those who realize the difficulties in bringing offenders to justice may well deem it wise that the exclusion of evidence should be confined to cases where rights under the Constitution would be violated by admitting it.

There is an impressive and persuasive internal logic to this argument. It affords an insight into what is loosely called "strict constructionism." The Fourth Amendment speaks only of material things; therefore, utterances and ideas cannot be brought within its penumbra. The emphasis is entirely on trespass, on physical invasion of private premises, without consideration for the larger interests that may be entailed in other forms of intrusion upon more subtle sorts of privacy such as confidential communication. In short, because the authors of the Fourth

Amendment had been unable to foresee the invention of the telephone and had stipulated protection only for "persons, houses, papers, and effects," the amendment's guarantee cannot be said to apply to the communication of confidences by electronic means. If this is not strict construction, it is certainly a narrow sort of literalism.

There is no doubt that the chief justice was right in his pronouncement regarding the common-law rule on the admissibility of illegally obtained evidence.[1] The question is whether it was a sound rule. When courts accept evidence gained by unlawful police conduct, they encourage the continuance of such conduct; the consequence may be to pollute the purity of the judicial process by making the courts accomplices of lawbreakers and so to diminish respect for the law in general. At least in part on this theory, the Supreme Court has, ever since 1914,[2] forbidden federal courts to accept evidence obtained in violation of the Fourth Amendment; and in 1961 it applied this rule to state courts as well.[3]

The Supreme Court was narrowly divided in the *Olmstead* case—5 to 4 for the Taft view. Justice Holmes wrote a brief and brilliant dissent in which, without committing himself on the constitutional question, he expressed strong distaste for the use of evidence obtained, and only obtainable, by criminal conduct on the part of government officers. "There is no body of precedents," he said, "by which we are bound, and which confines us to logical deduction from established rules. Therefore we must consider the two objects of desire, both of which

---

[1] The textbook case on this question is *Commonwealth* v. *Wilkins*, 243 Mass. 356, 138 N.E. 11, in which the Supreme Court of Massachusetts said in a search-and-seizure case in 1923: "It is a generally recognized principle of the law of evidence that courts do not pause in the trial of cases to investigate whether physical evidence . . . was obtained lawfully or unlawfully. That is regarded as a collateral inquiry. The only matter considered by the court is whether such evidence is pertinent to the issue. Courts do not impose an indirect penalty upon competent evidence because of illegality in obtaining it. . . ."

[2] Weeks v. United States, 232 U.S. 382 (1914).

[3] Mapp v. Ohio, 367 U.S. 643 (1961).

we cannot have, and make up our minds which to choose. It is desirable that criminals should be detected, and to that end that all available evidence should be used. It also is desirable that the Government should not itself foster and pay for other crimes, when they are the means by which the evidence is to be obtained. If it pays its officers for having got evidence by crime I do not see why it may not as well pay them for getting it in the same way, and I can attach no importance to protestations of disapproval if it knowingly accepts and pays and announces that in future it will pay for the fruits. We have to choose, and for my part I think it a less evil that some criminals should escape than that the Government should play an ignoble part."

It was in this opinion that Justice Holmes used the expression "dirty business" so frequently quoted and so commonly supposed to refer to wire tapping. But what Holmes condemned as "dirty" was not so much the tapping of Olmstead's telephones as the use of evidence collected in that way by a court of the United States when the state of Washington had made telephone tapping a crime. "If the existing code does not permit district attorneys to have a hand in such dirty business," he said, "it does not permit the judge to allow such iniquities to succeed." And he concluded his two-paragraph dissent by contradicting the chief justice's interpretation of the *Weeks* doctrine: "if we are to confine ourselves to precedent and logic, the reason for excluding evidence obtained by violating the Constitution seems to me logically to lead to excluding evidence obtained by a crime of the officers of the law."

It is a generally accepted practice of the Supreme Court to avoid reaching constitutional questions when it is possible to decide a case on simpler grounds. Perhaps it was this consideration that led Holmes to say, "While I do not deny it, I am not prepared to say that the penumbra of the Fourth and Fifth Amendments covers the defendant, although I fully agree that Courts are apt to err by sticking too closely to the words of a law where those words import a policy that goes beyond them." Justice Pierce Butler did not feel the same constraint. He dissented briefly, asserting that the wire tapping in this case "literally constituted a search for evidence" and thus violated both the Fourth and Fifth Amendments. In a one-paragraph dissent, Justice Harlan Stone expressed agreement with all the other dissenters.

It remained for Justice Louis D. Brandeis, in one of the most impassioned dissents in American legal literature, to give exhaustive examination to both of the great issues involved in the case. No less than Holmes a believer in the avoidance of any great constitutional question if a case could be disposed of on a lesser ground, Brandeis felt in this instance that the constitutional clash was inescapable. He pleaded for an application of the Fourth and Fifth Amendments not in their narrow, literal terms, but in their larger design as safeguarding a right of privacy essential to the idea of human dignity and personal integrity. Here, in part, is what he wrote:

When the Fourth and Fifth Amendments were adopted . . . force and violence were then the only means known to man by which a Government could directly effect self-incrimination. It could compel the individual to testify—a compulsion effected, if need be, by torture. It could secure possession of his papers and other articles incident to his private life—a seizure effected, if need be, by breaking and entry. Protection against such invasion of "the sanctities of a man's home and the privacies of life" was provided in the Fourth and Fifth Amendments by specific language. . . . But "time works changes, brings into existence new conditions and purposes." Subtler and more far-reaching means of invading privacy have become available to the Government. . . . by means far more effective than stretching upon the rack, to obtain disclosure in court of what is whispered in the closet. . . .

. . . The progress of science in furnishing the Government with means of espionage is not likely to stop with wire-tapping. Ways may some day be developed by which the Government, without removing papers from secret drawers, can reproduce them in court, and by which it will be enabled to expose to a jury the most intimate occurrences of the home. . . .

. . . The evil incident to invasion of the privacy of the telephone is far greater than that involved in tampering with the mails. Whenever a telephone line is tapped, the privacy of the persons at both ends of the line is invaded and all conversations between them upon any subject, and although proper, confidential and privileged, may be overheard. Moreover, the tapping of one man's telephone line involves the tapping of the telephone of every other person whom he may call or who may call him. As a means of espionage, writs of assistance and general warrants are but puny instruments of tyranny and oppression when compared with wire-tapping.

. . . The makers of our Constitution undertook to secure conditions favorable to the pursuit of happiness. . . . They conferred, as against the Government, the right to be let alone—the most comprehensive of rights and the right most valued by civilized men. To protect that right, every unjustifiable intrusion by the Government upon the privacy of the individual, whatever the means employed, must be deemed a violation of the Fourth Amendment. And the use, as evidence in a criminal proceeding, of facts ascertained by such intrusion must be deemed a violation of the Fifth.

. . . It is, of course, immaterial where the physical connection with the telephone wires leading into the defendant's premises was made. And it is also immaterial that the intrusion was in aid of law enforcement. Experience should teach us to be most on our guard to protect liberty when the Government's purposes are beneficent. Men born to freedom are naturally alert to repel invasion of their liberty by evil-minded rulers. The greatest dangers to liberty lurk in insidious encroachment by men of zeal, well-meaning but without understanding.[4]

Brandeis then turned his attention to the matter that had provoked Holmes's dissent—whether the government could properly use evidence obtained by violating the laws of the state of Washington. He closed his great opinion with this observation:

Decency, security and liberty alike demand that government officials shall be subjected to the same rules of conduct that are

---

[4] The full text of the Brandeis dissent can be found in the appendix.

*commands to the citizen. In a government of laws, existence of the
government will be imperilled if it fails to observe the law scrupulously. Our Government is the potent, the omnipresent teacher. For
good or for ill, it teaches the whole people by its example. Crime is
contagious. If the Government becomes a law-breaker, it breeds
contempt for law; it invites every man to become a law unto himself; it invites anarchy. To declare that in the administration of the
criminal law the end justifies the means—to declare that the Government may commit crimes in order to secure the conviction of a
private criminal—would bring terrible retribution. Against that
pernicious doctrine this Court should resolutely set its face.*

The idea of a right to privacy—a "right to be let alone,"
which he assessed in his *Olmstead* dissent as "the right most
valued by civilized men"—was a preoccupation with Louis D.
Brandeis, almost an obsession, throughout his life. When he
was a young man, he wrote for the *Harvard Law Review*, in
collaboration with his close friend and law partner, Samuel
Warren, an article entitled "The Right to Privacy," which
created a considerable stir when it was published in 1890 and
which has been recognized since as a classic statement of the
principle.[5] The article was concerned not with official eavesdropping, but with invasions of privacy by nongovernmental,
commercial enterprises—principally the press. The growth of
sensational journalism and the development of news photog-
raphy presented novel threats to personal dignity against
which Warren and Brandeis sought to develop some sort of
legal shield. The thesis they advanced in the article was that
the common law might be enlarged to embrace a protection
for a person's "emotions" and "spiritual nature" in much the
same way that the law had evolved to afford people protection
in the courts from assaults that might do injury to their bodies
or to their private property.

[5] Louis D. Brandeis and Samuel Warren, "The Right to Privacy," *Harvard
Law Review* Vol. 4 (1890), p. 193.

The 1890 article expressed a sensitivity and a concern for personal inviolability that were central to Brandeis's view of life as well as of the law. It foreshadowed his reaction thirty-eight years later to official intrusion into the asylum of the home and the confidences of private communication. The concept of the government of the United States as snooper and intruder in the name of law enforcement was utterly abhorrent to him. All this came to the surface in his *Olmstead* dissent.

Between Justice Brandeis and Chief Justice Taft there was a conflict that went beyond ideology. It had nothing to do with Taft's intemperate opposition when Brandeis's nomination was before the Senate for confirmation as an associate justice. That acerbity was healed by the experience of working together on the Court after the former president was chosen to be chief justice. But a gulf lay between them, growing out of their different natures and different backgrounds. Taft was a symbol and exemplar of the American establishment. Brandeis was basically an outsider, a critic, and a dissenter.

Justice Brandeis has sometimes been referred to as a modern Isaiah, and there is an aptness in the metaphor; undoubtedly he had a quality of the prophet in his style and in his idealism. If his background was less patrician (in a society-page sense) than Taft's, it was undoubtedly far richer in intellectual tradition. He grew up in a milieu that accorded the utmost respect to the individual personality, that regarded the home and family life as sacred, and that held, as Brandeis himself put it, that the final end of the state is simply "to make men free to develop their faculties." It is perhaps fair to say that out of his Jewish roots, Louis Brandeis drew an understanding of the significance of privacy that was never dreamed of in the philosophy of William Howard Taft.

Neither the opinion of the Court nor the Brandeis dissent appears to have stirred any great excitement at the time of the

Olmstead decision. Newspapers then tended to cover the Court only cursorily. Even *The New York Times* accorded the ruling scant attention. The law reviews and journals of the leading law schools commented on the case when the decision came down, of course. But they did not look upon it as a landmark in any way. At least one article, however—a Note in the *Notre Dame Lawyer* by Henry Hasley—presented a scathing criticism of the majority opinion and expressed warm sympathy for the force and majesty of Brandeis's dissent.

Most of the law-school publications took a conventional, law-and-order view of Chief Justice Taft's conventional, law-and-order justification of distasteful means to accomplish desirable ends. It was a period, somewhat like the present— perhaps somewhat like every period from the beginning of recorded history—in which there was great anxiety about the prevalence of crime. Prohibition had given rise to crime syndicates in every major American city, some of them a great deal more violent and more dangerous than Ralph Olmstead's friendly organization in Seattle. The warring bootleg mobs in New York and Chicago chilled the blood of citizens who regarded themselves as thoroughly law-abiding despite their persistent purchase of the illegal wares these lawless mobs purveyed—and over the profits of which they fought so bloodily.

The prevailing mood of the country was one of cynicism and a kind of world-weariness distrustful of the Wilsonian idealism that had taken the country into World War I. In that remarkably evocative "family album" he published in 1947, *I Remember Distinctly*, Frederick Lewis Allen summed it up in a paragraph that has a strikingly contemporaneous ring to it:

> *The widespread defiance of the prohibition laws was only one symptom of a pervasive change in American manners and customs during the post-war years. Great numbers of people had come out of their war experience feeling that ideals had been discredited, that those who talked about standards of conduct were old-fashioned and unrealistic, and that you might as well let the bars*

down and get yourself a good time whenever and wherever you could. Result: a rebellion against the puritan code of manners and morals, led by the "younger generation," who in great numbers went in for a new frankness of talk, an excited (if not obsessed) interest in sex, a tolerant acceptance of alcoholic conduct, and acceptance, too, of the permissibility of the petting-party (to use the favored term of that day), and a general lapse from gentility into rowdiness.

There is a paradoxical conjunction here of "permissiveness" on the one hand and acceptance of repressive governmental action on the other. But the paradox is more apparent than real. Then, as now, "permissiveness" was not much more than a euphemism for apathy or complacency. A similar sense that "anything goes"—that ethical standards no longer have relevance, that any means the government may choose to employ are permissible if they are resorted to in the name of law and order or national security—appears to have sprouted out of the soil of disillusionment following the Vietnam war.

In the country, as in the Court, at the time of the *Olmstead* decision, there probably was no more than a minority in sympathy with Louis Brandeis's austere standards for the conduct of law-enforcement officers and for the protection of an old-fashioned sort of privacy that might too easily serve as a shelter for criminals. The dominant view was expressed succinctly by George Ragland, Jr., in a Note on the *Olmstead* decision in the December, 1928, issue of the *Michigan Law Review*. His comment concluded as follows: "Nor need we seriously fear lest those who do not violate the law be deprived of their substantial right of being let alone, for even the most violent opponents of the majority opinion in the wiretapping case admit that thus far few persons other than the most flagrant of criminals have actually been molested. When this ceases to be true, it will be time enough for the courts to adjust the law to Mr. Justice Brandeis's 'new conditions.' "

In the decades that have followed, Justice Brandeis's nightmare vision of the potentialities of electronic eavesdropping has been terrifyingly fulfilled. Bugging and wire tapping have become almost universal law-enforcement devices with instruments of a sophistication unimagined in the 1920s. "Private eyes" have bugged and tapped at will, confident that they would not be molested by governmental authorities engaged in the same illegal practices. Industrial espionage, the collection of material for divorce proceedings or for blackmail, and political surveillance have reached epidemic proportions in the United States.

New techniques have made it easy to tap telephones without any physical trespass on the premises where the telephones are located. A variety of sensitive instruments have been perfected, capable of picking up conversations in homes or offices when the participants supposed they were speaking in complete confidence. A lugubrious insight into the capacities of these new tools for invading privacy is given by Alan F. Westin in his authoritative study of surveillance practices, *Privacy and Freedom:* "Any of the tiny mikes presently available can be attached by adhesive to the underside of furniture or by magnetic force to metal objects. They can also be installed inside telephones, intercoms, doorbell units, radios, TV's, water coolers, desk sets, clocks, picture frames, lamps, mattresses, flower pots, ash trays, cellophane-tape dispensers, bulletin boards, air conditioners, and a hundred other common objects within the room. A special microphone and transmitter have been built into a light bulb so that the transmitter begins broadcasting when the light switch is turned on and stops when it is turned off."[6]

In 1934, a few years after the *Olmstead* decision, Congress attempted to impose limits on the proliferating use of wiretaps by adopting the Federal Communications Act. Unfor-

[6] Alan F. Westin, *Privacy and Freedom* (New York: Atheneum, 1967), p. 74.

tunately, it incorporated into this law some extremely befud-
dling language from the Radio Act of 1927. Section 605 of the
Federal Communications Act of 1934 provided in part:

*No person not being authorized by the sender shall intercept
any communication and divulge or publish the existence, contents,
substance, purport, effect, or meaning of such intercepted communication to any person. . . .*

There were several things wrong with this statute. First, the
term "sender" was full of ambiguity. Second, the use of the
conjunctive "and" between "intercept" and "divulge" gave law-
enforcement authorities a pretext of a sort for contending that
the law could be violated only if a telephone conversation was
both intercepted *and* divulged and that, therefore, interception by itself was not unlawful. Third, law-enforcement authorities argued that the term "person" as used in the act did not
refer to an officer of the government. The Supreme Court was
obliged in 1937 to deal with these fictions in another case arising out of enforcement of the Prohibition law. Speaking for the
Court, Justice Owen J. Roberts said:

*The plain words of Sec. 605 forbid anyone, unless authorized by
the sender, to intercept a telephone message, and direct in equally
clear language that "no person" shall divulge or publish the message
or its substance to "any person." To recite the contents of the message in testimony before a court is to divulge the message. . . .*[7]

The opinion went on to say that government agents are
unmistakably *persons.* Although this ruling served to keep evidence gleaned through telephone tapping from being used in
federal courts—an exclusion that crime fighters found particularly galling—it did not *end* tapping. And it imposed no restraint of any kind on bugging.

In 1942, the Supreme Court dealt for the first time with a
case[8] in which evidence was obtained not by tapping a tele-

[7] Nardone v. United States, 302 U.S. 379 (1937). Italics in the original.
[8] Goldman v. United States, 316 U.S. 129 (1942).

phone, but by placing a sensitive listening device, called a detectaphone, on the wall of a room adjacent to an office in which a small group of lawyers were working out the details of a swindle in connection with a bankruptcy proceeding. The defendants, when they came to trial, tried to have this evidence suppressed, in part on the ground that it violated the Fourth Amendment. But Justice Roberts, writing for the Court majority, concluded that "No reasonable or logical distinction can be drawn between what federal agents did in the present case and what state officers [sic] did in the Olmstead case." Chief Justice Stone and Justice Frankfurter appended a note to the decision: "Had a majority of the Court been willing at this time to overrule the *Olmstead* case, we should have been happy to join them. But as they have declined to do so, and as we think this case is indistinguishable in principle from *Olmstead*'s, we have no occasion to repeat here the dissenting views in that case with which we agree."

For several years after the *Goldman* decision, the Court wrestled with half a dozen other cases involving aspects of electronic eavesdropping and squirmed uncomfortably in and out of acceptance of evidence obtained in this unsavory way. But always it found itself impaled on the prong of its 1928 decision in the *Olmstead* case. If the extension of an official ear by an electronic device—and for the purpose of obtaining evidence—into premises that citizens could reasonably regard as private, did not constitute a search within the meaning of the Fourth Amendment, then the Constitution afforded no safeguard against this kind of intrusion.

The nub of the problem lay in the "trespass doctrine" laid down by Chief Justice Taft in *Olmstead*—the assumption that a search occurred only when there was a physical intrusion upon private premises such as a house or an office. This interpreted the Fourth Amendment as intended to protect the premises rather than to protect the persons on those premises in the enjoyment of their privacy, particularly regarding the communication of their thoughts.

The anomaly was made almost ludicrously evident by a case that the Supreme Court decided in 1961.[9] The case concerned a man named Julius Silverman and some associates who were convicted of operating a gambling establishment in the District of Columbia. The District police gained evidence against Silverman by entering a house next door to his and driving an instrument called a "spike mike"—a microphone with a spike about a foot long attached to it—through a party wall until the spike touched a heating duct in the Silverman house that served as an excellent sound conductor.

The Supreme Court was unanimous in upsetting this conviction, distinguishing this case from *Goldman* on the ground that here the eavesdropping had involved a physical intrusion, a trespass. Justice Douglas in a concurring opinion asked a pertinent and illuminating question:

An electronic device on the outside wall of a house is a permissible invasion of privacy according to Goldman v. United States, *while an electronic device that penetrates the wall, as here, is not. Yet the invasion of privacy is as great in one case as in the other. The concept of "an unauthorized physical penetration into the premises," on which the present decision rests, seems to me to be beside the point. Was not the wrong in both cases done when the intimacies of the home were tapped, recorded, or revealed?*

The Court by this time was manifestly troubled by the contradictions and inadequacies of its position on electronic eavesdropping. And this unease was aggravated by knowledge that instruments, such as parabolic microphones and sonic-wave devices, had been developed to overhear conversations in a room without entering it physically in any way. Moreover, bugging and tapping in various forms by a great number of government agencies—often for purposes of sheer political surveillance—had become so widespread and so notorious as to

[9] Silverman v. United States, 365 U.S. 505 (1961).

warrant genuine anxiety about the state of civil liberty.[10] Justice William J. Brennan expressed this anxiety forcefully in a dissent that he wrote in another electronic-eavesdropping case decided by the Court in 1963.[11] Joined by Justice Douglas and Justice Goldberg, he articulated the grave threat that unregulated surveillance of this sort presented to all freedom of communication:

> *Electronic surveillance, in fact, makes the police omniscient; and police omniscience is one of the most effective tools of tyranny. . . . It must be plain that electronic surveillance imports a peculiarly severe danger to the liberties of the person. To be secure against police officers' breaking and entering to search for physical objects is worth very little if there is no security against the officers' using secret recording devices to purloin words spoken in confidence within the four walls of home or office. Our possessions are of little value compared to our personalities. . . . Electronic surveillance strikes deeper than at the ancient feeling that a man's home is his castle; it strikes at freedom of communication, a postulate of our kind of society. . . . If electronic surveillance by government becomes sufficiently widespread, and there is little in prospect for checking it, the hazard that as a people we may become hagridden and furtive is not fantasy. . . . This Court has, by and large, steadfastly enforced the Fourth Amendment against physical intrusions into person, home, and property by law enforcement officers. But our course of decisions, it now seems, has been outflanked by the technological advances of the very recent past. I cannot but believe that if we continue to condone electronic surveillance by federal agents by permitting the fruits to be used in evidence in the federal courts, we shall be contributing to a climate of official lawlessness and conceding the helplessness of the Constitution and this Court to protect rights "fundamental to a free society. . . ."*

At last, in 1967, the Court abandoned its "trespass" approach

---

[10] The formidable reach of such surveillance has subsequently been abundantly documented by the hearings of the U.S. Senate Subcommittee on Constitutional Rights in 1971 and the "Watergate" hearings of the Senate Select Subcommittee on Campaign Practices in 1973.

[11] Lopez v. United States, 373 U.S. 427 (1963).

to electronic surveillance and in two significant decisions embraced Justice Brandeis's view that such surveillance entails a search within the meaning of the Fourth Amendment. The Court also shifted its ground significantly, declaring that the purpose of the Fourth Amendment is to protect people, not merely places.

The first of the cases involved a test of a New York State law that sought to deal with the problem of electronic eavesdropping by recognizing it as a search and making it permissible as a law-enforcement tool only when, as in the case of an ordinary search, it was authorized in advance by a neutral judicial officer.[12] The case concerned a man named Berger, convicted on two counts of conspiracy to bribe the chairman of the New York State Liquor Authority. Berger's conviction was set aside by the Court and the New York law declared invalid because it entirely failed to meet the Fourth Amendment's insistence upon a warrant "particularly describing the place to be searched and the persons or things to be seized." Writing for the Court, Justice Tom C. Clark said, "New York's broadside authorization rather than being 'carefully circumscribed' so as to prevent unauthorized invasions of privacy actually permits general searches by electronic devices." While not explicitly overturning the *Olmstead* and *Goldman* decisions of the past, Justice Clark declared that "conversation was within the Fourth Amendment's protection" and "the use of electronic devices to capture it was a search within the meaning of the Amendment."

In his opinion in the *Berger* case, Justice Clark remarked that "It is said that neither a warrant nor a statute authorizing eavesdropping can be drawn so as to meet the Fourth Amendment's requirements. If that be true then the 'fruits' of eavesdropping devices are barred under the Amendment." In the *Katz* case (to be discussed presently), however, Justice Potter Stewart said that the surveillance conducted there had been

[12] Berger v. New York, 388 U.S. 41 (1967).

so narrowly circumscribed that it would have been valid had it been duly authorized in advance by a magistrate. Just how specific court orders authorizing electronic eavesdrops must be to make them constitutional remains to be determined. Following the Court's rather pointed suggestion in the *Berger* case, this is the direction in which Congress has chosen to move. As part of its Omnibus Crime Law, enacted in 1968, Congress provided in Title III for a court-authorization system for bringing electronic surveillance under reasonable control. Its constitutionality has yet to be tested. The dragnet character of this kind of investigation, the fact that anybody who happens to be in a bugged room or using a tapped telephone may be overheard, whether or not he has any connection with the crime being investigated and whether or not the subject of his conversation is wholly innocent and personal, all operate to make electronic surveillance, as Justice Brandeis foresaw, almost incurably injurious to reasonable rights of privacy.

Not long after the *Berger* decision—in fact, in the same year —the Court decided a case called *Katz* v. *United States*[13] in which, with only a single dissent by Justice Black,[14] the trespass doctrine was finally laid to rest. The case concerned a gambler who transmitted wagering information by telephone from Los Angeles to Miami and Boston, using a public telephone booth to the outside of which FBI agents had attached an electronic listening and recording device. Delivering the Court's opinion, Justice Stewart said:

[13] 389 U.S. 347 (1967).
[14] Justice Black's own peculiar brand of strict constructionism made him consistently "antilibertarian" where searches were concerned. The Fourth Amendment, he reminded his associates repeatedly, forbade only "unreasonable" searches. In his *Katz* dissent, he said: "Since I see no way in which the words of the Fourth Amendment can be construed to apply to eavesdropping, that closes the matter for me. In interpreting the Bill of Rights, I willingly go as far as a liberal construction of the language takes me, but I simply cannot in good conscience give a meaning to words which they have never before been thought to have and which they certainly do not have in common ordinary usage. I will not distort the words of the Amendment in order to 'keep the Constitution up to date' or 'bring it into harmony with the times.' It was never meant that this Court have such power, which in effect would make us a continuously functioning constitutional convention."

. . . Although a closely divided Court supposed in Olmstead that surveillance without any trespass and without the seizure of any material object fell outside the ambit of the Constitution, we have since departed from the narrow view on which that decision rested. Indeed, we have expressly held that the Fourth Amendment governs not only the seizure of tangible items, but extends as well to the recording of oral statements overheard without any "technical trespass under . . . local property law." Once this much is acknowledged, and once it is recognized that the Fourth Amendment protects people—and not simply "areas"—against unreasonable searches and seizures it becomes clear that the reach of that Amendment cannot turn upon the presence or absence of a physical intrusion into any given enclosure.

We conclude that the underpinnings of Olmstead and Goldman have been so eroded by our subsequent decisions that the "trespass" doctrine there enunciated can no longer be regarded as controlling. The Government's activities in electronically listening to and recording the petitioner's words violated the privacy upon which he justifiably relied while using the telephone booth and thus constituted a "search and seizure" within the meaning of the Fourth Amendment. The fact that the electronic device employed to achieve that end did not happen to penetrate the wall of the booth can have no constitutional significance.

When one rereads Justice Brandeis's moving dissent in the *Olmstead* case, written thirty-nine years before the Supreme Court embraced its essential ideas, one is struck first by the imaginative and genuinely prophetic quality of its warning about the ugly potentialities of electronic snooping. The evils about which Brandeis warned quickly became grim realities. The true importance of his dissent lies, however, in its visualization of privacy as an essential human value and in its broad reading of the Fourth Amendment as designed to guarantee that value, treating it as an integral aspect of human liberty.

A literal or strict constructionist reading of the Fourth Amendment can logically and rationally conclude that it was meant by its authors to do no more than forfend the general warrants and writs of assistance with which they were so painfully familiar—and to guarantee no more than the accepted English view that a man's home is his castle, secure against unwarranted entry by the king's men or by any governmental authority.

But the danger today is not that redcoats will cross the castle's threshold. The danger free men face is that their intimacies, their private sanctuaries, will be invaded by means of sophisticated scientific devices. The compelling need of free men in modern times is to keep intact some shelter, some sanctuary, some "castle" that is the symbol of privacy. Free men must still say to governmental authority: "So far and no farther."

This is what Louis Brandeis recognized and understood. The trouble with too literal a view of the Constitution is that it fails to take account of changes in the environment. What happened, as Justice Brennan astutely observed in his *Lopez* dissent, was that the Court's decisions regarding electronic surveillance were "outflanked by the technological advances of the very recent past."

If the Constitution says nothing about privacy, it says a great deal about liberty. Electronic eavesdropping is unmistakably a limitation of liberty. It puts a damper on the freedom most fundamental to a civilized and self-governing people—freedom of communication. It makes people fearful of talking with each other, fearful of voicing the criticism or scorn of official policy and performance which is the dynamo of the democratic process.

It is impossible to say precisely what effect Brandeis's dissent had upon changing the opinion of the Supreme Court in regard to privacy. Certainly it impelled reflection; more significantly, it invited a fresh breadth of outlook. His great contribution was that he looked beyond the Fourth Amendment's words—and discerned their meaning; he read the letter of the Constitution—and saw its spirit.

IV

"EQUAL JUSTICE UNDER THE LAW"

Betts v. *Brady*, Hugo L. Black dissenting[*]

None of the safeguards of the Bill of Rights is more wreathed in ambiguity than the Sixth Amendment's assurance of the right to counsel. What the Sixth Amendment says in plain, simple English is that "in all criminal prosecutions, the accused shall enjoy the right . . . to have the assistance of counsel for his defense." What it does *not* say is whether the enjoyment of that right shall depend upon the ability of the defendant to pay for a lawyer. If a lawyer is needed by an affluent defendant, he is no less needed, one would suppose, by an indigent defendant.

In 1942, the Supreme Court reviewed the conviction of a poor and luckless outcast who had been sentenced to prison for a robbery without enjoying any legal assistance at his trial. No one, of course, forbade him this assistance; the unlucky fact, so far as he was concerned, was simply that he could not afford it. The Supreme Court concluded that he had not been deprived of any constitutional right. Justice Hugo Black, sup-

[*] 316 U.S. 455 (1942).

ported by Justices Douglas and Murphy, vehemently dissented.[1] Reviewing a strikingly similar case twenty-one years later, the Court ruled, in an opinion written for it by the same Justice Black, that the assistance of counsel appointed at public expense when a defendant charged with a felony could not afford to retain a lawyer himself was an essential element of the due process assured by the Fourteenth Amendment.[2] The two cases, substantially alike in circumstances and indistinguishable respecting the constitutional question they raised, afford a pretty good insight into the process of constitutional evolution.

The first case concerned an unemployed farm worker named Smith Betts, forty-three years old and on relief at the time, who was charged with committing an armed robbery on Christmas Eve, 1938, near a country store in Carroll County, Maryland. According to the indictment against him and the testimony of prosecution witnesses, he had, in the dusk of the late winter afternoon, accosted a young employee of the store, named Norman Bollinger, who had just gotten into his car with the day's receipts. The bulk of these receipts were in a brown envelope, which Bollinger had put down on the car seat. In his hand was a brown paper bag containing $50 in coins. A man came to the side of the car, drew a pistol from his overcoat pocket, and ordered him to hand over the money. According to his testimony at the trial, Bollinger at first refused, but on hearing the click of what he took to be the pistol hammer or safety catch, handed over the bag of coins, though not the more valuable envelope. The man walked over to another car, with a driver in it apparently waiting for him, and drove away.

Smith Betts was speedily arrested as a suspect in the case, was indicted for armed robbery and assault, and was brought to trial in May, 1939, before Judge William H. Forsythe, Jr., in

---

[1] The complete text of Justice Black's dissent can be found in the appendix.

[2] Gideon v. Wainwright, 372 U.S. 335 (1963). A Supreme Court decision in 1972 extended this protection to a defendant charged with a misdemeanor. Argersinger v. Hamlin 407 U.S. 25 (1972).

the Circuit Court for Carroll County. At his arraignment, Betts pleaded not guilty and asked Judge Forsythe to appoint a lawyer to advise and help him, asserting that he could not afford to pay for a lawyer himself. The judge advised him that it was the practice in Carroll County to appoint counsel for indigent defendants only in cases of murder and rape—that is, in cases where a death penalty might be the consequence of conviction—and therefore refused to appoint counsel in this case. Betts had initially said he wanted to be tried by a jury but, on learning that he would not have a lawyer to represent him, changed his mind and waived a jury trial. He continued staunchly, however, to insist that he was innocent.

Norman Bollinger was, of course, the prosecution's first and principal witness. After telling about the holdup itself, he gave this description of the robber:

It was fairly dark but I could see that the man had on a dark overcoat and a handkerchief around his chin and a pair of dark amber glasses. The handerchief was not over his chin. He also had on a hat. I am employed by Medford Grocery Company, and he got the change bag, which had exactly fifty dollars in it. There was another fellow in his car with him but I couldn't identify him because his car was opposite mine and I didn't see him, and he stayed in the car and kept it ready to get away, and he didn't get out of the car.

Then, after testifying that he called the police to report the robbery and to ask for help, young Mr. Bollinger said something rather remarkable:

Subsequently I was called to jail, where the State police asked me if I could identify this man. I told them that I wasn't sure I could identify him without the glasses and the handkerchief, after seeing him when it was almost dark that evening. Smith Betts put on the glasses and then I could identify him.

At this point Judge Forsythe intervened briefly and the following colloquy took place:

Q. *(by the Court) Did you identify him?*
A. *Yes, sir.*
Q. *Are you positive that is the man?*
A. *Yes, sir.*

The state's attorney, George N. Fringer, then sought to establish another mode of identification:

Q. *Before you saw Smith Betts over at the jail, did you hear anything? Did you hear him speak or anything like that?*
A. *Yes, sir, as we stood out in the hall they had him in there and asked him questions to see if I could identify his voice. I told them before he had an awful determined voice, rough sort of voice, and I could identify that as I stood in the hall as the voice that was there that evening.*

The state called three other witnesses to identify Smith Betts, two of them employees of the Medford Grocery Company, the third a customer who happened to be in the store when Betts allegedly appeared there on the afternoon of December 24, shortly before the robbery. All of them noted Betts's "rough voice" and all of them recognized him as the man they had seen on that afternoon, although none of them, of course, had witnessed the crime itself. One of them, a witness named Harry W. Poole, was particularly forceful in his identification.

I work for the Medford Grocery Company, and about closing time on December 24th, 1938, I saw Mr. Betts in the main building of the grocery department where I worked. He was with another fellow and they bought a few things. I am sure that it was Smith Betts, because I have known him before. His father used to live and farm not very far from where I lived. I hadn't seen him for four or five years, but I have no doubt that it was he.

Cross-examined by Betts, acting as his own attorney, Poole added:

I could identify the clothes you had on and I knowed your voice as soon as I heard it. That was the first thing that drawed my attention to you, your voice. It may be possible that I haven't seen you since 1923; I couldn't tell you just how long it's been; it's been a long time, I know that.

That was the whole of the state's case, and a powerful case it was. Betts, acting perforce without any professional legal counsel, assumed the heavy burden of proving it mistaken. He made several strategic decisions the wisdom of which might be called into question by men more sophisticated in the law. To begin with, he decided to waive his right to a jury trial. There are pros and cons to that decision; Betts's judgment of them may have been colored in some degree by a feeling that his ignorance of legal forms and procedures would be more disadvantageous to him before a jury.

Second, although Betts pleaded not guilty, he chose not to take the witness stand in his own defense. No doubt his judgment on this point was strongly influenced by the fact that in 1935 he had been convicted of larceny and had been sentenced to serve three years in the Maryland House of Correction on a plea of guilty. Had he elected to testify, this damaging facet of his past would surely have been exposed and stressed by the prosecution, a serious consideration in a jury trial; but the judge, schooled in the law, might more confidently have been counted on to ignore it in deciding between guilt and innocence of the current crime.

Among jailhouse lawyers—among those convicts in prison who acquire a certain shrewdness about the law through frequent brushes with it and from whom Betts probably learned what little he knew about legal procedures—it is axiomatic that the witness stand should be avoided at all costs by defendants with a record and, of course, by a defendant with a consciousness of guilt. The costs, however, are likely to be pretty high, and it may be that in Betts's case they were disastrous.

Third, Betts chose to base his defense on an alibi supported by personal associates and acquaintances of unimpressive reputation who were obviously biased in his behalf, instead of making a frontal attack on the reliability of the prosecution's witnesses. A lawyer skilled in cross-examination might have done a great deal to expose contradictions and uncertainties among the men who identified Betts as the robber—at least to the extent of raising a reasonable doubt as to his complicity. But Betts cross-examined the witnesses against him only cursorily. He entirely failed to capitalize on the fallibility of eyewitness testimony and on the fact that the single witness who placed him at the scene of the crime saw him (if, indeed, it was he) only in semi-darkness and then identified not so much the defendant as the clothing and the amber glasses that the robber had been wearing.

Finally, and most important of all, Betts made no protest, as any lawyer surely would have done, against the quite outrageous police-station identification of him without even a lineup and with him attired to look like the robber. And he did not demand exclusion of the prosecution's witnesses at the trial so that they would not hear—and repeat—each other's testimony. He did not try to show that the prosecution witnesses had been materially helped in identifying him by the police, who may have shown them photographs of him as a convict.

One exceptionally astute and careful critic of the trial, Professor Yale Kamisar of the University of Michigan Law School, said, "I think the Betts record cries out for the talents of trained defense counsel."[3] He placed particular emphasis on the use of the clothing the robber was supposed to have worn:

Although the matter is not free from doubt,—because neither trial judge nor prosecutor seemed to care much and Betts evidently failed to realize how this would weaken the state's case—it is difficult to avoid the conclusion that the following "bootstrap" operation

[3] Yale Kamisar, "The Right to Counsel and the 14th Amendment," *University of Chicago Law Review* 30, no. 1, p. 1.

occurred: Bollinger described to the police the various items the
robber was supposed to have worn; the police simply went out,
begged or borrowed the requisite coat, glasses and handkerchief,
and slapped them on Betts; Bollinger made his identification, based
largely on the coat, glasses and handerchief the police put on
Betts. . . .[4]

To establish his alibi, Betts (who was in jail for want of the
means to pay a bondsman's fee and was therefore unable to
go out and interview witnesses himself) asked the state to
subpoena and produce at his trial thirteen witnesses. Subpoenas
were issued for all of them but, for some undisclosed reason,
three of them were not actually summoned. Conceivably they
could have made a difference. In any case, the succession of
down-at-the-heel witnesses put on by Betts seemed more pa-
thetic than persuasive. The first of them was Mary Emerson,
a woman who was living with Betts. The nub of her testimony
was expressed very briefly in response to cross-examination by
the state's attorney:

He was home on the day before Christmas and was home all day
up until along about four or four-thirty. He goes down the street
and gets the groceries and then comes back. About five o'clock Mrs.
Fletcher come over and asked him to do a favor for her, and I went
instead of him. Then, about five-thirty, when we came downstairs to
go out, the wife of the people we rent from was gone out, and then
we went down the street and he got a shave and haircut and then
come on down after me to come home and we was back home any-
where from nine to ten o'clock. . . .
Smith Betts has no occupation. He was applying for work on
WPA. He and I live together but we are not married.

Libby Uhler, the woman in whose house Betts and Mary
Emerson rented a room, testified that she "saw Smith Betts in
and around the house all day the Saturday before Christmas
of 1938, that is up until I left the house, about five-thirty in the

⁴ *Ibid.*, p. 49.

afternoon." Then, upon being cross-examined by Mr. Fringer, she said:

I know it was about five-thirty on the Saturday before Christmas because I left the house to buy the children some toys. I had not done my Christmas shopping earlier because I had no money, and on that day Smitty gave me $5 out of his welfare check, to go downtown on Saturday evening to get the children's toys with. That is, he gave it to my husband sometime Friday afternoon, after my husband came from work, because my husband gave it to me when I came from work in the evening. . . .

I did not see him with any money after Christmas but he gave my husband half of his welfare check before Christmas. . . .

None of this was of much avail. Immediately following the trial, the court found Smith Betts guilty as charged and sentenced him to confinement in the Maryland Penitentiary for a period of eight years.

From his prison cell a year or so later, Betts sought a writ of *habeas corpus* against Patrick J. Brady, warden of the penitentiary of Maryland, alleging that he had been denied his constitutional right to the assistance of counsel. His petition was heard by Judge Carroll T. Bond, chief judge of the Court of Appeals of Maryland and one of the most respected jurists in the state. Betts told the judge that he had friends in Carroll County, having been born there; that his father had been a minister in Carroll County; that his sister lived there, but that she refused to obtain counsel for him; that he could read and write English; that he was forty-three years of age. On October 6, 1941, Judge Bond issued an opinion, the essence of which follows:

The issue tried in the present case was one of identity of the robber. There was no dispute of the robbery. . . .

It is sufficiently proved that Betts was unable to employ counsel. But in this case, it must be said, there was little for counsel to do on either side. . . . Betts briefly cross-examined the witnesses who identified him, and the situation seems to have been such that counsel

*could have done little more than prolong the cross-examination
without advantage . . . .*

*There was no helplessness in the accused. He is forty-three years
old, and appears to have at least an ordinary amount of intelligence,
and the ability to take care of his own interests on a trial of this
narrow issue. I conclude that there is no such case as the Supreme
Court of the United States would hold lacking in due process of
law.*

It turned out that Judge Bond was quite right about the
Supreme Court of the United States. Dividing 6 to 3, the Court,
in an opinion written by Justice Owen J. Roberts and supported
by Chief Justice Stone and Justices Reed, Frankfurter, Jackson,
and Byrnes, upheld the view expressed by Judge Bond.

To understand the reasoning and the logic that lay behind
Judge Bond's opinion and that of the Supreme Court majority
upholding it, one must look at the evolving interpretation of the
right to counsel in American courts. The idea that a lawyer
is needed by a defendant in a criminal trial is of fairly recent
origin. Under English common law in the eighteenth century,
a right to representation by counsel in criminal actions was
recognized only in connection with misdemeanors and then
only in regard to points of law. A defendant in a felony prosecution was not allowed a lawyer and had to rely for the mainte-
nance of his rights on the rulings of the trial judge.

The American colonies were well ahead of England in this
respect, and the right to counsel was so commonly established
among them that it was taken for granted as indispensable to
a fair trial by the time the Bill of Rights was adopted. At that
time, however, the right to counsel, like, say, the right to
travel, was available only to those who could afford it.

Whether the assistance of counsel was requisite to a fair
trial was a question never directly considered by the Supreme
Court until the notorious case of the "Scottsboro Boys" arose in
1931. The case grew out of an incident on a freight train mov-

ing south through Alabama. Nine black boys—and two white
women who happened to be riding the same freight—were
arrested by the sheriff of Jackson County, Alabama, as a result
of a fight in which the black boys had thrown some white
boys off the train. The matter did not seem very serious until
the two white women told the sheriff a lurid story that they
had been raped by all nine of the boys—the oldest of whom
was twenty-one and the youngest thirteen.

Within a fortnight, the boys found themselves indicted for
rape and on trial for their lives—alone, friendless, ignorant
of any rights that the Constitution assured to them, and without anyone, in any event, to assert those rights for them or to
organize and present a defense against the charges. In the
course of a single day, eight of the boys were found guilty and
sentenced to death. An appeal was taken to the Supreme Court
of Alabama, which upheld seven of the convictions, reprieving
only the thirteen-year-old. Widespread outrage at the drum-
head character of the trial led to an appeal to the Supreme
Court of the United States, which agreed to review the case.[5]

The opinion of the Supreme Court in the *Scottsboro* case
was written by Justice Sutherland, one of the Court's pillars of
conservatism, strict constructionism, and judicial restraint. It
is a remarkable opinion, redolent of the indignation the Court
must have felt over this cruel parody of the judicial process.
Justice Sutherland set forth in the opinion, as well as it has
been set forth anywhere, why the right to counsel is a right
of prime importance. It is, indeed, when one comes to think
about it, a right upon which the exercise of every other right
involved in a fair trial must necessarily rest.

*Even the intelligent and educated layman has small and some-
times no skill in the science of law. If charged with crime, he is
incapable, generally, of determining for himself whether the indictment is good or bad. He is unfamiliar with the rules of evidence.
Left without the aid of counsel he may be put on trial without a*

[5] Powell v. Alabama, 287 U.S. 45 (1932).

proper charge, and convicted upon incompetent evidence, or evidence irrelevant to the issue or otherwise inadmissible. He lacks both the skill and knowledge adequately to prepare his defense, even though he have a perfect one. He requires the guiding hand of counsel at every step in the proceedings against him. Without it, though he be not guilty, he faces the danger of conviction because he does not know how to establish his innocence. If that be true of men of intelligence, how much more true it is of the ignorant and illiterate, or those of feeble intellect.

With this as a premise and after reciting the peculiar and heavy handicaps that beset the black youths in the Alabama trial—"the ignorance and illiteracy of the defendants, their youth, the circumstances of public hostility, the imprisonment and the close surveillance of the defendants by the military forces, the fact that their friends and families were all in other states and communication with them necessarily difficult, and *above all that they stood in deadly peril of their lives*" (italics mine)—Justice Sutherland fashioned a narrow and careful rule for the future:

All that is necessary now to decide, as we do decide, is that in a capital case, where the defendant is unable to employ counsel, and is incapable adequately of making his own defense because of ignorance, feeble-mindedness, illiteracy, or the like, it is the duty of the court, whether requested or not, to assign counsel for him as a necessary requisite of due process of law; and that duty is not discharged by an assignment at such a time or under such circumstances as to preclude the giving of effective aid in the preparation and trial of the case. . . . In a case such as this, whatever may be the rule in other cases, the right to have counsel appointed, when necessary, is a logical corollary from the constitutional right to be heard by counsel.

This is a rule that does not go very far. It expresses revulsion at the racism and disregard for decency in the Alabama proceeding; but it is so tentative and limited a first step as to afford no adequate general rule for the future. Six years later, in 1938, the Court dealt with the application of the Sixth Amendment in a noncapital case in a federal court. The Court opinion was written by Hugo L. Black—his first major opinion in regard to the Bill of Rights. The case involved two enlisted men in the United States Marine Corps, on leave, charged with the felony offense of "uttering and passing four counterfeit twenty-dollar Federal Reserve notes and possessing twenty-one such notes." They pleaded not guilty, said that they had no lawyer, and were tried, convicted, and sentenced without the assistance of counsel. The Court overturned the conviction, Chief Justice Hughes and Justices Brandeis, Stone, and Roberts supporting the Black opinion, which said:

> The Sixth Amendment stands as a constant admonition that if the constitutional safeguards it provides are lost, justice will not "still be done." It embodies a realistic recognition of the obvious truth that the average defendant does not have the professional legal skill to protect himself when brought before a tribunal with power to take his life or liberty, wherein the prosecution is presented by experienced and learned Counsel. That which is simple, orderly, and necessary to the lawyer, to the untrained layman may appear intricate, complex and mysterious. . . . The Sixth Amendment withholds from Federal Courts in all criminal proceedings, the power and authority to deprive an accused of his life or liberty unless he has or waives the assistance of counsel.[6]

With all these testimonials on record to the importance of counsel in a criminal defense, how, then, could the Supreme Court come to the conclusion, as it did only four years later in the *Betts* case, that an indigent defendant in a state court could constitutionally be sent to prison for eight years without having any lawyer to assist and speak for him? The answer is to be found in the deference that a majority of the justices felt they owed to long-established judicial procedures in the states and to the judgment of lower courts that had had more direct

[6] Johnson v. Zerbst, 304 U.S. 458 (1938). Justice Reed concurred in the result.

experience with the testimony and arguments in cases tried before them. And the answer is to be found also in the prevailing view within the Supreme Court as to the scope and meaning of the Fourteenth Amendment's due process clause.

Justice Owen Roberts's opinion for the Court in the *Betts* case was replete with obeisances to Judge Bond's evaluation of the trial, wholly accepting its conclusion that Betts had had ample means and opportunity to defend himself, and that a lawyer could have done him no real good. But it gave scant attention to Justice Sutherland's compelling argument in the *Scottsboro* case as to the need of a layman for a lawyer. It stated clearly the central question in the case: "Was the petitioner's conviction and sentence a deprivation of his liberty without due process of law, in violation of the Fourteenth Amendment, because of the court's refusal to appoint counsel at his request?" And it answered the question in these words:

The Sixth Amendment of the national Constitution applies only to trials in federal courts. The due process clause of the Fourteenth Amendment does not incorporate, as such, the specific guarantees found in the Sixth Amendment although a denial by a state of rights or privileges specifically embodied in that and others of the first eight amendments may, in certain circumstances, or in connection with other elements, operate, in a given case, to deprive a litigant of due process of law in violation of the Fourteenth. Due process of law is secured against invasion by the Federal Government by the Fifth Amendment and is safe-guarded against state action in identical words by the Fourteenth. The phrase formulates a concept less rigid and more fluid than those envisaged in other specific and particular provisions of the Bill of Rights. Its application is less a matter of rule. Asserted denial is to be tested by an appraisal of the totality of facts in a given case. That which may, in one setting, constitute a denial of fundamental fairness, shocking to the universal sense of justice, may, in other circumstances, and in the light of other considerations, fall short of such denial. In the application of such a concept there is always the danger of falling into the habit of formulating the guarantee into a set of hard and fast rules

*the application of which in a given case may be to ignore the quali-
fying factors therein disclosed.*

What this verbal deluge amounted to, so far as Smith Betts
was concerned, was simply that the treatment accorded him
at his trial in Carroll County, Maryland, was not so shocking
to the majority's sense of justice as to lead them to reverse his
conviction. Although counsel for a defendant was mandatory in
any federal trial by reason of the Sixth Amendment, the question to be asked in connection with a state trial was simply
whether failure to assign counsel resulted in any fundamental
unfairness.

Whatever may have been the reaction of "the universal sense
of justice," this curtailment of the Sixth Amendment's reach,
this willingness to apply a less exacting standard to state trials,
was altogether shocking to Hugo Black's sense of justice. In his
dissent in the *Betts* case, he expressed tentatively, and for the
first time, a view—which was to become a cornerstone of his
judicial philosophy—that the due-process clause of the Fourteenth Amendment had been intended when it was adopted
to make the first eight articles of the Bill of Rights applicable
to the states. In Black's judgment, the prevailing view of the
Fourteenth Amendment's due-process clause, as set forth by
Justice Roberts, gave entirely too much leeway and discretion
to judges. Nothing in the Constitution, he contended, justified
a transient majority of the Court in deciding what constituted,
at any given time, "a denial of fundamental fairness shocking to
the universal sense of justice." The authors of the Constitution
themselves, he insisted, had expressly fixed in the Bill of Rights
the standards that judges were to apply to the determination of
fairness; and to allow judges to apply individual, personal
standards would be to reduce a written Constitution to a
nullity.

Quite apart from this view of due process, however, and accepting the majority's view, Black insisted in his dissent that

the conviction of Smith Betts still ought to be reversed. He reminded his colleagues of the argument that Justice Sutherland had advanced in the *Scottsboro* case respecting the importance of counsel in presenting a defense and concluded:

A practice cannot be reconciled with "common and fundamental ideas of fairness and right," which subjects innocent men to increased dangers of conviction merely because of their poverty. Whether a man is innocent cannot be determined from a trial in which, as here, denial of counsel has made it impossible to conclude, with any satisfactory degree of certainty, that the defendant's case was adequately presented. . . .

Denial to the poor of the request for counsel in proceedings based on charges of serious crime has long been regarded as shocking to the "universal sense of justice" throughout this country. In 1854, for example, the Supreme Court of Indiana said: "It is not to be thought of, in a civilized community, for a moment, that any citizen put in jeopardy of life or liberty, should be debarred of counsel because he was too poor to employ such aid. No Court could be respected, or respect itself, to sit and hear such a trial. The defense of the poor, in such cases, is a duty resting somewhere, which will be at once conceded as essential to the accused, to the Court, and to the public." . . . And most of the other States have shown their agreement by constitutional provisions, statutes, or established practice judicially approved, which assure that no man shall be deprived of counsel merely because of his poverty. Any other practice seems to me to defeat the promise of our democratic society to provide equal justice under the law.

Hugo Black's lively sympathy for the plight of poor and not-very-well-educated persons called upon to defend themselves against the panoply of governmental power—whether wielded by the nation or by a state—doubtless stemmed from his experience as a young lawyer in his native Alabama. After a year of practice in Ashland, Alabama, a town of about 350 people where he had grown up, he went to Birmingham in 1907 and rented a desk in an attorney's office for $7 a month. His first real case was a damage suit for fifteen days' pay for work done by a black convict leased to a steel mill and kept overtime on the job. He won an award of $137.50 for his client. He served for a while as a part-time police-court judge in Birmingham, dispensing justice as fairly and compassionately as he could to an endless succession of unfortunates, mostly black, charged with disorderly conduct, drunkenness, and other minor offenses. In 1914 he became solicitor of Jefferson County, Alabama, an office in which he discovered that the police department of Bessemer, a Birmingham suburb, was running a third-degree torture mill to force confessions from black defendants. He presented evidence to a grand jury, persuading it to charge the use of third-degree tactics "in a manner so cruel that it would bring discredit and shame upon the most uncivilized and barbarous community."

Hugo Black never forgot what he learned in Bessemer. The bulk of his law practice, even after he had become established and successful, involved very few corporate clients; for the most part he represented labor unions and individuals; he relished courtroom work and, especially, cross-examination of witnesses. He knew his way around county courthouses; and he knew the ways of provincial policemen, judges, and juries. Even Supreme Court justices can bring to judging no more than the content of their own experience. Black's was rich in concern for individuals, and especially the hapless and helpless. And so, perhaps, he saw Smith Betts more understandingly than other justices, as deserving the law's shield as much as its sword.

The *Betts* decision created no great stir around the country, the subtle distinction it drew being somewhat esoteric for the ordinary citizen. Among law professors and thoughtful lawyers, however, the Black dissent evoked echoes. One of these, as Anthony Lewis has recalled in his fine study of the *Gideon* case,[7] was a lengthy letter to *The New York Times* written by Benjamin V. Cohen, one of the most distinguished and influential members of Franklin Roosevelt's New Deal, and Erwin N.

[7] Anthony Lewis, *Gideon's Trumpet* (New York: Random House, 1964), p. 112.

Griswold, then a law professor who was to become dean of the Harvard Law School and later solicitor general of the United States. The time, remember, was when the United States had but recently become a belligerent in a war waged against totalitarian tyranny. "At a critical period in world history," Cohen and Griswold wrote, "*Betts v. Brady* tilts the scales against the safe-guarding of one of the most precious rights of man. For in a free world no man should be condemned to penal servitude for years without having the right to counsel to defend him. The right of counsel, for the poor as well as the rich, is an indispensable safeguard of freedom and justice under law."

The *Journal of the American Bar Association* accepted the view expressed by Justice Roberts as entirely reasonable and natural. But other law journals tended to be less complacent about it. The *Columbia Law Review*, for example, condemned the decision in an unsigned note, concluding with this observation: "By holding that the intelligence of the accused and the complexity of the issue must be examined, the instant case overemphasizes the facts of the individual case. It would seem that a supposed constitutional guaranty should not be made dependent on distinctions that are at best difficult of ascertainment and often tenuous."

A criminal trial under the American adversary system of justice is a sort of contest from which the truth is supposed to emerge through the opposition of the contending parties. There must be a reasonable measure of equality between the resources of the contenders if the theory is to work. If the prosecution requires the skill of a professional prosecutor, the defense cannot fairly be forced to present its case without the skill of a professional defender. To say that a trial is fundamentally fair when conducted *without* counsel for the defense is simply to guess at what course it might have taken had it been conducted *with* counsel for the defense.

The *Betts* ruling kept troubling not only the dissenters on the Court, but others as well—on the Court as well as off it.

The discrepancy it permitted between federal and state practice was even more marked two years after *Betts*—in 1944—when the Court adopted Rule 44 of the Federal Rules of Criminal Procedure, stating firmly that, "If the defendant appears in court without counsel, the court shall advise him of his right to counsel to represent him at every stage of the proceeding unless he elects to proceed without counsel or is able to obtain counsel." The Court also made it clear that a waiver of the right to counsel could be considered valid only if it were made knowingly and responsibly.

This admirable rule applied only in federal courts, while an overwhelming majority of criminal prosecutions occurs, of course, in state courts. The states were moving in the direction indicated by the Supreme Court; a number of them by this time were providing counsel as a matter of right to indigent defendants in noncapital cases. Others, however, were not yet ready for so drastic a reform. A Supreme Court ruling summarily requiring all of them to conform to the federal standard would have raised an exceedingly difficult practical problem; applied retroactively, it might have required the sudden release from prison of an undeterminable number of more or less dangerous convicts who had been found guilty in trials where they had had no help from a lawyer. Writing for the Court in a 1947 decision, Justice Frankfurter raised this specter as a consideration to be weighed in regard to the right to counsel. "It does not militate against respect for the deeply rooted systems of criminal justice in the states," he wrote, "that such an abrupt innovation as recognition of the constitutional claim here made implies, would furnish opportunities hitherto uncontemplated for opening wide the prison doors of the land."[8] To this, Justice Black made a sharp retort in another dissent, joined this time by Justices Douglas, Murphy, and Rutledge, a new member of the Court.

The Court's decision relies heavily on Betts v. Brady. . . . *That*

[8] Foster v. Illinois, 332 U.S. 134 (1947).

*case is precedent for this one. But it is the kind of precedent that I
had hoped this Court would not perpetuate.*

*One thing more. The Court seems to fear that protecting these
Defendants' right to counsel to the full extent defined in the Bill
of Rights would furnish "opportunities hitherto uncontemplated for
opening wide the prison doors of the land," because, presumably,
there are many people like Betts, Foster, and Payne behind those
doors after trials without having had the benefit of counsel. I do
not believe that such a reason is even relevant to a determination
that we should decline to enforce the Bill of Rights.*

A year later, in 1948, the Court, holding still to its flexible
rule, tried, through Justice Reed, to give it a somewhat more
precise definition:

*Where the gravity of the crime and other factors—such as the
age and education of the defendant, the conduct of the court or
prosecuting officials, and the complicated nature of the offense
charged, and the possible defenses thereto—render criminal proceedings without counsel so apt to result in injustice as to be
fundamentally unfair. . . . the accused must have legal assistance.[9]*

The trend now was toward insisting on counsel for indigent
defendants without yet making a rule of it. In 1949, Justice
Reed tried again to fix the focus of the Court's requirements
more sharply, this time in an opinion upsetting the conviction
of an uncounseled defendant in a larceny trial. But what he
produced amounted to little more than a disclaimer:

*We cannot offer a panacea for the difficulty. Such an interpreta-
tion of the Fourteenth Amendment would be an unwarranted
federal intrusion into state control of its criminal procedure. The
due process clause is not susceptible of reduction to a mathematical
formula. . . .[10]*

Justices Black and Douglas concurred in the judgment of the

[9] Uveges v. Pennsylvania, 335 U.S. 437 (1948).
[10] Gibbs v. Burke, Warden, 337 U.S. 773 (1949).

Court with a tart reminder that they "think that *Betts v. Brady* should be overruled." The Court's regard for states' rights was clearly giving way to its queasiness over convicting defendants without legal aid.

The Supreme Court changes its collective mind, as it should, slowly and with the gravest deliberation. If it confesses error, it wants to be pretty sure that it won't have to confess it again on the same subject. And usually, before confession, it goes through a period of penitence during which it twists and turns uncomfortably in a forlorn hope of squeezing through the bars behind which it has imprisoned itself. All through the 1950s, the Court, in a succession of cases, overturned convictions against defendants who had not had the assistance of counsel —always on the ground of "special considerations," never on the basis of a right to counsel as an essential element of due process. By 1960, with new justices on the Court and several members calling publicly in dissenting opinions for rejection of the *Betts* rule, the time was plainly more than ripe for opening the doors of the cage.

The opportunity came in 1962 when the Supreme Court received a handwritten petition addressed to it by a prisoner in the Florida state prison, a fifty-one-year-old man named Clarence Earl Gideon. His case had great significance, first, because it so closely paralleled the *Betts* case and, second, because it became the vehicle for the Supreme Court's release, at last, from the *Betts* rule. Anthony Lewis of *The New York Times* has given a superlatively detailed and dramatic account of the *Gideon* case;[11] no more than a brief summary of it needs to be presented here.

Clarence Gideon was in prison for a five-year term because he had been convicted of breaking into the Bay Harbor Poolroom in Panama City, Florida, and stealing the cash contents of a cigarette vending machine and a jukebox he found there.

[11] Lewis, *op. cit.*

Some years older than Smith Betts at the time of that unhappy man's conviction in Maryland, Gideon had served time for four previous felonies although he had never been involved in any crime of violence. He seemed, as Lewis described him, to be a "perfectly harmless human being, rather likeable, but one tossed aside by life." Like Betts, he had insisted that he was not guilty of the offense charged to him; he had asked the trial court to assign a lawyer to help him in his defense and had been told that "under the laws of the state of Florida, the only time the court can appoint counsel to represent a Defendant is when that person is charged with a capital offense." And, like Betts, Gideon had undertaken to act as his own lawyer, utilizing such legal techniques as he had observed in various court-rooms and learned in various prisons—all without much success.

The crime charged to him being petit larceny, Gideon was tried on August 4, 1961, before a six-man jury in a court presided over by Judge Robert L. McCrary, Jr. Gideon was told that he could challenge any of the jurors but not that he could question them individually to determine if they were biased in any way or likely to be hostile to him. He accepted the jury as impaneled without any question. The state's case against him, like the case against Betts in Maryland, turned on the testimony of a single eyewitness, one Henry Cook, who swore that he knew Gideon and, standing outside the Bay Harbor Poolroom at 5:30 in the morning, had seen Gideon inside, had watched him come out of the place with a bottle of wine in his hand, make a telephone call at the street corner, and then enter a taxi that he had apparently summoned. Cook said he went back to the poolroom and "saw it had been broken into." Obviously, this was testimony that, as Professor Kamisar observed about the identification testimony in the *Betts* case, "cries out for the talents of trained defense counsel."

Gideon asked Cook, on cross-examination, what Cook was doing outside the poolroom at 5:30 in the morning—a good question, as the cliché puts it. But he did not press the point and his interrogation meandered aimlessly. The witnesses he produced in his own behalf contributed nothing to his defense, and one wonders what he had in mind in calling them. Like Betts, he declined to testify himself. The jury appears to have had little difficulty in finding him guilty. And Judge McCrary, after looking at Gideon's past record and without hearing any argument for leniency or probation, imposed the maximum sentence of five years.

The Supreme Court of the United States, granting a writ of certiorari in response to Gideon's simple, handwritten plea, reached down to Judge McCrary's court in Florida and, without any intermediate adjudication, brought Gideon's case before it. The Court requested counsel, who, in due course, would appear before it to argue the case, to discuss, among other questions, in their briefs and oral argument, the question: "Should this Court's holding in *Betts v. Brady*, 316 U.S. 455, be reconsidered?"

To represent Clarence Gideon in the Supreme Court of the United States, the Court appointed one of the most eminent lawyers in Washington, Abe Fortas, who subsequently became an associate justice of that Court. Fortas brought all the resources of a great law firm to the support of his own rich legal knowledge and skill in preparing briefs and argument in the *Gideon* case. In the end, the Court ruled—without any expression of dissent—that "the right of an indigent in a criminal trial to have the assistance of counsel is a fundamental right essential to a fair trial, and petitioner's trial and conviction without the assistance of counsel violated the Fourteenth Amendment."

Hugo Black, who twenty-one years earlier, had dissented so vigorously when *Betts v. Brady* was decided, wrote the Court's opinion in *Gideon v. Wainwright*. It must have been a singular satisfaction to him. After reciting the facts of the *Gideon* case and remarking that they were hardly distinguishable from the facts of the *Betts* case, he said flatly for the Court, "Upon full reconsideration we conclude that *Betts v. Brady* should be overruled." Then, after reciting the development of doctrine regarding the right to counsel, he went on in these words:

*The fact is that in deciding as it did—that "appointment of coun-
sel is not a fundamental right, essential to a fair trial"—the Court
in Betts v. Brady made an abrupt break with its own well-con-
sidered precedents. In returning to these old precedents, sounder
we believe than the new, we but restore constitutional principles
established to achieve a fair system of justice. Not only these precedents but also reason and reflection require us to recognize that in
our adversary system of criminal justice, any person haled into
court, who is too poor to hire a lawyer, cannot be assured a fair
trial unless counsel is provided for him. This seems to us to be an
obvious truth. Governments, both state and federal, quite properly
spend vast sums of money to establish machinery to try defendants
accused of crime. Lawyers to prosecute are everywhere deemed
essential to protect the public's interest in an orderly society. Similarly, there are few defendants charged with crime, few indeed,
who fail to hire the best lawyers they can get to prepare and present their defenses. That government hires lawyers to prosecute and
defendants who have the money hire lawyers to defend are the
strongest indications of the widespread belief that lawyers in criminal courts are necessities, not luxuries. The right of one charged
with crime to counsel may not be deemed fundamental and essential to fair trials in some countries, but it is in ours. From the very
beginning, our state and national constitutions and laws have laid
great emphasis on procedural and substantive safeguards designed
to assure fair trials before impartial tribunals in which every defendant stands equal before the law. This noble ideal cannot be
realized if the poor man charged with crime has to face his accusers
without a lawyer to assist him.*

The immediate effect of the Court's ruling, as far as Clarence
Gideon was concerned, was to send his case back to Florida for
a new trial to be conducted in accordance with the new rule
laid down by the Court. In August, 1963, Gideon went on trial
again in the Panama City courthouse, before the same judge
who had presided over his trial in August, 1961—this time with
a local lawyer appointed by Judge McCrary to represent him.
That lawyer, in cross-examining the state's chief witness, Henry
Cook, pointedly suggested that Cook might well have robbed

the Bay Harbor Poolroom himself. In one way and another, at any rate, he created enough doubt in the minds of jurors respecting Gideon's culpability so that when they filed back into the courtroom at the end of the trial and after about an hour's deliberation, their verdict was not guilty. Clarence Gideon was a free man. Smith Betts, too, might have won "the benefit of the doubt" had he had a skilled lawyer to assist him in his defense.

What were the factors that brought about the change in the Supreme Court's view of due process from *Betts* to *Gideon?* As usual, no doubt, they were complex and varied. They are worth guessing at, perhaps, as a way of suggesting the course of constitutional development.

One patent factor, it goes almost without saying, was the change in the Court's composition. Of the justices who had sat on the Supreme Court at the time *Betts* v. *Brady* was decided, only two remained when the Court came to consider *Gideon* v. *Wainwright*—Black and Douglas, both of them dissenters in the earlier case. Justice Murphy, who had agreed with them, was long gone. But so were all the justices who had constituted the majority in 1942—Justice Roberts, who had written the majority opinion; Chief Justice Stone; and Justices Reed, Frankfurter, Jackson, and Byrnes, all of whom had supported it. This amounted to more than a change of personality; it amounted to something rather like a generational or philosophical change. Collectively and individually, the men who sat on the Court in 1963 were less deferential to "states' rights" and more responsive to individual rights as opposed to the authority of the state than the men who had sat on the Court two decades earlier. Moreover, by the 1960s, the Court was already well launched upon a comprehensive reform of the criminal-justice system through a process of "selective incorporation," under which certain protections of the Bill of Rights were made binding upon the states by virtue of the Fourteenth Amendment; and doubtless it was emboldened by these precedent-shattering decisions to plow still further along this furrow.

A second factor of indubitable importance was a thoroughly pragmatic one. After twenty years of experience with the flexible rule laid down by Justice Roberts for determining the need to appoint counsel for indigent defendants in criminal prosecutions, the Court came to realize that it simply wasn't working very well. Its boundaries were so fluid as to create nothing but confusion and to leave state authorities uncertain as to what was expected of them. And all through the 1950s the Court found fault, anyhow, with all those cases brought before it in which the assistance of counsel had been withheld from an indigent defendant desiring it.

This was a kind of deference to state sovereignty that the states found they could get along very well without. The very flexibility that the Court had intended as a concession to states' rights proved much more of an irritant than a balm. It entailed, in case after case, the considerable cost as well as the discomfiture of having to retry defendants because a remote tribunal in Washington found imperfections in state trial procedures.

The most influential factor in turning the Court around was simply the steady process of growth or evolution that keeps the Constitution a living force in the life of a nation that is itself in the process of growth or evolution. There was clear evidence of this process in the fact that when the assistant attorney general of Florida in charge of the state's case circularized state attorneys general all over the country asking them to support his cause by filing briefs as *amici curiae*, only two did so. The governments of twenty-three states and commonwealths, on the contrary, as well as the American Civil Liberties Union, filed *amicus* briefs supporting Gideon's plea and urging reversal of the *Betts* rule as "an anachronism."[12]

The central truth of the matter is that by 1963 the time had

[12] By 1963, thirty-seven states furnished counsel for indigents in all felony trials; eight more frequently did so.

become ripe for the adoption of a reform, an advance in the administration of criminal justice, which the states of the Union were not yet prepared to accept in 1942 because the need for it had not yet been made evident. It seems likely that this is what lies behind a rather touching anecdote told by Anthony Lewis:

> *Shortly after the* Gideon *case was decided, Justice Black visited Justice Frankfurter at home and told his ailing colleague about the conference at which the case had been discussed. He had told the other members of the Court, Justice Black said, that if Felix had been there he would have voted—faithful to his own view of due process—to reverse the conviction of Clarence Earl Gideon and overrule* Betts. v. Brady.
> *Justice Frankfurter said: "Of course I would."*[13]

It is, to be sure, a great deal easier to assure the assistance of counsel in theory than it is to provide it in practice. In 1967, the President's Crime Commission painted an unattractive picture of the lawyers who "assist" most criminal defendants. "In many of our larger cities," the commission's task force on the courts reported, "there is a distinct criminal bar of low legal and dubious ethical quality. These lawyers haunt the vicinity of the criminal courts seeking out clients who can pay a modest fee. Some have referral arrangements with bondsmen, policemen, or minor court officials. They negotiate guilty pleas and try cases without investigation, preparation, or concern for the particular needs of their clients."[14]

It is, to a considerable extent, from this bar that court appointments of defense counsel are made. No doubt this has a good deal to do with the crime commission's finding that "most defendants who are convicted—as many as 90 percent in

[13] Lewis, *op. cit.*, pp. 221–222.
[14] Task Force Report, *The Courts, the President's Commission on Law Enforcement and Administration of Justice* (Washington, D.C.: U.S. Government Printing Office, 1967), p. 57.

some jurisdictions—are not tried. They plead guilty, often as the result of negotiations about the charge or the sentence."[15] The development of federal and state public-defender systems has dramatically ameliorated this condition. Public defenders commonly do a conscientious and thoroughly effective job of defending indigents charged with crime. So do a growing number of "public service" law firms. Nevertheless, in 1972, nearly a decade after the Supreme Court's decision in the *Gideon* case, one of the most thoughtful and sensitive appellate court judges in the United States felt constrained to say, "What I have seen in 23 years on the bench leads me to believe that a great many—if not most—indigent defendants do not receive the effective assistance of counsel guaranteed them by the Sixth Amendment."[16] It remains, still, to lift performance up to promise.

While the *Gideon* decision was a triumph for Justice Black, it should be noted that it did not embrace his belief that the Fourteenth Amendment had made the right-to-counsel guarantee of the Sixth Amendment, along with all the other specifics of the Bill of Rights, binding upon the states. It was bottomed, rather, upon a recognition that the assistance of counsel is one of those fundamental rights that are an essential element of due process. Justice Black accepted this rationale as the basis of his opinion for the sake of the unanimity it procured among members of the Court. And indeed it represents a more plastic and creative concept than a literal and limited application of the precise terms of the Bill of Rights. Justice Frankfurter, in another context, gave this concept an illuminating definition:

Due process of law . . . conveys neither formal nor fixed nor narrow requirements. It is the compendious expression of all those

[15] Report by the President's Commission on Law Enforcement and Administration of Justice, *The Challenge of Crime in a Free Society* (Washington, D.C.: U.S. Government Printing Office, 1967), p. 134.

[16] David L. Bazelon, chief judge, U.S. Court of Appeals for the District of Columbia Circuit, the Robert S. Marx Lectures in the College of Law, University of Cincinnati, December 6, 1972.

*rights which the courts must enforce because they are basic to our
free society. But basic rights do not become petrified as of any one
time, even though, as a matter of human experience, some may not
too rhetorically be called eternal verities. It is of the very nature of
a free society to advance in its standards of what is deemed reasonable and right. Representing as it does a living principle, due
process is not confined within a permanent catalogue of what may
at a given time be deemed the limits or the essentials of fundamental rights.*[17]

When one considers how standards of fairness—which is to
say, concepts of due process—have evolved over centuries, one
must recognize that the Constitution could hardly have been
meant to crystallize them forever in a static formulation. There
was a time when men believed that due process could best be
found in trial by combat or by ordeal; and at another time they
thought that the thumbscrew and the rack were appropriate
devices for the discovery of truth. The march called "civilization" forced abandonment of those ideas. They did not work
very well; and they were at odds with a developing sense of
humanity and human dignity. Maybe that is the very definition
of progress. Maybe the best thing that can be said for the
Constitution of the United States and for the system of law
that it sustains is that they afford opportunity for change consonant with the rising ideals of a vital community.

[17] Wolf v. Colorado, 338 U.S. 25 (1949).

V

"FREEDOM OF MIND AND SPIRIT MUST BE PRESERVED"

Minersville School District v. *Gobitis*, Harlan Fiske Stone dissenting[*]

On November 6, 1935, the Board of Education of the Minersville, Pennsylvania, School District formally adopted a regulation intended to instill love of country and respect for its symbols in youthful minds. The regulation, which no doubt seemed routine at the time of its adoption, laid the basis for a great constitutional controversy, affording a rather beautiful illustration of the clash of conflicting constitutional principles. It provided, "That the Superintendent of the Minersville public schools be required to demand that all teachers and pupils of said schools be required to salute the flag of our country as a part of the daily exercises. That refusal to salute the flag shall be regarded as an act of insubordination and shall be dealt with accordingly."

This requirement was far from a novelty in America at that time. The ritual of pledging allegiance to the flag had become common in public schools—as a profession of patriotism in reaction to the growing threat of totalitarian aggression in Europe

[*] 310 U.S. 586 (1940).

and Asia. People not infrequently turn themselves into a mirror image of what they most abhor and fear.

Adoption of the flag-salute regulation by the Minersville school board appears to have been a reaction as well to a small, special problem that had arisen in one of the schools there. Even without the adoption of a board regulation, the Minersville superintendent of schools, Charles E. Roudabush, had instituted the practice of saluting the flag and pledging allegiance to it at the opening of school each morning. The observance had been marred in some degree, however, by three children who had quietly and respectfully, but with unregenerate obstinacy, refused to participate in it.

These children were: Lillian Gobitis, aged twelve; William Gobitis, aged ten; and Edmund Wasliewski, whose age does not appear upon the record. They had been taught by their parents, members of a fundamentalist Christian sect known variously as Jehovah's Witnesses or as Russellites or, colloquially, as Earnest Bible Students, that to salute a flag would be a violation of the divine commandment set forth in the twentieth chapter of Exodus, declaring that "Thou shalt not make unto thee any graven image, or any likeness of any thing that is in heaven above, or that is in the earth beneath, or that is in the water under the earth; / Thou shalt not bow down thyself to them, nor serve them."

These children had been taught to believe that saluting a flag ascribes salvation and protection to it or to the power that the flag represents and that, as a spokesman for their creed put it in explanation of their attitude, "since the flag and the government which it symbolizes is of the world and not of Jehovah God, it is wrong to salute the flag, and to do so denies the supremacy of God, and contravenes His express command as set forth in Holy Writ."

At almost exactly the same time, Adolf Hitler dealt even more summarily with much the same problem in the new Germany against which Americans were preparing to defend themselves. "I consider them quacks," he declared in a pronouncement on April 4, 1935. "I dissolve the 'Earnest Bible Students' in Germany; their property I dedicate to the people's welfare; I will have all their literature confiscated."

Superintendent Roudabush's authority was not quite so sweeping. He merely arose at the school-board meeting in Minersville on November 6, 1935, immediately after adoption of the new regulation and, suggesting pretty plainly that this had been the board's particular purpose in adopting the regulation, announced: "I hereby expel from the Minersville Schools Lillian Gobitis, William Gobitis and Edmund Wasliewski for this act of insubordination, to wit, failure to salute the flag in our school exercises."

Pennsylvania had a compulsory-school-attendance law. So, expulsion from the public schools meant for these children that they had to seek an education at a private school with all that that entailed for their parents in terms of expenses for their tuition and transportation. After suffering in silence for a couple of years, Walter Gobitis, father of two of the three children, brought a lawsuit to recover the money he had paid out for Lillian's and William's schooling as the result of what he deemed an unlawful exclusion of them from the public schools.

At the trial, which took place on February 15, 1938, Mr. Gobitis declared: "I am a true and sincere follower of Christ Jesus, the Son of Jehovah God." Interrogated by the court, he said that he was born in this country, loved the country, wanted to be a good citizen and to do everything he could to be a good citizen of the United States. When asked about his belief as to the act of saluting a flag, he said he considered it "contrary to the commandment of God" as set forth in the second commandment and as stated in the third and fourth verses of Exodus, which he recited for the court's enlightenment. He had, he said, taught his children "to believe and study the Bible for a long time, and they were baptized to serve God, too, and as we were talking things over at home, no doubt they got a lot of knowledge in that respect concerning idolatry, we have talked about that." And he expressed, in addition, his conviction that "As the flag is used today, it is an image of something, and is worshiped, and the commandments of God are that we should not worship images or partake of idolatry."[1]

The lawyer for the Gobitis children brought to the trial as an expert witness Frederick William Franz, an official in the editorial department of the Watchtower Bible and Tract Society, the authoritative voice of Jehovah's Witnesses, and asked him the following question: "Now, Mr. Franz, what would be the penalty, if any, to a Christian, or one of Jehovah's Witnesses, who disobey such commandments?"

Mr. Franz answered the question with perfect simplicity and perfect certainty: "Eternal annihilation, destruction."

To a little girl and her even littler brother, this prospect must have seemed rather more terrifying than any form of expulsion Superintendent Roudabush could possibly threaten. The superintendent himself testified that Lillian and William were "very good children" but that, in his opinion, the public welfare and safety would be imperiled if some of the children in the school were allowed to refrain from saluting the flag, even on conscientious grounds.

The trial was conducted by Judge Albert B. Maris in the United States District Court for the Eastern District of Pennsylvania. He appeared to have very little difficulty in making up his mind about it. The authority of the school board, he said at the outset, was only to adopt "such regulations as are reasonable." The regulation adopted here, he went on, "although undoubtedly adopted from patriotic motives, appears to have become in this case a means for the persecution of children for conscience's sake. Our beloved flag, the emblem of religious liberty, apparently has been used as an instrument to impose a religious test as a condition of receiving the benefits of public education. And this has been done without any compelling necessity of public safety or welfare."

Judge Maris also dealt with the contention of the school

---

[1] Testimony of Walter Gobitis, Trial Record, pp. 50–51.

authorities that the belief regarding a salute to the flag held by
Jehovah's Witnesses was unreasonable and nonsensical, however sincere, and that a pledge of allegiance to the flag could
not seriously be regarded as a religious act of any sort—that it
amounted, as Adolf Hitler put it so succinctly, to mere quack-
ery. He said in his opinion:

*No one who heard the testimony of the plaintiffs and observed
their demeanor upon the witness stand could have failed to be im-
pressed with the earnestness and sincerity of their convictions.
While the salute to our national flag has no religious significance to
me and while I find it difficult to understand the plaintiffs' point
of view, I am nevertheless entirely satisfied that they sincerely believe that the act does have a deep religious meaning and is an act
of worship which they can conscientiously render to God alone. . . .*

*If an individual sincerely bases his acts or refusals to act on
religious grounds, they must be accepted as such and may only be
interfered with if it becomes necessary to do so in connection with
the exercise of the police power, that is, if it appears that the public
safety, health or morals or property or personal rights will be prej-
udiced by them. To permit public officers to determine whether the
views of individuals sincerely held and their acts sincerely undertaken on religious grounds are in fact based on convictions religious
in character would be to sound the death knell of religious liberty.*

The case was appealed to the Third Circuit Court of Appeals,
which unanimously sustained Judge Maris in a long, learned,
and often eloquent opinion by Judge William Clark. Despite
these redundant and really humiliating rebuffs, the Minersville
school authorities were encouraged to seek review in the
Supreme Court of the United States—by the fact, one surmises,
that on three previous occasions the justices had disposed of
the problem by *per curiam* opinion for want of a substantial
federal question, leaving in force state supreme court decisions
that upheld the validity of compulsory flag salutes.

At any rate, the issue came to the Supreme Court at a time
when that tribunal was experiencing a special sensitivity with
regard to the overturning of legislative judgments. The country

had gone through a long and exasperating period during which the Court had recklessly frustrated efforts by the national Congress and by state legislatures to cope with pressing social and economic problems. There was a widespread feeling that the Court had become an impassable roadblock to progress or, indeed, to any effective action by the other branches of government. President Franklin D. Roosevelt's Court-enlargement or "Court-packing" plan failed; but by the time the *Gobitis* case came up for review, the president had been able to put five of his own nominees on the Court: Black, Reed, Frankfurter, Douglas, and Murphy.

This majority was, of course, peculiarly aware that the Court ought not to operate as a superlegislature, second-guessing as it were, and imposing its will and judgment upon elected representatives directly responsive and accountable to the public. In the years when the Court obdurately obstructed the most important elements of the New Deal program, Justice Harlan F. Stone had urged again and again that it be governed by a sense of judicial restraint. And off the Court, Professor Frankfurter's voice had been among the most forceful and influential in criticizing the Court for interference in policy matters outside its proper jurisdiction.

The flag-salute case arose during Felix Frankfurter's first term on the Court. Apparently he saw it, when the writing of the Court's opinion was assigned to him, as a splendid opportunity to give expression and illustration to the meaning of judicial restraint. The entire Court shared this view, with a single exception. The exception, to Frankfurter's astonishment and dismay, was Harlan F. Stone, who had joined his colleagues just a year earlier in one of the *per curiam* decisions (i.e., by the Court as a whole without any individual opinion) denying an appeal from the Supreme Court of California, thus upholding a flag-salute requirement.

Frankfurter wrote a five-page letter to Stone tactfully setting forth his concern about the *Gobitis* case and the reasoning by which he had come to the conclusion that the expulsion of the

Gobitis children should be held to be within the authority of
the Minersville school board.[2] "We are not exercising an independent judgment," he pointed out to his colleague. "We are
sitting in judgment upon the judgment of the legislature." And
he emphasized his strong sense of the need to avoid exercising
"our judicial power unduly, as though we ourselves were legislators by holding with too tight a rein the organs of popular
government." In the letter to Stone, Frankfurter went on:

*Nothing has weighed as much on my conscience, since I have
come on this Court, as this case. All my bias and pre-disposition are
in favor of giving the fullest elbow room to every variety of religious, political, and economic view. . . . I want to avoid the mistake
comparable to that made by those whom we criticized when dealing
with the control of property. . . . My intention . . . was to use this
opinion as a vehicle for preaching the true democratic faith of not
relying on the Court for the impossible task of assuring a vigorous,
mature, self-protecting, and tolerant democracy by bringing the
responsibility for a combination of firmness and toleration directly
home where it belongs—to the people and their representatives
themselves.*

A defense of this position—an avoidance of any judicial interference in the formation of public policy when constitutional
commandments were not clearly violated—formed the principal theme of Justice Frankfurter's thoughtful and impressive
opinion for the Court. It was an opinion rendered, it must be
remembered, in the year 1940, a year in which the nation was
drawing itself together for participation in a world war against
Axis powers that seemed to threaten an engulfment of all the
institutions of liberty. "The precise issue, then, for us to decide,"
Frankfurter said in his opinion, "is whether the legislatures of
the various states and the authorities in a thousand counties

[2] The Frankfurter-Stone exchange is set forth in Alpheus Thomas Mason's
fine biography, *Harlan Fiske Stone: Pillar of the Law* (New York: Viking,
1956), pp. 526–7.

and school districts of this country are barred from determining the appropriateness of various means to evoke that unifying sentiment without which there can ultimately be no liberties, civil or religious." To a question stated in these exclusionary terms, there could be—at least for Felix Frankfurter and for most of those who had gone through the long struggle against interference with legislative judgments—but a single answer. The opinion said:

The wisdom of training children in patriotic impulses by those compulsions which necessarily pervade so much of the educational process is not for our independent judgment. Even were we convinced of the folly of such a measure, such belief would be no proof of its unconstitutionality. For ourselves, we might be tempted to say that the deepest patriotism is best engendered by giving unfettered scope to the most crotchety beliefs. Perhaps it is best, even from the standpoint of those interests which ordinances like the one under review seek to promote, to give to the least popular sect leave from conformities like those here in issue. But the courtroom is not the arena for debating issues of educational policy. It is not our province to choose among competing considerations in the subtle process of securing effective loyalty to the traditional ideals of democracy, while respecting at the same time individual idiosyncrasies among a people so diversified in racial origins and religious allegiances. So to hold would in effect make us the school board for the country. That authority has not been given to this court, nor should we assume it. . . .

What the school authorities are really asserting is the right to awaken in the child's mind considerations as to the significance of the flag contrary to those implanted by the parent. In such an attempt the state is normally at a disadvantage in competing with the parent's authority, so long—and this is the vital aspect of religious toleration—as the parents are unmolested in their right to counteract by their own persuasiveness the wisdom and rightness of those loyalties which the state's educational system is seeking to promote. Except where the transgression of constitutional liberty is too plain for argument, personal freedom is best maintained—so long as the remedial channels of the democratic process remain

*open and unobstructed—when it is ingrained in a people's habits
and not enforced against popular policy by the coercion of ad-
judicated law.*

Justice Frankfurter concluded this statement with a reminder
that Stone himself had given to the Court but a few years
before. "Judicial review, itself a limitation on popular government, is a fundamental part of our constitutional scheme," he
noted. "But to the legislature no less than to courts is committed the guardianship of deeply-cherished liberties. . . .
Where all the effective means of inducing political changes are
left free from interference, education in the abandonment of
foolish legislation is itself a training in liberty. To fight out the
wise use of legislative authority in the forum of public opinion
and before legislative assemblies rather than to transfer such
a contest to the judicial arena, serves to vindicate the self-
confidence of a free people."

Well aware, for his own part, of the dangers of judicial
meddling in the tempting fields of legislative policy, Justice
Stone nonetheless saw in the First Amendment an overriding
barrier to a compelled profession of allegiance to the flag that
trenched upon the domain of conscience. "I am truly sorry not
to go along with you," he wrote back to Justice Frankfurter.
"The case is peculiarly one of the relative weight of imponderables, and I cannot overcome the feeling that the Constitution
tips the scales in favor of religion."[3] In short, Stone's emphasis
was on the Constitution as a protector of individual and minority rights against majority demands.

Just two years before *Gobitis* was decided, Justice Stone had
appended his now-famous "Footnote 4" to his opinion for the
Court in a case called *United States* v. *Carolene Products Company*,[4] a case in which the Court declined to interfere with a
challenged statute regulating business practices. This was an
instance of judicial restraint, evidencing the Court's traditional

[3] Quoted by Mason, *op. cit.*, p. 527.
[4] 304 U.S. 144 (1938).

presumption of constitutionality for legislation enacted by Congress or by a state legislature. Stone added a caveat, however, in his footnote:

> *There may be narrower scope for operation of the presumption of constitutionality when legislation appears on its face to be within a specific prohibition of the Constitution, such as those of the first ten amendments, which are deemed equally specific when held to be embraced within the Fourteenth. It is unnecessary to consider whether legislation which restricts political processes which can ordinarily be expected to bring about repeal of undesirable legislation, is to be subjected to a more exacting judicial scrutiny under the general prohibitions of the Fourteenth Amendment than are most other types of legislation. Nor do we enquire whether similar considerations enter into the review of statutes directed at particular religious, national or racial minorities, whether prejudices against discrete and insular minorities may be a special condition which tends seriously to curtail the operation of those political processes ordinarily to be relied upon to protect minorities and which may call for a correspondingly more searching judicial inquiry.*

What this rather marvelously murky effusion comes down to in translation is simply that a distinction may be made between laws governing commercial activity and laws limiting the exercise of individual freedoms guaranteed by the Bill of Rights. Stone proposed, or asserted, a "preferred position" for personal liberty—and especially for individuals or minority groups unable to defend themselves effectively through the normal operation of the political process. In short, he contended that the Court should examine more carefully, require greater justification for, laws affecting speech, association, and religion than for laws affecting business interests. By and large the Court has embraced this preference, although some justices, most notably Felix Frankfurter, have argued against it vociferously on the ground that there is no warrant for giving one part of the Constitution greater weight than another. In the *Gobitis* case, at any rate, Stone himself followed the philosophy of "Footnote 4."

Stone was not in the habit of writing a separate dissenting opinion when he found himself in disagreement with a majority of the Court; usually he was content to record his dissent without articulating his premises. On this occasion, however, after some indecision, he made up his mind to write a dissenting opinion and, having written it, he took the rather extraordinary step, for him, of reading it aloud from the bench in full. He did so in a manner redolent of the intensity of his feelings on this occasion. The nub of his argument follows:

The guaranties of civil liberty are but guaranties of freedom of the human mind and spirit and of reasonable freedom and opportunity to express them. They presuppose the right of the individual to hold such opinions as he will and to give them reasonably free expression, and his freedom, and that of the state as well, to teach and persuade others by the communication of ideas. The very essence of the liberty which they guaranty is the freedom of the individual from compulsion as to what he shall think and what he shall say, at least where the compulsion is to bear false witness to his religion. If these guaranties are to have any meaning they must, I think, be deemed to withhold from the state any authority to compel belief or the expression of it where that expression violates religious convictions, whatever may be the legislative view of the desirability of such compulsion.

History teaches us that there have been but few infringements of personal liberty by the state which have not been justified, as they are here, in the name of righteousness and the public good, and few which have not been directed, as they are now, at politically helpless minorities. The framers were not unaware that under the system which they created most governmental curtailments of personal liberty would have the support of a legislative judgment that the public interest would be better served by its curtailment than by its constitutional protection. I cannot conceive that in prescribing, as limitations upon the powers of government, the freedom of the mind and spirit secured by the explicit guaranties of freedom of speech and religion, they intended or rightly could have left any latitude for a legislative judgment that the compulsory expression of belief which violates religious convictions would better serve the public interest than their protection. The Constitution may well elicit expressions of loyalty to it and to the government which it created, but it does not command such expressions or otherwise give any indication that compulsory expressions of loyalty play any such part in our scheme of government as to override the constitutional protection of freedom of speech and religion. . . .

The Constitution expresses more than the conviction of the people that democratic processes must be preserved at all costs. It is also an expression of faith and a command that freedom of mind and spirit must be preserved, which government must obey, if it is to adhere to that justice and moderation without which no free government can exist.

It was a deep disappointment to Stone that no other member of the Court joined in his dissent. Professor Mason quotes a letter that Stone wrote to Judge Henry Edgerton of the Court of Appeals for the District of Columbia Circuit, saying that "one of the difficulties with the opinion is that it is not moving enough."

The American Civil Liberties Union had filed a careful and impressive *amicus* brief with the Court on behalf of the Gobitis children. So had the Committee on the Bill of Rights of the American Bar Association. It was hardly a surprise that the reaction to the outcome of the case was one of extreme disagreement and dismay in intellectual and libertarian circles.

The law journals, reflecting, it is fair to say, the most informed and thoughtful professional reaction to the decision, were heavily weighted against it. In a comment signed by Louis Levene, the *Cornell Law Quarterly*, for instance, observed: "The present war has brought to the United States a feeling of insecurity and an emphasis upon national defense. It has brought also an attitude of suspicion toward non-conformists within our ranks. And, as we begin to divide the population into those who are with us and those who are against us, there has come the danger that patriotism will degenerate into a popular fetish. This danger the recent decision of the United

States Supreme Court in *Minersville School District* v. *Gobitis* does not mitigate."[5]

A note by William F. Andersen in the *Michigan Law Review* took much the same dyspeptic view: "The required flag salute would seem to be of little efficacy when applied to persons sincerely believing it to be a sinful act, and it is extremely doubtful whether it is desirable even when applied to children having no such beliefs. It is premature to conclude that the Court has succumbed to a spirit of superpatriotism. If individual liberties are something more than the by-product of a democratic process, if in fact they have an intrinsic value worthy of protection, it is difficult to justify a decision which subordinates a fundamental liberty to a legislative program of questionable worth."[6]

No note or comment on the decision appeared in the *Harvard Law Review*, the organ of that prestigious law school at which Felix Frankfurter had been among the most prestigious professors until his elevation to the Court but a year or so before. Perhaps this was because it had published a note on the merits of the flag-salute issue not long before the *Gobitis* case was decided: "Regardless of the constitutionality of the compulsory flag salute, however, the advisability of imposing it upon religious objectors seems extremely questionable. It is true that to give free rein to religious freedom might lead to a substantial impairment of government authority. But when there is no overbalancing public necessity, an indulgence of the religious beliefs of a minority seems more desirable than a futile attempt to compel a loyalty which can not be artificially stimulated, at a time when the United States is respected, more than ever, for the breadth of its tolerance and liberty."[7]

In the daily press, at least in the major cities, sentiment was overwhelmingly sympathetic to the Stone dissent and critical

---

[5] Louis Levene, in the *Cornell Law Quarterly*, 26 (December, 1940), 127–30.

[6] William F. Andersen, in the *Michigan Law Review* 39 (November, 1940), 149.

[7] *Harvard Law Review* 51 (June, 1938), 1418.

of the Frankfurter opinion. Professor Mason says that "one hundred and seventy-one leading newspapers promptly condemned the decision; only a handful approved it." The St. Louis *Post-Dispatch*, to pick one of the most vehement, called it "terrible" and "a surrender to popular hysteria." *The New Republic*—to which journal Frankfurter was a primary contributor in the 1920s and early 1930s—printed the majority and dissenting opinions in full and then, in an editorial entitled "Frankfurter v. Stone," commented that the Court itself appeared to be verging on hysteria when it "says in effect that we must imperil religious liberty in the interest of the American state, which is worth preserving because it guarantees religious liberty. . . ."[8]

In less academic circles, however, the outcome of the *Gobitis* case won a great deal of hyperpatriotic applause that spilled over in a number of places into vigilante violence. At the time of the Court ruling, one lower federal court and three top state courts had unconditionally held compulsory flag salutes to be constitutional; and at least twelve states had expelled pupils for refusing to salute the flag. The prevailing rationale of the court decisions was not deference to legislative judgments, but, rather, a flat rejection of the possibility that reasonable minds could see any religious significance in a salute to the flag and an oath of allegiance. The Supreme Court opinion, while not endorsing this view, nevertheless gave respectability and encouragement to it—and gave impetus as well to a great deal of meanness and folly in the name of patriotism.

In the wake of the decision, there was a wave of ugly attacks upon members of the Jehovah's Witnesses sect. All over the country, self-appointed guardians of "Americanism" paid homage to the Constitution by taking the law into their own hands. During the fortnight that followed the Court's ruling on June 3, 1940, literally hundreds of attacks on the Witnesses were reported to the Department of Justice. And in innumerable

---

[8] *The New Republic*, 102 (June 24, 1940), 843, 852–855.

communities, local school officials made the flag-salute requirements more stringent and even, in some instances, sent the
children of Witnesses to state reform schools as delinquents for
refusing to pledge allegiance to the flag of freedom.

There is in the record, however, a single electrifying instance
of common sense that perhaps more genuinely reflects the spirit
of America than any of the genuflections to the flag. In Ro-
chester, Michigan, where nineteen children had been expelled
from school for refusing on religious grounds to salute the flag,
a compromise was tried, so simple and obvious that one wonders why it was not universally adopted. A certain Judge
Moore, of Pontiac, Michigan, suggested that if the children of
Jehovah's Witnesses were unwilling to pledge allegiance to the
flag of the United States because they regarded it as a form
of graven image, they might, nevertheless, be perfectly willing
to pledge allegiance to the United States itself. It turned out
that the children and their parents, being thorough patriots,
every one of them, had no conscientious qualms whatever
about doing this. So, they enthusiastically pledged allegiance
to the United States of America, one nation indivisible, with
liberty and justice for all (we were not yet "under God"), and
went quietly back to school the following day.

If there is difficulty in understanding the rationale by which
Justice Frankfurter was led to strike the balance as he did between a compelled declaration of faith and judicial deference
to the elected representatives of the people, that difficulty is
compounded when one tries to understand what led such colleagues on the Court as Hugo Black, William O. Douglas, and
Frank Murphy to go along with him. As the successor on the
Court to Benjamin Cardozo, Justice Frankfurter occupied what
had come to be known as "The Scholar's seat"; and possibly
this fact, combined with the immense prestige he brought with
him to the bench as the country's most distinguished law pro-

fessor, had something to do with persuading these fellow new-comers to the Court to accept his view.

Even Supreme Court justices may be subject in some degree to the pull of patriotism and to a sense of the flag as a symbol of the land they love. In Justice Frankfurter's case, moreover, it is possible that he was moved unconsciously by a special devotion to America that grew out of his being Jewish and having come here in early childhood as an immigrant in search of freedom; he had an intense love for the land of his adoption and perhaps a special reverence for the flag that symbolized it. Intellectually, however, he was undoubtedly as much repelled as any of the others at the idea of a forced obeisance to the flag. In any case, the avoidance of personal or policy preferences in the decision of judicial issues was a prime article of faith with him. Indeed, one can hardly help wondering whether some strong moral strain—some sense that duty was synonymous with self-denial—did not at times make him teeter backward and impel him, precisely because it was painful to him to do so, to take judicial positions that were directly opposed to his own naturally warm and tolerant impulses. He appears to have been determined in his first years on the Court to erase the image of himself as an inveterate "liberal" that he had acquired as a law professor and as a result of his valorous fight to save the lives of the convicted anarchists Sacco and Vanzetti. A distinguished Harvard Law School colleague wrote about him after he had been on the Court but a few years: "Those who have wrongly assumed . . . that Mr. Justice Frankfurter is a fallen liberal angel should at least be convinced . . . that liberalism in a judge is not to be tested solely by the result of a particular adjudication and that one facet of liberalism in a judge may be the insistence that courts should not interpose their vetoes except under the strongest constitutional compulsions."[9]

Whatever the reasons that led Justices Black, Douglas, and

[9] Thomas Reed Powell, *Iowa Law Review* 29 (March, 1944), 383.

Murphy to support Justice Frankfurter in the *Gobitis* case, they took advantage of the very first opportunity to recant. Just two years later, on June 8, 1942, the Court decided a case called *Jones* v. *Opelika* in which Justice Stanley Reed delivered a 5-to-4 majority opinion sustaining the constitutionality of municipal ordinances under which members of the Jehovah's Witnesses were convicted for not paying license taxes on the sale of their tracts and other religious publications. Harlan Stone, who by this time had become chief justice, dissented. Black, Douglas, and Murphy not only joined his dissent but, in addition, filed a single dissenting paragraph of their own, designed simply to disclose their repentance in an entirely different matter. What they wrote follows in full:

> The opinion of the Court sanctions a device which in our opinion suppresses or tends to suppress the free exercise of a religion practiced by a minority group. This is but another step in the direction which Minersville School District v. Gobitis *took against the same religious minority and is a logical extension of the principles upon which that decision rested. Since we joined in the opinion in the* Gobitis *case, we think this is an appropriate occasion to state that we now believe that it was also wrongly decided. Certainly our democratic form of government functioning under the historic Bill of Rights has a high responsibility to accommodate itself to the religious views of minorities however unpopular and unorthodox those views may be. The First Amendment does not put the right freely to exercise religion in a subordinate position. We fear, however, that the opinions in this and in the* Gobitis *case do exactly that.*[10]

Outright reversal of the *Gobitis* decision was evidently on the way. It came with unique speed in another flag-salute case, *West Virginia State Board of Education* v. *Barnette,* decided only a year later, on June 14, 1943[11] In the course of that intervening year, Wiley Rutledge took his seat on the Court,

[10] Jones v. Opelika, 316 U.S. 584 (1942).
[11] 319 U.S. 624 (1943).

replacing James F. Byrnes; and Justice Robert H. Jackson, who had come to the Court just in time to join the majority in the *Opelika* decision, found that he could not approve a compulsory flag salute. Indeed, it was Justice Jackson to whom the writing of the Court opinion was assigned.

Justice Jackson brought to the Court a long experience in political activity and in law enforcement. He had been both solicitor general and attorney general of the United States and one of President Roosevelt's most trusted counselors. He was an intensely pragmatic man, ordinarily disinclined to interfere with police or other state authorities in the handling of local problems. Temperamentally and philosophically, he was much more akin to Justice Frankfurter than to Justices Black and Douglas. He wrote brilliantly and often quite mordantly. In *West Virginia State Board of Education,* he produced one of the most moving and memorable pleas for the tolerance of heterodoxy and eccentricity in the whole of the Court's literature.

Justice Jackson's opinion for the Court expressly overruled *Gobitis* and, indeed, the very rationale on which it had been decided. In the view of the new majority, the vital question was whether the state has power to compel an affirmance of any belief; and it applied to the determination of this question the clear-and-present-danger test, holding that compulsion could not be exacted without a showing that avoidance of it presented an imminent and serious threat to the public welfare and safety. The opinion rejected the view set forth in the *Gobitis* decision that the matter was one which could properly be left to local school boards acting under state legislative authorizations; it asserted instead that in respect to rights guaranteed by the Constitution the Court had an overriding obligation. Justice Jackson brought his forceful opinion to a conclusion with these words:

National unity as an end which officials may foster by persuasion and example is not in question. The problem is whether under our

*Constitution compulsion as here employed is a permissible means
for its achievement.*

*Struggles to coerce uniformity of sentiment in support of some
end thought essential to their time and country have been waged by
many good as well as by evil men. Nationalism is a relatively recent
phenomenon but at other times and places the ends have been
racial or territorial security, support of a dynasty or regime, and
particular plans for saving souls. As first and moderate methods to
attain unity have failed, those bent on its accomplishment must
resort to an ever-increasing severity. As governmental pressure
toward unity becomes greater, so strife becomes more bitter as to
whose unity it shall be. Probably no deeper division of our people
could proceed from any provocation than from finding it necessary
to choose what doctrine and whose program public educational officials shall compel youth to unite in embracing. . . . Those who begin
coercive elimination of dissent soon find themselves exterminating
dissenters. Compulsory unification of opinion achieves only the
unanimity of the graveyard.*

*It seems trite but necessary to say that the First Amendment to
our Constitution was designed to avoid these ends by avoiding these
beginnings. . . . There is no mysticism in the American concept of
the State or of the nature or origin of its authority. We set up
government by the consent of the governed, and the Bill of Rights
denies those in power any legal opportunity to coerce that consent. Authority here is to be controlled by public opinion, not
public opinion by authority.*

*The case is made difficult not because the principles of its deci-
sion are obscure but because the flag involved is our own. Nevertheless, we apply the limitations of the Constitution with no fear
that freedom to be intellectually and spiritually diverse or even
contrary will disintegrate the social organization. To believe that
patriotism will not flourish if patriotic ceremonies are voluntary and
spontaneous instead of a compulsory routine is to make an unflatter-
ing estimate of the appeal of our institutions to free minds. We can
have intellectual individualism and the rich cultural diversities that
we owe to exceptional minds only at the price of occasional eccentricity and abnormal attitudes. . . .*

*If there is any fixed star in our constitutional constellation, it is
that no official, high or petty, can prescribe what shall be orthodox*

in politics, nationalism, religion, or other matters of opinion or force
citizens to confess by word or act their faith therein. . . .

To this, Justice Frankfurter offered a dogged dissent, asserting once more, perhaps with a sense of hopelessness, the doctrine that judges are not empowered to pass upon the wisdom
of legislation deemed desirable by elected representatives of
the people, and may invalidate it only when it is manifestly
contrary to the Constitution. The depth and intensity of his
feeling about this case found expression in the very opening
line of this Jewish immigrant's opinion: "One who belongs to
the most vilified and persecuted minority in history is not
likely to be insensible to the freedoms guaranteed by our Constitution. . . . Were my purely personal attitude relevant I
should wholeheartedly associate myself with the general libertarian views in the Court's opinion, representing as they do
the thought and action of a lifetime." He went on, however,
to restate with immensely impressive force the sense of self-
discipline which was the cornerstone of his judicial philosophy:

As a member of this Court I am not justified in writing my pri-
vate notions of policy into the Constitution, no matter how deeply
I may cherish them or how mischievous I may deem their disregard.
The duty of a judge who must decide which of two claims before
the Court shall prevail, that of a State to enact and enforce laws
within its general competence or that of an individual to refuse
obedience because of the demands of his conscience, is not that
of the ordinary person. It can never be emphasized too much that
one's own opinion about the wisdom or evil of a law should be
excluded altogether when one is doing one's duty on the bench.
The only opinion of our own even looking in that direction that is
material is our opinion whether legislators could in reason have
enacted such a law. . . .

The reason why from the beginning even the narrow judicial
authority to nullify legislation has been viewed with a jealous eye
is that it serves to prevent the full play of the democratic process.
The fact that it may be an undemocratic aspect of our scheme of

*government does not call for its rejection or its disuse. But it is the
best of reasons, as this Court has frequently recognized, for the
greatest caution in its use. . . .*

Frankfurter then went on to offer his colleagues one more
pointed reminder of how mischievously the Court had super-
imposed its authority on the judgment of legislatures during
the early years of the New Deal:

*In the past this Court has from time to time set its views of policy
against that embodied in legislation by finding laws in conflict with
what was called the "spirit of the Constitution." Such undefined
destructive power was not conferred on this Court by the Constitution. Before a duly enacted law can be judicially nullified, it must
be forbidden by some explicit restriction upon political authority
in the Constitution. Equally inadmissable is the claim to strike
down legislation because to us as individuals it seems opposed to
the "plan and purpose" of the Constitution. That is too tempting
a basis for finding in one's personal views the purposes of the
Founders. . . .*

*I think I appreciate fully the objections to the law before us. But
to deny that it presents a question upon which men might reasonably differ, appears to me to be intolerance. And since men may
so reasonably differ, I deem it beyond my constitutional power to
assert my view of the wisdom of this law against the view of the
State of West Virginia.*

And he struck again the note he had sounded in his *Gobitis*
opinion, decrying the unwillingness of his colleagues to rely
upon the political arena for the determination of political issues. He concluded his impassioned dissent with these words:

*Of course patriotism cannot be enforced by the flag salute. But
neither can the liberal spirit be enforced by judicial invalidation of
illiberal legislation. Our constant preoccupation with the constitutionality of legislation rather than with its wisdom tends to preoccupation of the American mind with a false value. The tendency
of focussing attention on constitutionality is to make constitutionality synonymous with wisdom, to regard law as all right if it is*

constitutional. Such an attitude is a great enemy of liberalism. Particularly in legislation affecting freedom of thought and freedom of speech, much which should offend a free-spirited society is constitutional. Reliance for the most precious interests of civilization, therefore, must be found outside of their vindication in courts of law. Only a persistent positive translation of the faith of a free society into the convictions and habits and actions of a community is the ultimate reliance against unabated temptations to fetter the human spirit.

The Frankfurter dissent dealt, in addition, with the merits of the controversy—the question whether state insistence upon a pledge of allegiance to the flag constituted a violation of religious liberty as guaranteed by the First Amendment. It did not do so, Frankfurter contended, because it was not aimed at any religious belief or activity, but only at the accomplishment of a legitimate legislative aim, the furtherance of national unity. He said on this score:

The constitutional protection of religious freedom terminated disabilities, it did not create new privileges. It gave religious equality, not civil immunity. Its essence is freedom from conformity to religious dogma, not freedom from conformity to law because of religious dogma. . . .

The prohibition against any religious establishment by the government placed denominations on an equal footing—it assured freedom from support by the government to any mode of worship and the freedom of individuals to support any mode of worship. Any person may therefore believe or disbelieve what he pleases. He may practice what he will in his own house of worship or publicly within the limits of public order. But the lawmaking authority is not circumscribed by the variety of religious beliefs, otherwise the constitutional guaranty would be not a protection of the free exercise of religion but a denial of the exercise of legislation.

Justice Jackson's opinion for the Court was joined, of course, by Chief Justice Stone, the lone dissenter in *Gobitis*, and by the newcomer to the Court, Justice Rutledge; and it was joined also by Justices Black, Douglas, and Murphy. Black and Douglas together submitted a concurring opinion, which offered little more than an explanation of their change. "Reluctance to make the Federal Constitution a rigid bar against state regulation of conduct thought inimical to the public welfare was the controlling influence which moved us to consent to the *Gobitis Decision.* Long reflection convinced us that although the principle is sound, its application in the particular case before us fails to accord full scope to the freedom of religion secured to the appellees by the First and Fourteenth Amendments."

So, in the very brief span of three years—unprecedentedly brief, as such transformations go—Justice Stone's dissent in the flag-salute controversy won majority acceptance. Whether or not it entailed, as Justice Frankfurter so strongly felt, an improper judicial incursion into an area of policy reserved by the Constitution for legislative determination, it sounded, nevertheless, a note of tolerance for heterodox belief, of compassion for eccentricity, highly becoming to a powerful, pluralistic society. If it was questionable constitutional law, it was, nevertheless, judicial morality much more consonant with the great ideals of freedom than a forced profession of patriotism by unwilling children. Perhaps, as Justice Stone suggested in his Footnote 4, there is a special justification for judicial invasion of the legislature's province when it is undertaken not in behalf of economic doctrines and property interests, but in championship of individual resistance to the clamor of majorities and the overpowering majesty of the state. For this, surely, it is the Court's special province to protect.

VI

"EQUAL REPRESENTATION
OF CITIZENS"

Colegrove v. *Green*, Hugo L. Black dissenting *

Equality among citizens—equality at least in the making of
the laws under which they are to live—is the premise of any
democracy. And when a democracy is to be ruled by a representative government, it follows necessarily that it must be
bottomed upon equality in the voting booth. This much seems
implicit in the very first of the truths that the authors of the
American Declaration of Independence deemed "self-evident"
—"that all men are created equal."

Political equality was the basis of the Leveller movement
in seventeenth-century England, from the seeds of which the
American political system flowered. "For really," said Colonel
Thomas Rainborough, one of the leaders of the Levellers, "I
think that the poorest he that is in England hath a life to live,
as the greatest he; and therefore truly, sir, I think it's clear,
that every man that is to live under a government ought first
by his own consent to put himself under that government; and
I do think that the poorest man in England is not at all bound
in a strict sense to that government that he hath not had a

* 328 U.S. 549 (1946).

voice to put himself under.[1] Thus was conceived the doctrine
brought to birth somewhat more than a century later in the
American Declaration of Independence, that the just powers
of government are derived from the consent of the governed—
all of the governed.

The history of representative government has been in no
small part a history of struggles to achieve equality of representation. In 1646, John Lilburne, the greatest of the Levellers,
was already complaining bitterly about the rotten-borough
system that made the Long Parliament in England so unrepre-
sentative of the country. "It is," he declared, "unrighteous that
Cornwall should choose fifty members and Yorkshire, twice
as big and three times as populous and rich, not half so many
and my own poor county, the Bishopric of Durham, none at
all." Their underrepresented inhabitants, he went on, are
"mere vassals and slaves" like the peasants in France or
Turkey."[2]

To the English colonists who migrated to the New World—
many of them direct descendants of the English Levellers—
equality of representation in the colonial legislatures was the
essence of self-government. When the government of the
United States was established by these colonists, equal participation in its affairs was their underlying assumption. Thomas
Jefferson wrote in 1816 that "a government is republican in
proportion as every member composing it has his equal voice
in the direction of its concerns . . . by representatives chosen
by himself. . . ."[3] And in 1819, he wrote: "Equal representation
is so fundamental a principle in a true republic that no prejudice can justify its violation because the prejudices themselves cannot be justified."[4] And obviously this was the essence

[1] The Putney Debates, 1647, quoted in *Fountainheads of Freedom*, ed.
Irwin Edman (New York: Reynal and Hitchcock, 1941), p. 288.
[2] Quoted by H. N. Brailsford, *The Levellers and the English Revolution*
(London: The Cresset Press, 1961), p. 115.
[3] Jefferson to Samuel Kercheval, in *The Writings of Thomas Jefferson*,
ed. Paul A. Ford, 10 vols. (New York: 1829–1899), X (1899), p. 38.
[4] Jefferson to William King, Thomas Jefferson Papers, Vol. 216, p. 38616,
Library of Congress, Washington, D.C.

of what Abraham Lincoln had in mind when he spoke of "government of the people, by the people. . . ."

That equality of political power among citizens was to be a cornerstone of the American political system can be seen plainly enough from the words of Article I, Section 2, of the Constitution:

Representatives and direct Taxes shall be apportioned among the several States which may be included within this Union, according to their respective Numbers, which shall be determined by adding to the whole Number of free Persons, including those bound to Service for a Term of Years, and excluding Indians not taxed, three-fifths of all other Persons. The actual Enumeration shall be made within three Years after the first Meeting of the Congress of the United States, and within every subsequent Term of ten Years, in such manner as they shall by Law direct.

The section went on to provide that, pending the first enumeration, or census, the several states should be entitled to representation roughly in proportion to their estimated respective populations—New Hampshire, 3; Massachusetts, 8; Connecticut, 5; and so on. Black persons, as is well known, were not then considered citizens. Article I, Section 2, was subsequently modified by the second section of the Fourteenth Amendment when it was adopted in 1868—a section that, unfortunately, was left largely unenforced. It reads:

Representatives shall be apportioned among the several States according to their respective numbers, counting the whole number of persons in each State, excluding Indians not taxed. But when the right to vote at an election for the choice of electors for President and Vice President of the United States, Representatives in Congress, the Executive and Judicial officers of a State, or the members of the Legislature thereof, is denied to any of the male inhabitants of such State, being twenty-one years of age, and citizens of the United States, or in any way abridged, except for participation in rebellion, or other crime, the basis of representation therein shall be reduced in the proportion which the number of such male citi-

*zens shall bear to the whole number of male citizens twenty-one
years of age in such State.*

It is quite true that this says nothing about election by districts, let alone about how districts should be designed. It was
recognized from the outset, however, that division of the
states into electoral units afforded an essential means of obtaining fair and balanced representation; and federal law early
stipulated that election to the House of Representatives should
be from districts in each state. State constitutions and laws had
similar provisions designed to assure equal representation of
their citizens, at least in the lower house of the state legislatures. As the country began to grow, however, and as industrialization of the economy accelerated the movement of
population from rural areas to urban centers, gross imbal-
ances developed between legislative districts. Along with this
development, unfortunately, there grew also for the representatives of the less populous districts a vested interest in perpetuation of the imbalance. When disproportion develops between
electoral districts, the vote of an elector in the larger district
of course carries proportionately less weight than the vote of
an elector in the smaller district.

There are obvious advantages in this situation not only for
the voters in the smaller district, but for their representatives
as well; it is easier for them to campaign, to stay in office, and
to reflect the interests and wishes of a relatively small and
homogeneous electorate. It enables them to perpetuate their
advantage through ingenious gerrymanders. In addition to using the imbalance for perpetuation of their own power, they
have used it in many states to apportion financial benefits and
burdens to the advantage of their rural constituents. It is probably fair to say that no single factor has contributed so much
to the neglect of urban problems by state legislatures and the
federal Congress as the rural domination that has worked
persistently against attention to those problems or the alloca-
tion of resources for their solution.

More and more, those who sought by normal political means
to deal with the pressing and multiplying needs of cities in
decay—by providing public housing, improved public schools,
clearance of slums, enlargement of recreational and park facilities, improved transportation, and the like—found themselves
frustrated by the indifference or actual hostility of legislators
who wielded dominance because they held "safe" seats and
committee chairmanships through long tenure, and because
they outnumbered the delegates of city dwellers. The normal
and appropriate way to deal with this inequality was, of course,
through the political process; as the beneficiaries of inequality
were always ready to point out, the proper remedy for malapportionment was to elect state legislatures that would apportion fairly. The only trouble with this counsel was that it was
doomed to failure; although efforts to accomplish reform in
this way were made again and again in many states—by political action, by petition, by appeals to reason—the people who
held power were quite unwilling to relinquish it. Decade after
decade following the turn of the nineteenth into the twentieth
century, they let the inequities fester and enlarge.

It was this awareness of impasse, this sense that the political
process held no real hope of salvation, that in 1945 led a
group of political scientists at Northwestern University and
the University of Chicago to seek a remedy in the courts. Led
by Professor Kenneth Wallace Colegrove, they brought a suit
against the governor of Illinois, Dwight H. Green, charging
that gross inequality in districting violated the Constitution of
the United States and seeking an at-large election of all congressmen from the state. Governor Green himself had not long
before appealed, vainly, to the Illinois legislature to "correct
the inequities of our congressional apportionment under which
Illinois now has both the largest and smallest congressional
districts in the United States, one nine times the size of the
other."

Professor Colegrove lived in Chicago, in a district that, at
the time of the lawsuit, had a population of 914,053, as com-

pared with the smallest congressional district in Illinois, downstate, with a population of 112,116. Each of these districts sent
one representative to Congress with an absolutely equal voice
and vote in the deliberations there. The individual citizen in
the downstate district had, in short, nearly nine times the political clout of the individual citizen in the city district.

The population of Illinois, according to the census of 1940,
was 7,897,241. The state was entitled to twenty-six representatives in the United States House of Representatives, which
meant, if the state had been divided into equal districts, that
each of them would have had a population of 303,740. The
Illinois legislature had not, however, redrawn the boundaries
of either congressional or state legislative districts since 1901
—despite a specific directive in the state constitution that this
must be done decennially. Illinois's largest state legislative district had, in fact, a population sixteen times as great as the
population of its smallest state legislative district.

Five of the six largest congressional districts in the country
were in the state of Illinois at this time; and so were the country's three smallest districts. In the Illinois state legislature, an
assemblyman represented, on an average, 213,860 persons;
downstate, the average was 119,809 persons for each representative. Put differently, the Chicago districts, aggregating 52 per
cent of the state's population, elected only 37 per cent of the
state legislators.[5] No one pretended that this inequality reflected anything but the realities of political power in the state
assembly.

The suit brought by Professor Colegrove and his associates
was argued before a special three-judge federal court composed of Evan A. Evans, Michael L. Igoe, and Walter J. La-
Buy. These judges reacted to it with the liveliest indignation:

*Petitioners base their argument on the sound and elementary
proposition that all the electors should have an equal voice and that*

[5] The figures are taken from the *Yale Law Journal*, 56, no. 11 (November,
1946), 127, 132–3.

none should be disfranchised. A failure to redistrict the State of Illinois after each census results in either disfranchisement or inequality of franchise strength. In short, the voice of one citizen carries more weight than that of another in another district, solely because the State of Illinois has refused and continues to refuse to reapportion the state in accordance with the population facts showing of the last census. Not only has the State of Illinois failed to redistrict the state according to population after the last census, but it has failed to do so for over forty years. Its action is apparently deliberate and defiant of both Federal and State Government and the principles upon which they are founded.

Defendants do not defend this action. Their defense is that this gross misrepresentation of Illinois citizens is due to certain legislators who, to retain political strength greater than they are entitled to, or would be entitled to, if equality in representation occurred, refuse to act or to grant relief to this existing disgraceful situation in Illinois.

Defendants rely chiefly on their alleged unusual and unique immunity from legal process, both state and Federal. The citizens have sought relief in both tribunals. As representative of the legislative branch, the Legislature of Illinois has taken a defiant and arbitrary position quite at variance with the theory of a representative democracy.

Their refusal to grant relief is as obstinate as it is unpatriotic. It [is a violation of] the spirit of citizen obligation to state and Federal Government which is as surprising as it is happily unusual. It is apparently modeled after the action of South Carolina in the days of President Jackson. Its continuance provokes, if it does not invite, the resort to arms if appeals to reason or the patriotism of the individuals are too long ignored. . . .

Having delivered themselves of this resounding condemnation of the legislature and its failure to do its duty, the judges concluded sorrowfully that they could do nothing about it. What stood in the way was a 5-to-4 Supreme Court decision in a case known as *Wood* v. *Broom*.[6] This was a 1932 case in which the Court dismissed a suit for equitable apportionment

[6] 287 U.S. 6 (1932).

on the ground that the Reapportionment Act of 1929 had no
provision in it analogous to that of the Reapportionment Act
of 1911, which earlier statute explicitly required that election
districts be drawn with compactness of territory and approx-
imate equality of population. From the failure to restate these
requirements, the Court drew the deduction that Congress
had meant to rescind them. The special three-judge court
in Illinois felt obliged, however reluctantly, to follow this
directive:

*Our study of the opinion of the Supreme Court in the case of
Wood. v. Broom has resulted in our reaching a conclusion contrary
to that which we would have reached but for that decision. We are
an inferior court. We are bound by the decision of the Supreme
Court, even though we do not agree with the decision or the reasons which support it. . . . In the absence of this decision we would
assume that such requirement arose necessarily from the Constitution. Inequality in population of the districts is so contrary to the
spirit of the Government and of the Constitution that we would
assume it was a required condition to representation in the Congress
of the United States. There is little or no difference between an unequal voice in election of members to Congress and a denial altogether of participation in the election of Congressmen. It is at
most a matter of degree. The right to vote, however, is not one of
those boasted guarantees of the Constitution, if it appears that one
voter has eight times as many votes as another. . . .*

The academic plaintiffs in Illinois appealed to the Supreme
Court of the United States, the only instrumentality affording
any realistic possibility of relief from their unjust predicament.
Their awareness that this was, in the most literal sense, the
court of last resort—the ultimate hope, as it were, for a restoration of their rights—was expressed in the somewhat unconven-
tional nature of the brief they filed. Headed "An 'Appeal to
Caesar,'" it began as follows:

*We think it may not be out of order to begin our Argument, in
this particular case, with a sort of introductory parable which we
feel is apt and has a clear cogency to the case at bar:*

*It will be recalled that when St. Paul sought justice from
the Scribes and Pharisees in Jerusalem, he proclaimed with
pride that he was a native of Tarsus, "no mean city"; but they
bound him with thongs. He then appealed to the Roman
Tribune and said to him: "I am a Roman citizen and was born
so"; but still they refused him a hearing and turned him away.
Later, he was taken before the Council where he tried to
speak, but the High Priest commanded that he be struck upon
the mouth. Again they sent him away to Felix, the Governor.
And after a long wait Paul was finally taken before the succeeding Governor, Festus. And then at last they took him
before King Herod Agrippa himself. There he again made a
valiant fight, and when once more he was denied justice, Paul
uttered the famous words, "I appeal to Caesar."*

*It is after a somewhat similar experience in search of justice
denied, that these Appellants stand before this Court, as a final
expedient, and figuratively make their "Appeal to Caesar." They
have been denied their Constitutional rights for a generation by the
State of Illinois, and specifically by the General Assembly of that
State, and by its Supreme Court. If this final appeal to this Court,
as the highest Reviewing Authority in the Land, is refused, then
all is lost.*

There developed in the Supreme Court of the United States,
however, a conflict of very much the same sort that had developed in the flag-salute cases discussed in the preceding
chapter. It was a conflict in which, again, the issue revolved
around differing ideas of judicial restraint and a prudent limitation of judicial authority.

Justice Frankfurter wrote the opinion of the Court in the
case, which came to be known as *Colegrove* v. *Green*. Only
seven of the Court's nine members participated in the decision
of the case; Justice Jackson was in Nürnberg as chief American
prosecutor of the principal Nazi war criminals; and the chief
justice, Harlan F. Stone, suffered a heart attack on the bench
while the case was being argued and died prior to its decision.
Only two other members of the Court joined in Justice Frankfurter's opinion, Justices Reed and Burton. Justice Rutledge,

following a somewhat different line of reasoning, concurred
in the result, which served to give a 4-to-3 majority to rejection
of the *Colegrove* appeal. Justice Black, supported by Justices
Douglas and Murphy, dissented.

Once more, as in the flag-salute cases, Justice Frankfurter
had no uncertainty about the unfairness and undesirability of
the situation that the suit sought to correct. He simply felt that
the legislature, not the Court, was the appropriate instrument
for correction. The intrusion of judicial authority into matters
of public policy would, he felt, be at once injurious to the
Court and to the democratic process. His own words set forth
his conviction with great clarity:

*We are of opinion that the appellants ask of this Court what is
beyond its competence to grant. This is one of those demands on
judicial power which cannot be met by verbal fencing about
"jurisdiction." It must be resolved by considerations on the basis of
which this Court, from time to time, has refused to intervene in
controversies. It has refused to do so because due regard for the
effective working of our Government revealed this issue to be of a
peculiarly political nature and therefore not meet for judicial
determination.*

*This is not an action to recover for damage because of the dis-
criminatory exclusion of a plaintiff from rights enjoyed by other
citizens. The basis for the suit is not a private wrong, but a wrong
suffered by Illinois as a polity. . . . In effect this is an appeal to the
federal courts to reconstruct the electoral process of Illinois in order
that it may be adequately represented in the councils of the
Nation. Because the Illinois legislature has failed to revise its
Congressional Representative districts in order to reflect great
changes, during more than a generation, in the distribution of its
population, we are asked to do this, as it were, for Illinois.*

*Of course no court can affirmatively re-map the Illinois districts
so as to bring them more in conformity with the standards of
fairness for a representative system. At best we could only declare
the existing electoral system invalid. The result would be to leave
Illinois undistricted and to bring into operation, if the Illinois legislature chose not to act, the choice of members for the House of*

Representatives on a statewide ticket. The last stage may be worse than the first. The upshot of judicial action may defeat the vital political principle which led Congress, more than a hundred years ago, to require districting. . . . Assuming acquiescence on the part of the authorities of Illinois in the selection of its Representatives by a mode that defies the direction of Congress for a selection by districts, the House of Representatives may not acquiesce. In the exercise of its power to judge the qualifications of its own members, the House may reject a delegation of Representatives-at-large. . . . Nothing is clearer than that this controversy concerns matters that bring courts into immediate and active relations with party contests. From the determination of such issues this Court has traditionally held aloof. It is hostile to a democratic system to involve the judiciary in the politics of the people. And it is not less pernicious if such judicial intervention in an essentially political contest be dressed up in the abstract phrases of the law. . . .

The short of it is that the Constitution has conferred upon Congress exclusive authority to secure representation by the State in the popular House and left to that House determination whether States have fulfilled their responsibility. If Congress fails in exercising its powers, whereby standards of fairness are offended, the remedy ultimately lies with the people. Whether Congress faithfully discharges its duty or not, the subject has been committed to the exclusive control of Congress.

Justice Frankfurter brought this trenchant argument to a conclusion in a paragraph that summed up his philosophy of judicial restraint and, at the same time, imprisoned the issue of equal representation for nearly two decades in an ironclad constitutional doctrine:

To sustain this action would cut very deep into the very being of Congress. Courts ought not to enter this political thicket. . . . The Constitution has left the performance of many duties in our governmental scheme to depend on the fidelity of the executive and legislative action and, ultimately, on the vigilance of the people in exercising their political rights.

Justice Rutledge saw the situation similarly but not in pre-

cisely the same way as Justice Frankfurter. He did not deny
that courts had jurisdiction in the matter, but he concurred
in the result because he believed that the relief sought "pitches
this Court into delicate relation to the functions of state officials and Congress"; the shortness of the time remaining
"makes it doubtful whether action could, or would, be taken
in time to secure for petitioners the effective relief they seek";
and to force an election at large would deprive Illinois citizens
of "representation by districts which the prevailing policy of
Congress demands."

Justice Black saw it altogether differently. In his view, the
case presented an intolerable wrong, violating a fundamental
premise of the American Constitution and calling imperatively,
therefore, for remedial action by the Supreme Court. Between
the Black and Frankfurter views of the judicial function, there
was, in short, a diametric and dramatic antagonism.[7]

Black began his dissent with a summary of the facts relating
to malapportionment in Illinois and a recital of the vain efforts
made to find relief in the state legislature and the state courts.
He regarded the arbitrary reduction of the effectiveness of
ballots cast by the plaintiffs in the case as amounting to a
denial of the equal protection of the laws and an abridgment
of "their privilege as citizens of the United States to vote for
Congressmen, a privilege guaranteed by Article I of the Constitution." He then asserted an outright opposition to virtually
all of the Frankfurter assumptions: "It is my judgment," he
wrote, "that the District Court had jurisdiction; that the complaint presented a justiciable case and controversy; and that
appellants had standing to sue, since the facts alleged show
that they have been injured as individuals. Unless previous
decisions of this Court are to be overruled, the suit is not one
against the State but against state officials as individuals."
Arguing that the 1901 State Apportionment Act itself consti-

[7] The complete text of the Black dissent can be found in the Appendix.

tuted a denial of the equal protection of the laws, he presented the following rationale:

Had Illinois passed an Act requiring that all of its twenty-six Congressmen be elected by the citizens of one county, it would clearly have amounted to a denial to the citizens of the other counties of their constitutionally guaranteed right to vote. And I cannot imagine that an Act that would have apportioned twenty-five Congressmen to the State's smallest county and one Congressman to all the others, would have been sustained by any court. Such an Act would clearly have violated the constitutional policy of equal representation. The 1901 Apportionment Act here involved violates that policy in the same way. The policy with respect to federal elections laid down by the Constitution, while it does not mean that the courts can or should prescribe the precise methods to be followed by state legislatures and the invalidation of all Acts that do not embody those precise methods, does mean that state legislatures must make real efforts to bring about approximately equal representation of citizens in Congress. Here the Legislature of Illinois has not done so. Whether that was due to negligence or was a wilful effort to deprive some citizens of an effective vote, the admitted result is that the constitutional policy of equality of representation has been defeated. Under these circumstances it is the Court's duty to invalidate the state law.

It is contended, however, that a court of equity does not have the power, or even if it has the power, that it should not exercise it in this case. To do so, it is argued, would mean that the Court is entering the area of "political questions." I cannot agree with that argument. . . .

. .It is true that voting is a part of elections and that elections are "political." But as this Court said in Nixon v. Herndon [273 U.S. 536], it is a mere "play upon words" to refer to a controversy such as this as "political" in the sense that courts have nothing to do with protecting and vindicating the right of a voter to cast an effective ballot. The Classic case,[8] among myriads of others, refutes the con-

---

[8] *United States* v. *Classic,* 313 U.S. 299 (1941), held that primary elections are an integral part of the election process and that the right of voters at a primary to have their votes counted, regardless of race or color, is a right secured by the Constitution.

*tention that courts are impotent in connection with evasions of all
"political" rights. . . .*

*. . . It is true that declaration of invalidity of the State Act and
the enjoining of state officials would result in prohibiting the State
from electing Congressmen under the system of the old congressional districts. But it would leave the State free to elect them from
the State at large, which . . . is a manner authorized by the Constitution. It is said that it would be inconvenient for the State to
conduct the election in this manner. But it has an element of virtue
that the more convenient method does not have—namely, it does
not discriminate against some groups to favor others, it gives all the
people an equally effective voice in electing their repesentatives as
is essential under a free government, and it is constitutional.*

The *Colegrove* decision brought to a halt efforts in a dozen
states to achieve more equitable arrangement of election districts through the courts. "If this final appeal to this Court, as
the highest Reviewing Authority in the Land, is refused, then
all is lost," the *Colegrove* plaintiffs had declared in their brief
to the Supreme Court. All seemed lost, indeed. A large part
of the frustration stemmed, however, from a misconception as
to just what the Court had decided in *Colegrove.*

If Justice Frankfurter's view was the Court's view, there
was no longer any use at all in seeking a judicial remedy for
malapportionment. The Court would never venture into this
"political thicket." But the fact of the matter was that Justice
Frankfurter had spoken only for himself and two other justices,
as far as the denial of jurisdiction was concerned. Apparently
this important fact was not clearly or generally appreciated.

Sixteen years elapsed before another test came to the Court.
It arose this time in Tennessee where, as in Illinois, a rural-dom-
inated state legislature left dramatically expanded urban communities of the state helpless and hopeless, contemptuously
spurning their pleas for recognition of a right to equal representation. For half a century the General Assembly of Tennessee had tyrannically ignored two provisions of the state

constitution. Article II, Section 5, provided that "the number of Representatives shall at the several periods of making the enumeration [every ten years by requirement of Section 4], be apportioned among the several counties or districts, according to the number of qualified voters in each. . . ." And Section 6 made the same stipulation for the apportionment of state senators.

Gene Graham, a reporter for the *Nashville Tennessean,* has recounted in illuminating detail the patient, painstaking, and resourceful efforts of a group of doughty and determined Tennesseans (American Levellers, he calls them) to obtain, through the assembly and through the state courts, a reasonable implementation of these constitutional commands.[9] The assembly leadership simply laughed at them. The courts simply concluded that jurisdiction had been foreclosed by *Colegrove* v. *Green.*

Charles W. Baker, chairman of the Shelby County Quarterly Court, lived in that county, which embraced a part of the city of Memphis and one of its suburbs, Millington. Shelby County had grown mightily in population during the 1950s and had also grown mightily in the urban problems that had come along with a population boom. On the basis of its population, Shelby County was probably entitled to about twenty representatives, including senators, in the General Assembly. All it had, however, was nine. And as a direct consequence of this underrepresentation in the state legislature, the county was comparably underrepresented in the Congress of the United States as well. The congressman from this Memphis district represented about three times as many persons as the two congressmen who were sent to Washington by two adjoining west Tennessee districts, rural and sparsely populated.

Joined by the mayor of Nashville, by a number of thoughtful and enterprising young lawyers, by some older citizens with a fervor for justice, Baker filed a suit against the Tennessee

[9] Gene Graham, *One Man One Vote* (Boston: Little, Brown, 1972).

secretary of state, Joseph Cordell Carr, a suit that came to be known as *Baker* v. *Carr*[10] and that wrought a revolution in the politics of the United States. The suit was, in short, hardly distinguishable from *Colegrove* v. *Green*, except that it directly involved apportionment of a state legislature rather than congressional districting. But the constitutional question was essentially the same. The problem for the plaintiffs was to get around the barrier Justice Frankfurter had erected to keep the judiciary out of the "political thicket."

As in Illinois in the *Colegrove* case, *Baker* v. *Carr* was argued in Tennessee before a special three-judge United States District Court. This made possible a direct appeal to the Supreme Court. The judges agreed unanimously on December 21, 1959, that a great wrong had been perpetrated by the Tennessee legislature but that, in the light of the Supreme Court's *Colegrove* ruling, nothing could be done about it by the judicial department of the government. Declaring that it lacked jurisdiction, the court would not even listen to arguments on the merits of the controversy.

Disappointed but not entirely daunted, the Tennessee plaintiffs sought a review by the Supreme Court of the United States. They took two effective steps. They retained Charles S. Rhyne, a prestigious Washington lawyer and former president of the American Bar Association, as their chief attorney. And they persuaded the solicitor general of the United States, Archibald Cox, to enter the case on their side as a friend of the Court.

Of the three members of the Court who had joined in the Frankfurter opinion in the *Colegrove* case, only Justice Frankfurter himself was still on the bench. Justices Reed and Burton, who had supported him, were gone, and so was Justice Rutledge whose concurrence in the result had enabled the Frankfurter doctrine to prevail. Justices Black and Douglas, dissenters in *Colegrove*, were still sitting. Chief Justice Warren

[10] 369 U.S. 186 (1962).

and Associate Justices Clark, Harlan, Brennan, Whittaker, and Stewart had all come to the Court since *Colegrove.* Justice Whittaker, however, did not participate in the decision of *Baker* v. *Carr.*

The argument before the Supreme Court was conducted in an atmosphere charged with emotion and full of tension. Justice Frankfurter seemed determined, from the very outset, to defend his doctrine against all comers. Charles Rhyne's overriding need was to persuade the Court that it had not, in fact, denied jurisdiction in its *Colegrove* decision. "Our interpretation of *Colegrove,*" he told the Court, "simply is that it is not a decision against us on jurisdiction, but it is for us on jurisdiction; that the decision of this Court was not against jurisdiction, but for jurisdiction. . . . We say that the lower court here, and the other courts that have cited it as holding that no jurisdiction exists, are in error."[11]

With some assistance from Justice Black in the course of questioning from the bench, Rhyne succeeded in wresting from Justice Frankfurter an acknowledgment that this was so. In fact, four members of the Court—the three dissenters and Justice Rutledge—had thought there was jurisdiction, but Rutledge had joined Frankfurter in holding that relief should not be granted on the mere basis of the Court's equity powers.

The Supreme Court announced its decision in *Baker* v. *Carr* on March 26, 1962, in an opinion written by Justice William Brennan. It was an exceptionally long opinion, yet it came to exceedingly simple, definite conclusions. The Court held that the district court had jurisdiction of the subject matter of the federal constitutional claim that had been presented to it, that the plaintiffs had standing to maintain their suit, and that their charges of a denial of equal protection constituted a justiciable cause of action upon which they were entitled to a trial and a decision. In short, the Supreme Court decided only that the

[11] Quoted by Gene Graham, *op. cit.,* p. 231.

district court had authority to decide the matter on its merits. Once this was settled, however, there was hardly any question as to how the controversy would be concluded. The district court had already declared that "Tennessee is guilty of a clear violation of the state constitution and of the [federal] rights of the plaintiffs. . . ."

Six distinct opinions were delivered by members of the Supreme Court. Justices Douglas, Clark, and Stewart wrote individual concurrences, each finding something special he wanted to say about jurisdiction and justiciability. Justice Frankfurter wrote an outraged sixty-four-page dissenting opinion in which Justice Harlan (grandson of the John M. Harlan who had dissented in *Plessy* v. *Ferguson* sixty-five years earlier) joined, and Justice Harlan wrote a twenty-page dissenting opinion, hardly less vehement, in which Justice Frankfurter joined.

The Frankfurter dissent began by denouncing the Court's decision as "a massive repudiation of the experience of our whole past" and warned that "it may well impair the Court's position as the ultimate organ of 'the supreme Law of the Land' in that vast range of legal problems, often strongly entangled in popular feeling, on which this Court must pronounce." And he went on to declare that "The Court's authority —possessed of neither the purse nor the sword—ultimately rests on sustained public confidence in its moral sanction. Such feeling must be nourished by the Court's complete detachment, in fact and in appearance, from political entanglements and by abstention from injecting itself into the clash of political forces in political settlements."

It must have been some degree of pique that led Justice Frankfurter to inject into this dissent a long and novel argument—an argument not mentioned in his *Colegrove* opinion for the Court—that representation proportioned to population has the support neither of history nor of logic—that "it was not the English system, it was not the colonial system, it was not the system chosen for the national government by the Constitution, it was not the system exclusively or even predominantly practiced by the States at the time of adoption of the Fourteenth Amendment, it is not predominantly practiced by the States today." There is, to be sure, an element of truth in all this; but it is essentially beside the truth.

The very heart of his dissent, however, is again the "political thicket" doctrine. "Apportionment battles," he concludes, "are overwhelmingly party or intra-party contests. It will add a virulent source of friction and tension in federal-state relations to embroil the federal judiciary in them." Here is a strong reflection, and an inescapably respectable one, of the lesson learned in the early days of the New Deal when the Court's obduracy and recklessness led to FDR's almost successful attack upon it. To undertake a role redolent of politics and peculiarly the province of the Congress and the state legislatures would be, in Frankfurter's view, needlessly to embroil the Court in a conflict with adversaries far more powerful than itself.

This argument was echoed effectively by Justice Harlan, who brought his scholarly dissent to a close with these words: "In conclusion, it is appropriate to say that one need not agree, as a citizen, with what Tennessee has done or failed to do, in order to deprecate, as a judge, what the majority is doing today. Those observers of the Court who see it primarily as the last refuge for the correction of all inequality or injustice, no matter what its nature or source, will no doubt applaud this decision and its break with the past. Those who consider that continuing national respect for the Court's authority depends in large measure upon its wise exercise of self-restraint and discipline in constitutional adjudication, will view the decision with deep concern."

This, then, is the case for judicial restraint, for a guardianship and conservation of the Court's tenuous authority, presented by two of the ablest jurists in the Court's long history. Perhaps the best rebuttal to this view was stated by Justice Clark at the very end of his concurring opinion:

As John Rutledge (later Chief Justice) said 175 years ago in the course of the Constitutional Convention, a chief function of the Court is to secure the national rights. Its decision today supports the proposition for which our forebears fought and many died, namely, that to be fully conformable to the principle of right, the form of government must be representative. That is the keystone upon which our government was founded and lacking which no republic can survive. It is well for this Court to practice self-restraint and discipline in constitutional adjudication, but, never in its history have those principles received sanction where the national rights of so many have been so clearly infringed for so long a time. National respect for the courts is more enhanced through the forthright enforcement of those rights rather than by rendering them nugatory through the interposition of subterfuges. In my view the ultimate decision today is in the greatest tradition of this Court.

Here is a clear clash between the philosophy of judicial restraint and the philosophy of judicial activism. Those who place their emphasis upon restraint tend to look upon the Court primarily as though it were the trustee of an estate, the limited assets of which it must jealously husband and conserve. Thus, for example, Justice Frankfurter spoke, in his *Baker* dissent, of a danger that the Court's intervention in the apportionment problem "may well impair the Court's position as the ultimate organ of 'the supreme Law of the Land.' . . ." And one of his most articulate disciples, Professor Alexander Bickel of the Yale Law School, a Frankfurter law clerk in 1952–53, has observed that "there is a natural quantitative limit to the number of major, principled interventions the court can permit itself per decade, let us say. It is a matter of credibility."[12]

The activists tend to believe, on the other hand, that the Court's credibility depends on its willingness to do battle, against whatever odds, for the constitutional rights it was established to uphold. No doubt there are limits to its capacity for intervention. But it is no less true that a failure to intervene

[12] Alexander M. Bickel, *The Supreme Court and the Idea of Progress* (New York: Harper & Row, 1970), p. 94.

in a time of crisis may take away forever the opportunity for intervention. Inaction may be as decisive as action. In an essay roundly critical of Professor Bickel, J. Skelly Wright, a distinguished judge of the United States Court of Appeals for the District of Columbia Circuit, wrote of "a new generation of lawyers" on whose thinking the Warren Court has exercised a "revolutionary influence" and who "were inspired by the dignity and moral courage of a man and an institution that was prepared to act on the ideals to which America is theoretically and rhetorically dedicated."

"The new generation of lawyers," Judge Wright went on to say, "the new professors as well as judges and practitioners, I might add—hope that the Supreme Court might resist a coup d'état. But they see no point in querulous admonitions that the Court should restrain itself from combatting injustice now in order to preserve itself to combat a coup later on. An institution that sits back, always emphasizing its weakness and its reasons for inaction, is unlikely to be in a fighting stance when the tanks roll down Pennsylvania Avenue. The young lawyers know that a country which hoards all of its moral capital in the form of windy rhetoric is likely to die rich—and soon."

The decision in *Baker* v. *Carr* acted like the opening of a sluice gate. Before the end of 1962—that is to say, within nine months of the decision—litigation attacking apportionment of state legislatures had been instituted in at least thirty-four states.

If equality of representation in state legislatures was a requirement of the equal-protection clause of the Fourteenth Amendment, the same must almost certainly be true of representation in the national House of Representatives. A case testing that question came up to the Court from Georgia in the fall of 1963 and was decided on February 17, 1964.[13] Its history was very like

---

[13] Wesberry v. Sanders, 376 U.S. 1 (1964).

the history of *Colegrove* v. *Green.* According to the 1960 census, the Fifth Congressional District of Georgia had a population of 823,680 as compared with the Ninth District, which had a population of 272,154. A three-judge district court found unanimously that this was "grossly out of balance." On the authority of the *Colegrove* decision—because this case concerned congressional districting—a majority of the district court dismissed the case, however, on the ground that it raised only "political" questions.

This time Justice Black, the dissenter in the *Colegrove* case, wrote the opinion of the Court. Referring to Justice Frankfurter's opinion of the Court in *Colegrove* as a "minority opinion," he said that the district court had erred in following it. "We hold," he wrote, "that, construed in its historical context, the command of Article I, Section 2, that Representatives be chosen by the People of the several States means that as nearly as is practicable one man's vote in a congressional election is to be worth as much as another's. . . . The history of the Constitution, particularly that part of it relating to the adoption of Article I, Section 2, reveals that those who framed the Constitution meant that, no matter what the mechanics of an election, whether state-wide or by districts, it was population which was to be the basis of the House of Representatives."

Justice Frankfurter had left the Court by this time and so was unable to protest; but Justice Harlan remained to warn again in dissent, as ardently as he could, that "the Constitution does not confer on the Court blanket authority to step into every situation where the political branch may be thought to have fallen short" and that "What is done today saps the political process."

Final vindication of Black's *Colegrove* dissent came a few months later when the Court dealt for the first time with the substantive issues of malapportionment in both houses of the legislature of Alabama. A suit had been filed in that state just three days after *Baker* v. *Carr* was decided. Relying on that decision rather than on *Colegrove*, a special three-judge district court held that the inequality of the existing representation in the Alabama legislature violated the equal-protection clause of the Fourteenth Amendment. One quarter of Alabama's population lived in districts that elected more than half of the members of the state senate and house of representatives. Population-variance ratios of up to about 41 to 1 existed in the senate and up to about 16 to 1 in the house. This time the district court had accepted jurisdiction, and it was its judgment rather than a refusal to judge that came up to the Supreme Court for review.

Chief Justice Warren himself wrote for the Court in the Alabama case *Reynolds* v. *Sims.*[14] Half a dozen cases were decided under that rubric, with Justice Harlan angrily dissenting and with brief concurring opinions noting differences of view by Justices Stewart and Clark. The gist of the chief justice's reasoning is contained in a single paragraph of his long opinion:

Legislators represent people, not trees or acres. Legislators are elected by voters, not farms or cities or economic interests. As long as ours is a representative form of government, and our legislatures are those instruments of government elected directly by and directly representative of the people, the right to elect legislators in a free and unimpaired fashion is a bedrock of our political system. It could hardly be gainsaid that a constitutional claim had been asserted by an allegation that certain otherwise qualified voters had been entirely prohibited from voting for members of their state legislature. And, if a State should provide that the votes of citizens in one part of the State should be given two times, or five times, or 10 times the weight of votes of citizens in another part of the State, it could hardly be contended that the right to vote of those residing in the disfavored areas had not been effectively diluted. . . . Overweighting and overvaluation of the votes of those living here has the certain effect of dilution and undervaluation of the votes of those living there. The resulting discrimination against those voters living in disfavored areas is easily demonstrable mathematically.

[14] 377 U.S. 533 (1964).

Their right to vote is simply not the same right to vote as that of those living in a favored part of the State. Two, five, or 10 of them must vote before the effect of their voting is equivalent to that of their favored neighbor. Weighting the votes of citizens differently, by any method or means, merely because of where they happen to reside, hardly seems justifiable.

From this foundation, the chief justice went forward to rule that "as a basic constitutional standard, the Equal Protection Clause requires that the seats in both houses of a bicameral state legislature must be apportioned on a population basis." He rejected out of hand the contention, drawn from an analogy with the federal government, that the upper chamber of a state legislature could fairly represent geographical subdivisions of the state if the lower chamber accurately represented equal population groups. The federal arrangement, under which each state of the Union, regardless of size and population, is entitled to two senators, grew, of course, out of the consideration that the former colonies that were to establish the American Republic regarded themselves as sovereign entities jealous of their independence and willing to relinquish a portion of it only if assured equality in one branch of the national legislature. Indeed, so insistent were they upon equality that the Constitutional Convention wrote into Article V of the Constitution the stipulation "that no State, without its Consent, shall be deprived of its equal Suffrage in the Senate." The arrangement under which the Senate represented the states as political entities while the House represented the people of the states was known as "the Great Compromise." It made possible a Union that might otherwise not have been achieved, and constituted a cornerstone of the American federal system. But, of course, the reasoning that justified giving Nevada and California equal representation in the Senate had no relevance to the geographical subdivisions of the states themselves. Chief Justice Warren said this about it:

Attempted reliance on the federal analogy appears often to be little more than an after-the-fact rationalization offered in defense of maladjusted state apportionment arrangements. The original constitutions of 36 of our States provided that representation in both houses of the state legislatures would be based completely, or predominantly, on population. And the Founding Fathers clearly had no intention of establishing a pattern or model for the apportionment of seats in state legislatures when the system of representation in the Federal Congress was adopted. . . .

Political subdivisions of States—counties, cities, or whatever— never were and never have been traditionally regarded as subordinate governmental instrumentalities created by the State to assist in carrying out of state governmental functions. . . . In summary, we can perceive no constitutional difference, with respect to the geographical distribution of state legislature representation, between the two houses of a bicameral state legislature.[15]

Warren's opinion proceeds, then, to allow a reasonable degree of flexibility for state apportionment:

By holding that as a federal constitutional requisite both houses of a state legislature must be apportioned on a population basis, we mean that the Equal Protection Clause requires that a State make an honest and good faith effort to construct districts, in both houses of its legislature, as nearly of equal population as is practicable. We realize that it is a practical impossibility to arrange legislative districts so that each one has an identical number of residents, or citizens, or voters. Mathematical exactness or precision is hardly a workable constitutional requirement.[16]

For all the forebodings of Justice Frankfurter and Justice Harlan, the Supreme Court seems to have survived the districting and apportionment decisions with its prestige and power unimpaired. There was a great deal of commotion, it is true, when these decisions were handed down. Indeed, there was rather boisterous talk of a constitutional amendment to

[15] 377 U.S. 533 at 573 and 575.
[16] *Id.,* at 577.

undo the Court's ruling. It came to nothing, however. Before very long, lawyers and law professors were hailing the changes produced by these decisions as the Warren Court's outstanding achievement. Professor Robert McKay, now dean of the New York University Law School, published a law-journal article entitled, "Reapportionment: Success Story of the Warren Court."[17] And Chief Justice Warren himself, in a television interview in 1972 after his retirement from the Court, said that he regarded *Baker* v. *Carr* as the most important case decided during his tenure as chief justice.

The clash of constitutional principle and of judicial philosophy reflected in these voting cases presents a dramatic dilemma. It is indisputably true that the Court needs to conserve its prestige and power, avoiding embroilment in transient contests for political advantage. And it is no less true that it needs to cast its weight upon the scales of justice whenever basic constitutional rights are in the balance. In these cases, the clash between competing truths was presented with great force by men of learning, conscience, and integrity.

Whatever the merits or demerits in constitutional theory of the triumph of the one-man, one-vote principle first championed with so much fire by Hugo Black in his *Colegrove* dissent, it has surely proved a liberating influence in state and national legislatures. Rural blocs in many legislative bodies remain tightly knit and formidable, clinging where they can to control and often voting against the big cities if only out of pique. Nevertheless, the restoration of equality in the voting booth has served, in some measure, to set the legislatures free from their bondage to rural rule. And it has afforded the country's urban communities at least a chance to deal with their problems. If it is true that the Court invaded the legislature's province in fashioning the one-man, one-vote rule, it is no less true, paradoxically, that the invasion gave the legislature a new birth of freedom, a fresh means of political usefulness.

[17] Robert McKay, "Reapportionment: Success Story of the Warren Court," *Michigan Law Review* 67 (1968), 223.

VII

"FREE SPEECH
IS THE RULE"

———

Dennis v. *United States*, William O. Douglas dissenting*

The meaning and boundaries of free expression—of that deceptively simple and seemingly unambiguous command contained in the very first article of the Bill of Rights, "Congress shall make no law . . . . abridging the freedom of speech or of the press"—have been in continuous controversy since the birth of the American Republic. It is sobering to recall that no more than a decade after the ratification of the Constitution the Congress of the United States adopted the Alien and Sedition Laws in 1798, which appear to be, on their face, a direct nullification of the amendment's promise.

When an American says pridefully that this is a free country, he means usually that it is a country in which anybody can say anything he pleases. But very few Americans have ever actually been willing to grant that degree of freedom respecting either political or aesthetic matters to ideas or opinions that they dislike or believe fraught with danger to the general welfare. There have always been limits on expression in the

* 341 U.S. 494 (1951).

United States, no matter how unequivocal the language of the First Amendment. And in times of crisis, the limits have been narrowly drawn and stringently enforced. In every period of this country's history there have been many Americans, perhaps a majority at times, who have deeply mistrusted heterodoxy of any sort, who have looked askance upon any challenge to duly constituted authority or to generally accepted doctrine, who have tended, in short, to equate dissent with disloyalty, to seek suppression of unwelcome views, and to punish nonconformity.

It is at once interesting and curious, indeed, to observe how frequently attacks upon unorthodox opinions are made in the name of patriotism, as though uniformity were the ultimate expression of national unity. People who pride themselves on being patriots often seem prone to question the patriotism of others who may disagree with them. They tend also to be extravagantly skeptical of the loyalty and good sense of nearly all their fellow citizens. Thus they seem almost invariably convinced that alien propaganda will subvert not themselves, but nearly everybody else, and that the political gospel according to Karl Marx will prove far more appealing than the gospel according to, say, Thomas Jefferson. Patriotism to these super-Americans, seems, in short, to combine a total want of confidence in their fellow citizens with a total lack of faith in the appeal of American traditions, institutions, and values.

Those who believe in freedom of expression as a vital element of any good society—as a positive asset rather than as a mere slogan or a luxury to be enjoyed only in untroubled times —may be cast, roughly, into two categories. One category is made up of those who seek as much freedom as they deem compatible with public safety—or with national security, a more usual contemporary term; the other comprises those who believe free speech is itself an indispensable contributor to security and the general welfare, the true source of national strength.

Those who belong in the first category see the problem as

one of striking a balance between the needs of the nation and the demands of its individual members for free expression, between the requirements of public order and the benefits of free discussion and debate. Those in the second category contend that the necessary balancing was done long ago by the authors of the First Amendment who weighed the risks inherent in untrammeled freedom against the risks involved in government control of public information and expression, opting for total freedom as the best way of preserving the public interest and the national strength.

In a noble book analyzing the incursions on free speech during the First World War and its aftermath—a period when the ideas of the Russian Revolution and the international machinations of the communist conspiracy seemed, to some Americans, a menace to this country's very foundations—Zechariah Chafee, Jr., gave a concise statement of the balancing theory, the recognition of free speech as vitally important, yet subject to restraint in the national interest:

The true boundary line of the First Amendment can be fixed only when Congress and the courts realize that the principle on which speech is classified as lawful or unlawful involves the balancing against each other of two very important social interests, in public safety and in the search for truth. Every reasonable attempt should be made to maintain both interests unimpaired, and the great interest in free speech should be sacrificed only when the interest in public safety is really imperiled, and not, as most men believe, when it is barely conceivable that it may be slightly affected. In war time, therefore, speech should be unrestricted by the censorship or by punishment, unless it is clearly liable to cause direct and dangerous interference with the conduct of the war.[1]

In a direct criticism of this statement, another distinguished philosopher of American freedom, Alexander Meiklejohn, sets forth the opposing position in these terms:

[1] Zechariah Chafee, Jr., *Free Speech in the United States* (Cambridge, Mass.: Harvard University Press, 1942), p. 35.

*The interest in the public safety and the interest in the search
for truth are, Mr. Chafee says, two distinct interests. And they may
be so balanced against each other, he says, that on occasion we must
choose between them. Is that the relation between public discussion
and the public welfare as it is conceived by the Constitution? I
do not think so. And I can find nothing in the Constitution which
justifies the assertion. . . . The First Amendment . . . is saying that,
as interests, the integrity of public discussion and the care for
the public safety are identical. We Americans, in choosing our
form of government, have made, at this point, a momentous
decision. We have decided to be self-governed. We have mea-
sured the dangers and the values of the suppression of the freedom
of public inquiry and debate. And, on the basis of that mea-
surement, having regard for the public safety, we have decided
that the destruction of freedom is always unwise, that freedom is
always expedient. The conviction recorded by that decision is not
a sentimental vagary about the "natural rights" of individuals. It is
a reasoned and sober judgment as to the best available method of
guarding the public safety. We, the People, as we plan for the
general welfare, do not choose to be "protected" from the "search
for truth." On the contrary, we have adopted it as our "way of
life," our method of doing the work of governing for which, as
citizens, we are responsible. Shall we, then, as practitioners of freedom, listen to ideas which, being opposed to our own, might destroy confidence in our form of government? Shall we give a hearing to those who hate and despise freedom, to those who, if they
had the power, would destroy our institutions? Certainly, yes! Our
action must be guided not by their principles, but by ours. We
listen, not because they desire to speak, but because we need to
hear. If there are arguments against our theory of government, our
policies in war or in peace, we the citizens, the rulers, must hear and
consider them for ourselves. That is the way of public safety. It
is the program of self-government.*[2]

Perhaps this difference of outlook between two great champions of liberty derived in some degree from the fact that Mr.
Chafee was a professor of law while Mr. Meiklejohn was a

[2] Alexander Meiklejohn, *Political Freedom* (New York: Harper & Brothers,
1948), pp. 56–57.

professor of philosophy. The distinction is too great to be ignored, however, and too fundamental to judicial interpretation of the First Amendment. In another portion of his book, Professor Meiklejohn offers a specific definition of what he means by political freedom and how, in practical terms, he would apply the First Amendment to dissent or to heretical belief:

If, then, on any occasion in the United States it is allowable to say that the Constitution is a good document, it is equally allowable, in that situation, to say that the Constitution is a bad document. If a public building may be used in which to say, in time of war, that the war is justified, then the same building may be used in which to say that it is not justified. If it be publicly argued that conscription for armed service is moral and necessary, it may likewise be publicly argued that it is immoral and unnecessary. If it may be said that American political institutions are superior to those of England or Russia or Germany, it may, with equal freedom, be said that those of England or Russia or Germany are superior to ours. These conflicting views may be expressed, must be expressed, not because they are valid, but because they are relevant. If they are responsibly entertained by anyone, we, the voters, need to hear them. When a question of policy is "before the house," free men choose to meet it not with their eyes shut, but with their eyes open. To be afraid of ideas, any idea, is to be unfit for self government. Any such suppression of ideas about the common good, the First Amendment condemns with its absolute disapproval. The freedom of ideas shall not be abridged.[3]

In general, it is Professor Chafee's view, rather than Professor Meiklejohn's view, that has prevailed in setting the limits of free expression in America. During the fledgling years of the Republic, when the excesses and extravagances of the French Revolution seemed, to the establishment of that time, a threat to the stability of this country, the Alien and Sedition Laws were enacted to contain them. John Marshall's Supreme Court

[3] *Ibid.*, pp.27–28.

was too preoccupied with defining the shape and scope of federalism to deal with the constitutionality of those enactments. Congress, as it turned out, dealt with them definitively as soon as Thomas Jefferson moved into the White House—by wiping them off the statute books and providing indemnification for the citizens who had been fined and thrown into jail for violating them.

The Civil War, naturally, brought its own inevitable incursions into civil liberty in general and freedom of expression in particular. It was not until the twentieth century, however—first during the excitement and anxiety of the First World War and later in the heyday of hysteria known as McCarthyism, when there was terror that Americans would be seduced and subverted by the lure of communist propaganda—that the attack on all dissident opinion reached the summit of its fury and folly in the United States.

The story of the Supreme Court's role as a guardian and guarantor of free speech has been, on the whole, an inglorious one, although it has produced some rather glorious rhetoric about the importance of freedom, mostly in dissenting opinions. In the panic period of the 1950s, the Court succumbed to the prevailing concern over communism to the extent of upholding a twentieth-century sedition law—a statute forbidding *advocacy* of any violent overthrow of the government.[4] Before the decade was out, however, the Court, as the country became more rational and sober, reconsidered and modified its ruling. Before examining the record of those midcentury cases, however, it is necessary to go farther back and look at some precursor issues that the Court dealt with in the years immediately following the First World War.

On the heels of American entry into the war—on June 15, 1917—Congress adopted the Espionage Act, a law that went beyond the prohibition of spying, sabotage, or other activity in aid of the enemy, establishing three new offenses:

---

[4] Dennis v. United States, 341 U.S. 494 (1951). The complete text of Justice Douglas's dissent in this case can be found in the appendix.

Whoever, when the United States is at war, shall willfully make or convey false reports or false statements with intent to interfere with the operation of or success of the military or naval forces of the United States or to promote the success of its enemies and whoever, when the United States is at war, shall willfully cause or attempt to cause insubordination, disloyalty, mutiny, or refusal of duty, in the military or naval forces of the United States; *or shall willfully obstruct the recruiting or enlistment service of the United States, to the injury of the service or of the United States, shall be punished by a fine of not more than $10,000 or imprisonment for not more than twenty years or both.*[5] *[Emphasis added.]*

In addition, the act was amended not quite a year later by a section, sometimes referred to as the Sedition Act, that forbade such things as saying or doing anything with intent to obstruct the sale of United States bonds, except by way of bona-fide and not disloyal advice; urging any curtailment of production of any things necessary to the prosecution of the war with intent to hinder its prosecution; or even uttering, printing, writing, or publishing any disloyal, profane, scurrilous, or abusive language, or language intended to cause contempt, scorn, contumely or disrepute as regards the form of government of the United States!

The Espionage Act did not come before the Supreme Court until 1919, when the war was already over. The first test of it involved Schenck, the general secretary of the Socialist party, who had had a hand in printing and mailing 15,000 leaflets declaring that the draft was unconstitutional and that it involved "a monstrous wrong against humanity in the interest of Wall Street's chosen few." The leaflets, many of which went to young men who had been summoned to military service by their draft boards, urged recipients to "assert your opposition to the draft."

The Court upheld the conviction of Schenck, and by a unanimous decision. Its opinion in the case was written by Justice

[5] Act of June 15, 1917, c. 30, Title I, Sec 3.

Oliver Wendell Holmes, Jr., and has tremendous significance in the development of American judicial doctrine about the limits of expression because it contains the first formulation of what has been known ever since as "the clear and present danger test."[6] Holmes said for the Court:

> . . . We admit that in many places and in ordinary times the defendants in saying all that was said in the circular would have been within their constitutional rights. But the character of every act depends upon the circumstances in which it is done. The most stringent protection of free speech would not protect a man in falsely shouting fire in a theatre and causing a panic. It does not even protect a man from an injunction against uttering words that may have all the effect of force. The question in every case is whether the words used are used in such circumstances and are of such a nature as to create a clear and present danger that they will bring about the substantive evils that Congress has a right to prevent. It is a question of proximity and degree. When a nation is at war many things that might be said in time of peace are such a hindrance to its effort that their utterance will not be endured so long as men fight and that no Court could regard them as protected by any constitutional right.

This did not afford much help or comfort for Schenck and his associates; but it offered hope, at least in time of peace, for radicals who thought of themselves as prophets of some new order and believed that Utopia was attainable only through revolution in some distant, rosy future. It aimed at sparing from imprisonment the rhetoricians whose rebellions were only verbal, the visionaries who strove to stir men's dreams, the reformers who sought change, but not violent overthrow, of the government. The Court's acceptance of the clear-and-present-danger test in the *Schenck* case was an important early victory for tolerance.

It was short-lived, however. In the very year in which *Schenck* was decided, the Court dealt with another case in-

---

[6] Schenck v. United States, 249 U.S. 47 (1919).

volving freedom of expression—dealt with it without any evidence of understanding the clear-and-present-danger doctrine it had itself adopted. The case arose under the Draconian provisions of the Espionage Act, which had been added to it by the 1918 amendment. The defendants were prosecuted for throwing from a window of a New York loft building some leaflets that denounced "The Hypocrisy of the United States and Her Allies" in dispatching American troops to Vladivostok and Murmansk in the summer of 1918. Seven members of the Court held their conviction to be entirely valid. Justice Brandeis joined in a superb dissent written by Justice Holmes. The opinion sets forth once more the justice's conviction that only grave and imminent danger can justify the suppression of speech and offers a beautifully eloquent argument for tolerance:

> . . . *I do not doubt for a moment that by the same reasoning that would justify punishing persuasion to murder, the United States constitutionally may punish speech that produces or is intended to produce a clear and imminent danger that it will bring about forthwith certain substantive evils that the United States constitutionally may seek to prevent. The power undoubtedly is greater in time of war than in time of peace because war opens dangers that do not exist at other times.*
>
> *But as against dangers peculiar to war, as against others, the principle of the right to free speech is always the same. It is only the present danger of immediate evil or an intent to bring it about that warrants Congress in setting a limit to the expression of opinion where private rights are not concerned. Congress certainly cannot forbid all effort to change the mind of the country. . . .*
>
> *Persecution for the expression of opinions seems to me perfectly logical. If you have no doubt of your premises or your power and want a certain result with all your heart you naturally express your wishes in law and sweep away all opposition. To allow opposition by speech seems to indicate that you think speech impotent, as when a man says that he has squared the circle, or that you do not care wholeheartedly for the result, or that you doubt either your power or your premises.*

But when men have realized that time has upset many fighting faiths, they may come to believe even more than they believe the very foundations of their own conduct that the ultimate good desired is better reached by free trade in ideas—that the best test of truth is the power of the thought to get itself accepted in the competition of the market, and that truth is the only ground upon which their wishes safely can be carried out. That, at any rate, is the theory of our Constitution. It is an experiment, as all life is an experiment. Every year if not every day we have to wager our salvation upon some prophecy based upon imperfect knowledge. While that experiment is part of our system I think that we should be eternally vigilant against attempts to check the expression of opinions that we loathe and believe to be fraught with death, unless they so imminently threaten immediate interference with the lawful and pressing purposes of the law that an immediate check is required to save the country.[7]

The second case arose five years later, not under the Espionage Act nor, indeed, under any federal statute, but under a New York State law forbidding advocacy of the doctrine that organized government should be overthrown by force or violence. Under this state law, a man named Benjamin Gitlow was convicted of advocating criminal anarchy because he had written a pamphlet, "The Left-Wing Manifesto," published by the left wing of the Socialist party. It was a ferocious, if insignificant, document, rejecting moderation or any possibility of achieving socialism through the electoral process and urging instead a "revolutionary dictatorship of the proletariat." Justice Sanford said for the Court that the New York law did not penalize "abstract doctrine" or academic discussion. Citing the final assertion of the pamphlet, "The Communist International calls the proletariat of the world to the final struggle!" he declared: "This is not the expression of philosophical abstraction, the mere prediction of future events; it is the language of direct incitement." Thus Sanford expressed his own

---

[7] Abrams et al. v. United States, 250 U.S. 616 (1919). The complete text of Justice Holmes's dissent in this case can be found in the Appendix.

conclusion that "The Left-Wing Manifesto" did, indeed, constitute a clear and present danger. Holmes and Brandeis again dissented, the former setting forth the views of both in another of his brilliantly terse opinions.

> . . . *It is said that this manifesto is more than a theory, that it was an incitement. Every idea is an incitement. It offers itself for belief and if believed it is acted on unless some other belief outweighs it or some failure of energy stifles the movement at its birth. The only difference between the expression of an opinion and an incitement in the narrower sense is the speaker's enthusiasm for the result. Eloquence may set fire to reason. But whatever may be thought of the redundant discourse before us it had no chance of starting a present conflagration.*
>
> *If in the long run the beliefs expressed in proletarian dictatorship are destined to be accepted by the dominant forces of the community, the only meaning of free speech is that they should be given their chance and have their way.*
>
> *If the publication of this document had been laid as an attempt to induce an uprising against the government at once and not at some indefinite time in the future, it would have presented a different question. The object would have been one with which the law might deal, subject to the doubt whether there was any danger that the publication could produce any result, or in other words, whether it was not futile and too remote from possible consequences. But the indictment alleges the publication and nothing more.*[8]

It is evident from the marked differences of opinion among members of the Court in these cases that "clear and present danger" can hardly be said to afford a precise standard for judgment. It left a great deal to the discretion of the judges at every level of the judiciary. Holmes, its creator, found himself ensnared by it; a test that he had conceived in the *Schenck* case as a safeguard for speech proved in *Gitlow* to be a rationale for its suppression. Only the long, slow judicial process

[8] Gitlow v. New York, 268 U.S. 652 (1924).

called "inclusion and exclusion"—determination by case after case—could serve to give it any clarity of content.

Another state case, *Whitney* v. *California*,[9] came before the Supreme Court in 1927. It concerned the conviction of Anita Whitney, a woman of almost sixty, a Wellesley graduate active in philanthropic and social causes, who had joined the Communist Labor party. This linked her in some manner to the IWW, an organization that at that time struck terror into the hearts of the respectable and caught her in the coils of a Criminal Syndicalism Act adopted in California, as in so many other states, in 1919 after the Supreme Court's *Schenck* decision of that year made such statutes seem valid and effective. Because Miss Whitney's attorney died during her trial and the clear-and-present-danger argument was not presented in such a way as to raise the constitutional issue, Holmes and Brandeis felt constrained to join the rest of the Court in sustaining the conviction. Together, however, they filed a concurring opinion— a vehement dissent from the Court's reasoning, in fact, much more than a concurrence. The opinion was written by Brandeis and affords a considerably more detailed and persuasive statement of the clear-and-present-danger doctrine than can be found in any of Holmes's own presentations of the idea. It embodies also what may well be the most enlightening and eloquent statement of the First Amendment's meaning—of the essential character of the American polity, indeed—that has ever been composed. A portion of the Brandeis opinion follows:

The right of free speech, the right to teach and the right of assembly are, of course, fundamental rights. . . . These may not be denied or abridged. But, although the rights of free speech and assembly are fundamental, they are not in their nature absolute. Their exercise is subject to restriction, if the particular restriction proposed is required in order to protect the State from destruction or from serious injury, political, economic or moral. That the nec-

---

[9] Whitney v. California, 274 U.S. 357 (1927). The complete text of Justice Brandeis's concurring opinion in this case can be found in the Appendix.

essity which is essential to a valid restriction does not exist unless speech would produce, or is intended to produce, a clear and imminent danger of some substantive evil which the State constitutionally may seek to prevent has been settled. See Schenck v. United States. . . .

This Court has not yet fixed the standard by which to determine when a danger shall be deemed clear; how remote the danger may be and yet be deemed present; and what degree of evil shall be deemed sufficiently substantial to justify resort to abridgement of free speech and assembly as the means of protection. To reach sound conclusions on these matters, we must bear in mind why a State is, ordinarily, denied the power to prohibit dissemination of social, economic and political doctrine which a vast majorty of its citizens believes to be false and fraught with evil consequences.

Those who won our independence believed that the final end of the State was to make men free to develop their faculties; and that in its government the deliberative forces should prevail over the arbitrary. They valued liberty both as an end and as a means. They believed liberty to be the secret of happiness and courage to be the secret of liberty. They believed that freedom to think as you will and to speak as you think are means indispensable to the discovery and spread of political truth; that without free speech and assembly discussion would be futile; that with them, discussion affords ordinarily adequate protection against the dissemination of noxious doctrine; that the greatest menace to freedom is an inert people; that public discussion is a political duty; and that this should be a fundamental principle of the American government. They recognized the risks to which all human institutions are subject. But they knew that order cannot be secured merely through fear of punishment for its infraction; that it is hazardous to discourage thought, hope and imagination; that fear breeds repression; that repression breeds hate; that hate menaces stable government; that the path of safety lies in the opportunity to discuss freely supposed grievances and proposed remedies; and that the fitting remedy for evil counsels is good ones. Believing in the power of reason as applied through public discussion, they eschewed silence coerced by law—the argument of force in its worst form. Recognizing the occasional tyrannies of governing majorities, they amended the Constitution so that free speech and assembly should be guaranteed.

*Fear of serious injury cannot alone justify suppression of free
speech and assembly. Men feared witches and burnt women. It is
the function of free speech to free men from the bondage of irrational fears. To justify suppression of free speech there must be a
reasonable ground to fear that serious evil will result if free speech
is practiced. There must be reasonable ground to believe that the
danger apprehended is imminent. There must be reasonable ground
to believe that the evil to be prevented is a serious one. . . .*

*Those who won our independence by revolution were not
cowards. They did not fear political change. They did not exalt
order at the cost of liberty. To courageous, self-reliant men, with
confidence in the power of free and fearless reasoning applied
through the processes of popular government, no danger flowing
from speech can be deemed clear and present, unless the incidence
of the evil apprehended is so imminent that it may befall before
there is opportunity for full discussion. If there be time to expose
through discussion the falsehoods and fallacies, to avert the evil
by the processes of education, the remedy to be applied is more
speech, not enforced silence. Only an emergency can justify repression. Such must be the rule if authority is to be reconciled with
freedom. Such, in my opinion, is the command of the Constitution.
It is therefore always open to Americans to challenge a law abridging free speech and assembly by showing that there was no emergency justifying it. . . .*[10]

In the decade following the Second World War, there developed in the American community, despite the magnitude
of its military triumph, despite its awareness of predominant
military power and its exclusive possession of an atomic ar-
senal, an extraordinary crisis of self-confidence. Freedom of
political expression was subjected to unprecedented legal restrictions and private pressures. Far-reaching loyalty-security

[10] In a case decided by the Supreme Court on June 9, 1969, *Brandenburg
v. Ohio,* 395 U.S. 444, *Whitney* v. *California* was expressly overruled in terms
manifestly based on Justice Brandeis's concurring opinion in the latter case.
The Ohio Criminal Syndicalism Statute, enacted in 1919 and essentially
similar to the California Criminal Syndicalism Act and the New York criminal
anarchy law under which Benjamin Gitlow was convicted, was held unconstitutional.

programs for screening federal employees were instituted. Numerous persons were condemned as "disloyal" or as "security risks" on the basis of uncorroborated accusations by unidentified informers. Legislation subsequently found to be in large part unconstitutional—notably the Smith Act of 1940, the McCarran Internal Security Act of 1950, and the Communist Control Act of 1954—was adopted by Congress to stifle and restrict ideas and associations that were considered "subversive." Congressional investigating committees probed ruthlessly into all sorts of activities and organizations previously considered outside the range of governmental regulation; these investigating bodies operated often as itinerant autos-da-fé, passing judgment on the guilt or innocence, the loyalty or disloyalty of individual citizens and subjecting them to punishment by publicity for offenses that were not constitutionally punishable by law. All this had an immeasurably chilling influence upon the exercise of the freedoms of speech and association.

Zechariah Chafee, Jr., wrote regarding the Alien Registration Act of 1940 (more commonly known as the Smith Act): "It is no more limited to the registration of aliens than the Espionage Act of 1917 was limited to spying. Most of the Alien Registration Act is not concerned with registration, and the very first part of it has nothing particular to do with aliens. Just as the 1917 Act gave us a war-time sedition law, so the 1940 Act gives us a peace-time sedition law—for everybody, especially United States citizens."[11] The Smith Act contained the following provisions:

Sec. 2. (a) It shall be unlawful for any person—

(1) to knowingly or willfully advocate, abet, advise, or teach the duty, necessity, desirability, or propriety of overthrowing or destroying any government in the United States by force or violence, or by the assassination of any officer of any such government;

(2) with the intent to cause overthrow or destruction of any

---

[11] Chafee, *op. cit.*, p. 441.

government in the United States, to print, publish, edit, issue, circulate, sell, distribute, or publicly display any written or printed matter advocating, advising, or teaching the duty, necessity, desirability, or propriety of overthrowing any government in the United States by force or violence;

(3) to organize or help to organize any society, or group, or assembly of persons who teach, advocate, or encourage the overthrow or destruction of any government in the United States by force or violence; or to be or become a member of, or affiliate with, any such society, group, or assembly of persons, knowing the purposes thereof. . . .

Sec. 3. It shall be unlawful for any person to attempt to commit, or to conspire to commit, any of the acts prohibited by the provisions of this title. . . .

Under the terms of this statute, twelve leaders of the American Communist party were indicted in July, 1948, at a time when the war in Europe and Asia had been triumphantly concluded and the cold war against the Soviet Union was just barely under way. When the defendants' case—known as the *Dennis* case, after the Communist party general secretary who was among them—came to trial a year later, their number was reduced to eleven by the severance of William Z. Foster from the group. They were charged "with willfully and knowingly conspiring (1) to organize as the Communist Party of the United States of America a society, group and assembly of persons who teach and advocate the overthrow and destruction of the Government of the United States by force and violence, and (2) knowingly and willfully to advocate and teach the duty and necessity of overthrowing and destroying the Government of the United States by force and violence." The key word in the indictment is the word "conspiring."

There were not only eleven defendants at the trial; there were also eleven lawyers representing the defendants. They turned it, whether intentionally or not, into a kind of barbaric orgy that reverberated through the halls of the United States District Court in New York for nine months through the sum-

mer and into the fall of 1949. United States District Judge
Harold R. Medina conducted the trial—at least for a long time
—with almost miraculous patience and forbearance. Had he
possessed the patience of a saint, however—and he did not—
he could hardly have overcome the endless and patently concerted efforts of the eleven defense lawyers to embroil and en-
rage him. Two or three of them—to offer but a single instance
—complained seriatim at one point in the proceeding that he
was scratching his head in a manner calculated to prejudice
the jury. "I want you gentlemen to understand," the judge
responded, "that when I scratch my head, I am just plain
scratching my head. I don't intend to stop doing that because
you make these statements here. I have a habit of doing that.
I am not going to stop just because you make these remarks."[12]

Group trials are notoriously disorderly and unsatisfying. It
says, perhaps, quite enough about this one to note that the
record, not including briefs, runs to 15,937 pages embraced in
thirteen large, very fat, buckram-bound volumes and that at
the conclusion of the trial Judge Medina summarily meted out
contempt sentences to all the lawyers who had so mercilessly
hazed, berated, and offended him during the trial—who had,
indeed, as he charged, obstructed justice. The Supreme Court
subsequently upheld his authority to do this, although later
rulings have indicated plainly that it would have been wiser
and better to have proceeded against them by indictment,
leaving judgment to a judge who was unbiased and unof-
fended.[13]

A verdict of guilty as to all the defendants was returned by
the jury on July 14, 1949. The court of appeals affirmed the
convictions. The Supreme Court agreed to review the case,
limiting its consideration to two questions—whether either
Section 2 or 3 of the Smith Act, inherently or as construed and
applied in the *Dennis* case, violates the First Amendment or
other provisions of the Bill of Rights; and whether either of

[12] Trial Record, p. 3318.
[13] Sacher v. United States, 343 U.S. 1 (1952).

these sections violates the First and Fifth Amendments because of indefiniteness. The Court upheld the validity of the convictions in an opinion written by the chief justice, Fred Vinson, and announced on June 4, 1951.[14] The opinion set forth, as an interpretation of the Smith Act, a fundamental premise in these terms:

> The obvious purpose of the statute is to protect existing Government, not from change by peaceable, lawful and constitutional means, but from change by violence, revolution and terrorism. That it is within the power of the Congress to protect the Government of the United States from armed rebellion is a proposition that requires little discussion. Whatever theoretical merit there may be to the argument that there is a "right" to rebellion against dictatorial governments is without force where the existing structure of the government provides for peaceful and orderly change. We reject any principle of government helplessness in the face of preparation for revolution, which principle, carried to its logical conclusion, must lead to anarchy. No one could conceive that it is not within the power of Congress to prohibit acts intended to overthrow the Government by force and violence. The question with which we are concerned here is not whether Congress has such power, but whether the means which it has employed conflict with the First and Fifth Amendments to the Constitution.

Having laid down these truisms, the chief justice propounded a distinction that may be more semantic than substantial. "The very language of the Smith Act . . . is directed," he said, "at advocacy, not discussion. . . . Congress did not intend to eradicate the free discussion of political theories, to destroy the traditional rights of Americans to discuss and evaluate ideas without fear of governmental sanction. Rather Congress was concerned with the very kind of activity in which the evidence showed these petitioners engaged."

The First Amendment, it would seem from this, protects the expression of ideas—so long as it is not accompanied by any

---

[14] Dennis v. United States, 341 U.S. 494 (1951).

expression of belief in their desirability or any indication of preference for them as opposed to contrary ideas. Such qualified freedom of expression has about it a certain pallor.

Reviewing the World War I cases and those that came soon after it, Chief Justice Vinson makes a bow to the clear-and-present-danger doctrine. "There is little doubt," he acknowledges, "that subsequent opinions have inclined toward the Holmes-Brandeis rationale." He prefers, however, a restatement of clear and present danger formulated in the Court of Appeals for the Second Circuit—which sustained the convictions—by its immensely esteemed chief judge, Learned Hand. "In each case," Chief Judge Hand wrote when the *Dennis* case was before him, courts "must ask whether the gravity of the 'evil,' discounted by its improbability, justifies such invasion of free speech as is necessary to avoid the danger." It is hard to see in this any real improvement on Justice Holmes's earlier formulation either in definiteness or in literary quality. Nevertheless, it pleased Chief Justice Vinson, who declared: "We adopt this statement of the rule. As articulated by Chief Judge Hand, it is as succinct and inclusive as any other we might devise at this time. It takes into consideration those factors which we deem relevant, and relates their significances. More we cannot expect from words." From this, then, he goes on:

Likewise, we are in accord with the court below, which affirmed the trial court's finding that the requisite danger existed. The mere fact that from the period 1945 to 1948 petitioners' activities did not result in an attempt to overthrow the Government by force and violence is of course no answer to the fact that there was a group that was ready to make the attempt. The formation by petitioners of such a highly organized conspiracy, with rigidly disciplined members subject to call when the leaders, these petitioners, felt that the time had come for action, coupled with the inflammable nature of world conditions, similar uprisings in other countries, and the touch-and-go nature of our relations with countries with whom petitioners were in the very least ideologically attuned, convince us that their convictions were justified on this score. And this analysis disposes of the contention that a conspiracy to advocate, as distinguished from the advocacy itself, cannot be constitutionally restrained, because it comprises only the preparation. It is the existence of the conspiracy that creates the danger. . . . Petitioners intended to overthrow the Government of the United States as speedily as the circumstances would permit. Their conspiracy to organize the Communist Party and to teach and advocate the overthrow of the Government of the United States by force and violence created a "clear and present danger" of an attempt to overthrow the Government by force and violence.

Justice Frankfurter wrote a long concurring opinion in affirmance of this judgment, arriving at his conclusion with a little more heartburn, a little less credulity about the magnitude of the Communist party threat to the government of the United States—and with his familiar obeisance to the judgment of the legislature. "It is not for us," he warns once more, "to decide how we would adjust the clash of interests which this case presents were the primary responsibility for reconciling it ours. Congress has determined that the danger created by advocacy of overthrow justifies the ensuing restriction on freedom of speech. The determination was made after due deliberation, and the seriousness of the Congressional purpose is attested by the volume of legislation passed to effectuate the same ends. Can we then say that the judgment Congress exercised was denied it by the Constitution?"

The justice gave, of course, a negative answer to his own rhetorical question and concluded with another short essay on the political process:

Civil liberties draw at best only limited strength from legal guaranties. Preoccupation by our people with the constitutionality, instead of with the wisdom of legislation or of executive action, is preoccupation with a false value. Even those who would most freely use the judicial brake on the democratic process by invalidating legislation that goes deeply against their grain, acknowledge, at least by paying lip service, that constitutionality does not exact a sense of proportion or the sanity of humor or an absence of fear.

Focusing attention on constitutionality tends to make constitution-ality synonymous with wisdom. When legislation touches freedom of thought and freedom of speech, such a tendency is a formidable enemy of the free spirit. Much that should be rejected as illiberal, because repressive and envenoming, may well be not unconstitu-tional. The ultimate reliance for the deepest needs of civilization must be found outside their vindication in court of law; apart from all else, judges, howsoever they may seek to discipline themselves against it, unconsciously are too apt to be moved by the deep undercurrents of public feeling. A persistent, positive translation of the liberating faith into the feelings and thoughts and actions of men and women is the real protection against attempts to straight-jacket the human mind. . . .

Justice Jackson also submitted a concurring opinion, the whole emphasis of which was focused on the fact of conspiracy. "What really is under review here," he wrote, "is a conviction of conspiracy, after a trial for conspiracy, on an indictment charging conspiracy, brought under a statute outlawing con-spiracy. . . ." And he went on:

I do not suggest that Congress could punish conspiracy to advo-cate something, the doing of which it may not punish. Advocacy or exposition of the doctrine of communal property ownership, or any political philosophy unassociated with advocacy of its imposi-tion by force or seizure of government by unlawful means could not be reached through conspiracy prosecution. But it is not forbid-den to put down force or violence, it is not forbidden to punish its teaching or advocacy, and the end being punishable, there is no doubt of the power to punish conspiracy for the purpose. . . .

There were two strong dissenting opinions, a brief one by Justice Black and a more detailed and extended discussion by Justice William O. Douglas. Justice Black's dissent expounds succinctly the thesis that freedom of speech affords the best and strongest safeguard against sedition. He said:

Undoubtedly, a governmental policy of unfettered communica-tion of ideas does entail dangers. To the Founders of this Nation, however, the benefits derived from free expression were worth the risk. They embodied this philosophy in the First Amendment's command that "Congress shall make no law . . . abridging the freedom of speech, or of the press. . . ." I have always believed that the First Amendment is the keystone of our Government, that the freedoms it guarantees provide the best insurance against destruction of all freedom. At least as to speech in the realm of public matters, I believe that the "clear and present danger" test does not "mark the furthermost constitutional boundaries of protected expression" but does "no more than recognize a minimum compulsion of the Bill of Rights." . . .

So long as this Court exercises the power of judicial review of legislation, I cannot agree that the First Amendment permits us to sustain laws suppressing freedom of speech and press on the basis of Congress' or our own notions of mere "reasonableness." Such a doctrine waters down the First Amendment so that it amounts to little more than an admonition to Congress. The Amendment as so construed is not likely to protect any but those "safe" or orthodox views which rarely need its protection. . . .

Justice Douglas's dissent took a line less absolutist than Justice Black's, yet ardent and eloquent in its championship of the utility and value of free expression; later, he would embrace the absolute view of the First Amendment unreservedly. He based his condemnation of the *Dennis* convictions, however, on the clear-and-present-danger test, acknowledging that "The freedom to speak is not absolute; the teaching of methods of terror and other seditious conduct should be beyond the pale along with obscenity and immorality." But the facts in this case, he contended, showed no such conduct. "So far as the present record is concerned, what petitioners did was to organize people to teach and themselves teach the Marxist-Leninist doctrine." He progressed, then, to a fresh exposition of clear and present danger:

Free speech has occupied an exalted position because of the high service it has given our society. Its protection is essential to the very existence of a democracy. The airing of ideas releases pressures which otherwise might become destructive. When ideas compete in the market for acceptance, full and free discussion exposes the false and they gain few adherents. Full and free discussion keeps a society from becoming stagnant and unprepared for the stresses and strains that work to tear all civilizations apart.

Full and free discussion has indeed been the first article of our faith. We have founded our political system on it. It has been the safeguard of every religious, political, philosophical, economic, and racial group amongst us. We have counted on it to keep us from embracing what is cheap and false; we have trusted the common sense of our people to choose the doctrine true to our genius and to reject the rest. This has been the one single outstanding tenet that has made our institutions the symbol of freedom and equality. We have deemed it more costly to liberty to suppress a despised minority than to let them vent their spleen. We have above all else feared the political censor. We have wanted a land where our people can be exposed to all the diverse creeds and cultures of the world.

There comes a time when even speech loses its constitutional immunity. Speech innocuous one year may at another time fan such destructive flames that it must be halted in the interests of the safety of the Republic. That is the meaning of the clear and present danger test. When conditions are so critical that there will be no time to avoid the evil that the speech threatens, it is time to call a halt. Otherwise, free speech which is the strength of the Nation will be the cause of its destruction.

Yet free speech is the rule, not the exception. The restraint to be constitutional must be based on more than fear, on more than passionate opposition against the speech, on more than a revolted dislike for its contents. There must be some immediate injury to society that is likely if speech is allowed.

Justice Douglas's opinion moves from this broad statement of principle to an evaluation of the Communist party in the United States as discredited and impotent. "Free speech," he says, "has destroyed it as an effective political party. . . . In days of trouble and confusion, when bread lines were long, when the unemployed walked the streets, when people were starving, the advocates of a short-cut by revolution might have a chance to

gain adherents. But today there are no such conditions. . . .
How it can be said that there is a clear and present danger that
this advocacy will succeed is, therefore, a mystery. Some nations
less resilient than the United States, where illiteracy is high and
where democratic traditions are only budding, might have to
take drastic steps and jail these men for merely speaking their
creed. But in America they are miserable merchants of unwanted ideas; their wares remain unsold. The fact that their
ideas are abhorrent does not make them powerful. . . . The First
Amendment reflects the philosophy of Jefferson 'that it is time
enough for the rightful purposes of civil government, for its
officers to interfere when principles break out into overt acts
against peace and good order.' "

The Supreme Court's decision in the *Dennis* case, upholding
the validity of the Smith Act, introduced an open season for
heresy hunting. "Loyalty" was to be ensured by law. The newly
created Subversive Activities Control Board, the subversive
activities committees of the House and Senate, the Internal
Security Division of the Department of Justice all went to work
with refreshed fervor. Having convicted the top echelon of
Communist party leaders, the Justice Department at once
undertook a new series of prosecutions in various parts of the
country and in Hawaii and Puerto Rico aimed at the party's
secondary leadership. Fifteen prosecutions, involving more than
a hundred individual defendants and requiring in each case
three to six months of trial time, were brought under the
conspiracy provisions of the Smith Act.

The fever peaked in the early years of the 1950s. While not
wholly burned out, it began to abate with the censure of
Senator McCarthy by the United States Senate at the end
of 1954. A regard for civil liberties began again to be respectable, if not actually in fashion. And in 1957 the Supreme Court
agreed to review the convictions of fourteen West Coast Communist party officials who had been found guilty of Smith Act

violations in the Southern District of California. The hope that Hugo Black had expressed in his *Dennis* dissent in 1951—the hope "that in calmer times, when present pressures, passions and fears subside, this or some later Court will restore the First Amendment liberties to the high preferred place where they belong in a free society"—was ripe for realization.

The case of the Southern California Communists was known as *Yates* v. *United States*,[15] and the Court's opinion in the case, while not explicitly overruling the *Dennis* decision, modified it so substantially as virtually to make the sedition sections of the Smith Act a dead letter. The case resulted in an acquittal of five of the fourteen defendants by direct order of the Supreme Court; and the indictment against the others was subsequently dismissed by the trial court when the government declared that "we cannot satisfy the evidentiary requirements laid down by the Supreme Court in its opinion reversing the conviction in this matter." No new prosecutions have been brought under the Smith Act since that time.

The essence of the Court's ruling in the *Yates* case was a recognition of a vital distinction "between advocacy of abstract doctrine and advocacy directed at promoting unlawful action." In his opinion for the Court, Justice Harlan stressed this distinction and quoted language in the *Gitlow* decision which declared of the Smith Act: "The statute does not penalize the utterance or publication of abstract 'doctrine' or academic discussion having no quality of incitement to any concrete action. . . . It is not the abstract 'doctrine' of overthrowing organized government by unlawful means which is denounced by the statute, but the advocacy of action for the accomplishment of that purpose." And he went on to say that "The legislative history of the Smith Act and related bills shows beyond all question that Congress was aware of the distinction between the advocacy or teaching of abstract doctrine and the advocacy and teaching of concrete action, and that it did not intend to disregard it. The statute was aimed at the advocacy and teach-

[15] 354 U.S. 298 (1957).

ing of concrete action for the forcible overthrow of the Government, and not of principles divorced from action. . . . The essential distinction is that those to whom the advocacy is addressed must be urged to *do* something, now or in the future, rather than merely to *believe* in something."

Thus, in this time of diminished tension, the clear-and-present-danger doctrine was restored to something like the meaning that Justice Holmes had intended it to have when he first formulated it nearly forty years earlier. If it did not protect all speech, it protected at least the advocacy of ideas. If it did not give the words of the First Amendment all the sweep and certainty that they seemed to suggest, it at least made them a substantial shield for the discussion of conflicting views and principles of government. This must be admitted, nevertheless, to be a far cry from the bold, uncompromising concept of the First Amendment offered once more by Justice Black in a separate opinion in the *Yates* case in which he was joined by Justice Douglas, concurring in part and dissenting in part:

> *Doubtlessly, dictators have to stamp out causes and beliefs which they deem subversive to their evil regimes. But governmental suppression of causes and beliefs seems to me to be the very antithesis of what our Constitution stands for. The choice expressed in the First Amendment in favor of free expression was made against a turbulent background by men such as Jefferson, Madison, and Mason—by men who believed that loyalty to the provisions of this Amendment was the best way to assure a long life for this new nation and its Government. Unless there is complete freedom for expression of all ideas, whether we like them or not, concerning the way government should be run and who shall run it, I doubt if any views in the long run can be secured against the censor. The First Amendment provides the only kind of security system that can preserve a free government—one that leaves the way wide open for people to favor, discuss, advocate, or incite causes and doctrines however obnoxious and antagonistic such views may be to the rest of us.*

For all of its appeal to idealism, faith in democracy, and

courage, the trouble with this construction of the First Amendment is that it seems to demand more tolerance than lies within human capacity. "Clear and present danger," for all its uncertainties and shortcomings, seems a test more in keeping with the pragmatic character of the American people. It has a flexibility, an adaptability to changing circumstances, that may better suit the American temperament. Perhaps it represents the outermost limits of the American aptitude for tolerance.

The trouble with "clear and present danger," however, is that its meaning is forever in flux. It means, as has been said of the Constitution as a whole, what the Supreme Court says it means. And what the Supreme Court says, as we have seen, depends a great deal upon the climate of opinion, the temperature of the body politic of the time wherein it speaks. "Clear and present danger" has already run the gamut from tolerance to constraint and back. It may run that gamut again. And so, alas, no one can define with any exactitude the boundaries of free expression in the United States—now or in the future. Yet those boundaries, more than any others, will shape America's destiny.

VIII

"IT IS A CONSTITUTION
WE ARE EXPOUNDING"

One characteristic common to the dissenting opinions discussed in this book is a disposition to construe the Constitution of the United States not so much in the precise terms of its provisions as in an imaginative sense of its spirit and its great purposes. It is, of course, a risky thing to invoke something so vague as the "spirit" of a written document in place of the words it embodies —and particularly so in regard to an instrument designed primarily to limit the powers of government. Yet it seems evident in considering the cases presented here—cases in which presumed errors committed by the Court were subsequently corrected by its own decision—that in most instances, the "error" arose out of too literal and narrow an interpretation of the Constitution and was amended by an interpretation of greater flexibility and scope. This has been true equally respecting the powers delegated to the national government by the Constitution and the specific restraints on government power contained in the Bill of Rights and other limiting clauses of the Constitution.

"The provisions of the Constitution," Justice Holmes once

wrote, "are not mathematical formulas having their essence in their form; they are organic living institutions transplanted from English soil." As such, they must need cultivation, nourishment, and opportunity for growth.

Perhaps the best text ever composed on how to construe a constitution—and the best argument for construing it with imaginative flexibility—was provided by Chief Justice John Marshall in the landmark decision of 1819 called *McCulloch* v. *Maryland.*[1] The seemingly simple question involved in this case was whether Congress had power to charter a national bank. There is no language in the Constitution explicitly conferring such power upon Congress. And for those at that time who believed that the national government should be no more than an agent of sovereign states discharging extremely limited, specifically delegated functions chiefly in the areas of interstate commerce, national defense, and foreign relations, this was an end to the matter; in the absence of any explicit authorization to Congress, the power to charter a bank was a power reserved to the states.

But the Constitution, in Article I, after setting forth the manner in which the Congress should be selected, the rules under which it should function, and the general areas in which it should legislate, provided that "The Congress shall have Power. . . . To make all Laws which shall be necessary and proper for carrying into Execution the foregoing Powers, and all other Powers vested by this Constitution in the Government of the United States, or in any Department or Officer thereof." To those who envisioned a national government capable of guiding a great nation, this seemed sufficient to authorize the establishment of a bank that would contribute, in the judgment of Congress, to the country's commerce and economic growth. The Constitution of the United States, they contended, implied many powers that, by reason of its character as a constitution, could not be explicitly enumerated. This contention was set

[1] 4 Wheaton's Reports 400 (1819).

forth with superb clarity in the *McCulloch* decision by the
chief justice, writing for a unanimous Supreme Court:

*A constitution, to contain an accurate detail of all the sub-
divisions of which its great powers will admit, and of all the means
by which they may be carried into execution, would partake of the
prolixity of a legal code, and could scarcely be embraced by the
human mind. It would probably never be understood by the public.
Its nature, therefore, requires, that only its great outlines should be
marked, its important objects designated, and the minor ingredients
which compose those objects be deduced from the nature of the
objects themselves. That this idea was entertained by the framers
of the American constitution, is not only to be inferred from the
nature of the instrument, but from the language. Why else were
some of the limitations, found in the ninth section of the 1st
article, introduced? It is also, in some degree, warranted by their
having omitted to use any restrictive terms which might prevent
its receiving a fair and just interpretation. In considering this
question, then, we must never forget, that it is* a constitution *we are
expounding. . . .*

*To have prescribed the means by which government should, in
all future time, execute its powers, would have been to change, entirely, the character of the instrument, and give it the properties
of a legal code. It would have been an unwise attempt to provide,
by immutable rules, for exigencies which, if foreseen at all, must
have been seen dimly, and which can be best provided for as they
occur. To have declared that the best means shall not be used,
but those alone without which the power given would be nugatory,
would have been to deprive the legislature of the capacity to
avail itself of experience, to exercise its reason, and to accommodate
its legislation to circumstances. If we apply this principle of construction to any of the powers of the government, we shall find it
so pernicious in its operation that we shall be compelled to dis-
card it. . . .*

*We admit, as all must admit, that the powers of the govern-
ment are limited, and that its limits are not to be transcended. But
we think the sound construction of the constitution must allow
to the national legislature that discretion, with respect to the
means by which the powers it confers are to be carried into execution, which will enable that body to perform the high duties as-*

signed to it, in the manner most beneficial to the people. Let the end be legitimate, let it be within the scope of the constitution, and all means which are appropriate, which are plainly adapted to that end, which are not prohibited, but consist with the letter and spirit of the constitution, are constitutional. . . .

Should Congress, in the execution of its powers, adopt measures which are prohibited by the constitution; or should Congress, under the pretext of executing its powers, pass laws for the accomplishment of objects not entrusted to the government; it would become the painful duty of this tribunal, should a case requiring such a decision come before it, to say that such an act was not the law of the land. But where the law is not prohibited, and is really calculated to effect any of the objects entrusted to the government, to undertake here to inquire into the degree of its necessity, would be to pass the line which circumscribed the judicial department, and to tread on legislative ground. This court disclaims all pretensions to such a power. . . .

This early decision of the Supreme Court, giving extensive implied powers to the newly established national government, evoked an instant outcry from the champions of "states' rights." Before the end of the month in which the *McCulloch* decision was announced, there appeared in the *Richmond Enquirer* two essays, signed "Amphictyon" and probably written by Judge William Brockenbrough of Virginia, where states' rights were the foundation of political orthodoxy. These essays attacked the decision bitterly as a perversion of the founding fathers' purposes.

John Marshall was alarmed by the vehemence of this attack and by the threat it seemed to present to the development of essential governmental powers. He proceeded, therefore, to do what has not been done, so far as is known, by any chief justice of the United States before or since—to write a vigorous defense of the Court's opinion under the pseudonym "A Friend to the Union," which appeared a month later in the *Philadelphia Union.*

Not long after, this was countered by a still more strident challenge, printed again in the *Richmond Enquirer*, signed this time "Hampden" and actually written by Judge Spencer Roane of the Virginia Court of Appeals, a leading exponent of the states' rights theory. Recognizing this as part of a concerted effort to thwart the federalism of the Supreme Court's view, John Marshall again took up the challenge. He wrote nine essays, or letters to the editor, signing them "A Friend of the Constitution." These were published in late June, 1819, in the *Alexandria Gazette*.[2] Hampden's own estimate of the importance of the controversy was summed up succinctly in the final sentence of his first letter: of the chief justice's opinion in the *McCulloch* case he said, "I consider that opinion as the '*Alpha and Omega*, the beginning and the *end*, the first and *last*—of federal usurpations.'"

The essence of the Hampden view can be summarized in another sentence from one of the Hampden essays: "The rights of the states ought not to be usurped and taken from them; for the powers delegated to the general government are few and defined, and relate chiefly to external objects, while the states retain a residuary and inviolable sovereignty over all other subjects; over all those great subjects which immediately concern the prosperity of the people." Whatever may be the merits of this view with regard to the welfare and liberties of Americans over the span of two centuries, it is not a view likely to have been conducive to the development of the United States as a great world power. Marshall's conception of the Constitution was at once more imaginative and more majestic.

Perhaps the most significant passage in Marshall's nine-part reply is a single, long paragraph summing up once more his understanding of the nature of a constitution and his reasons for believing that it must be open to flexible and creative interpretation by the Court constituted to determine its meaning.

[2] This remarkable debate has recently been brought together and published for the first time by Professor Gerald Gunther of the Stanford University Law School in a volume, *John Marshall's Defense of McCulloch v. Maryland* (Stanford, Calif.: Stanford University Press, 1969). It is Professor Gunther's scholarship that established the authorship of these letters. All quotations from them here are taken from his book.

It can scarcely be necessary to say, that no one of the circum-
stances which might seem to justify rather a strict construction in
the particular cases quoted by Hampden, apply to a constitution.
It is not a contract between enemies seeking each other's destruc-
tion, and anxious to insert every particular, lest a watchful adversary
should take advantage of the omission. —Nor is it a case where
implications in favor of one man impair the vested rights of another.
Nor is it a contract for a single object, every thing relating to which,
might be recollected and inserted. It is the act of a people, creating
a government, without which they cannot exist as a people. The
powers of this government are conferred for their own benefit, are
essential to their own prosperity, and are to be exercised for their
good, by persons chosen for that purpose by themselves. The
object of the instrument is not a single one which can be minutely
described, with all its circumstances. The attempt to do so, would
totally change its nature, and defeat its purpose. It is intended to
be a general system for all future times, to be adapted by those who
administer it, to all future occasions that may come within its own
view. From its nature, such an instrument can describe only the
great objects it is intended to accomplish, and state in general
terms, the specific powers which are deemed necessary for those
objects. To direct the manner in which these powers are to be
exercised, the means by which the objects of the government are to
be effected, a legislature is granted. This would be totally useless,
if its office and duty were performed in the constitution. This legis-
lature is an emanation from the people themselves. It is a part
chosen to represent the whole, and to mark, according to the judg-
ment of the nation, its course, within those great outlines which
are given in the constitution. It is impossible to construe such an
instrument rightly, without advertising its nature, and marking the
points of difference which distinguish it from ordinary contracts.

The conflict presented here is a conflict that has run through
the whole of American history. It is sometimes spoken of as a
conflict between "strict constructionism" on the one hand and
a more "creative" reading of the Constitution on the other,
between "judicial restraint" and "judicial activism." But such
designations obfuscate more than they define. How meaningless

they are is amply illustrated by the fact that when President Nixon sought to characterize the kind of jurist he proposed to place on the Supreme Court, he referred to Justice Frankfurter as an exemplar of strict constructionism. Yet Justice Frankfurter was fond of quoting—and always with the warmest approval—the Marshall observation in the *McCulloch* case that "It is a constitution we are expounding." Indeed, Justice Frankfurter said of this statement that "it bears repeating because it is, I believe, the single most important utterance in the literature of constitutional law—important because most comprehensive and comprehending."[3] And he demonstrated his devotion to this view in numerous liberal and libertarian opinions respecting due process, search, and the protection of privacy.

In contrast, Justice Black, widely considered the archetype of judicial activism, said in a summing up of his judicial philosophy:

> *Of course I realize "that it is a* constitution *we are expounding." But this does not mean that in order to obtain results thought to be desirable at the time, judges may rewrite our basic charter of government under the guise of interpreting it. . . . Judges take an oath to support the Constitution as it is, not as they think it should be. I cannot subscribe to the doctrine that consistent with that oath a judge can arrogate to himself a power to "adapt the Constitution to new times."[4]*

Do these contrasting expressions indicate that in 1819 Frankfurter would have approved the chartering of a bank by the federal government and Black would have condemned it? It would be a rash writer who said so. Each of them acted sometimes as a literalist and sometimes as an activist. So many imponderables enter into judicial decision making—the circum-

---

[3] Felix Frankfurter, "John Marshall," in *Government Under Law* (Cambridge, Mass.: Harvard University Press, 1956), p. 8; quoted by Helen Shirley Thomas in *Felix Frankfurter, Scholar on the Bench* (Baltimore: The Johns Hopkins University Press, 1969), p. 242.

[4] Hugo LaFayette Black, *A Constitutional Faith* (New York: Alfred A. Knopf, 1968), pp. 8, 20–21.

stances of the particular case; the social context in which it
arises; the arguments of counsel before the Court; and, even
more significantly, the arguments behind closed doors between
members of the Court in the judicial conference and the ways
in which differing opinions are presented, attracting or repelling concurrence—that guesswork about hypothetical situations
has little validity. Temperament plays at least as large a role
as philosophy in making up the minds of judges.

Judges of the caliber of Black and Frankfurter are not to be
sorted into comfortable categories in the way that a computer
drops punched cards into appropriate slots. As Justice Goldberg
remarked, "nearly every justice considers himself a strict constructionist in the sense that he tries to apply the Constitution
in accordance with the intent of the framers. But that intent is
not always easy to ascertain; historical materials rarely point
unambiguously to a single, particular disposition for an individual case."[5]

Probably the most egregious instance of strict constructionism in the Court's history is the doom that Chief Justice Roger
Taney pronounced upon the whole black race in the *Dred Scott*
case. Having declared that blacks were not thought of as citizens, or even as persons, at the time when the Constitution
was adopted, he went on to insist, in a sort of slide-rule style
of constitutional interpretation, that the letter rather than the
spirit of the charter must prevail:

> No one, we presume, supposes that any change in public
> opinion or feeling in relation to this unfortunate race, in the civil-
> ized nations of Europe or in this country, should induce the court
> to give to the words of the Constitution a more liberal construc-
> tion in their favor than they were intended to bear when the instru-
> ment was framed and adopted. Such an argument would be alto-
> gether inadmissible in any tribunal called on to interpret it. If any
> of its provisions are deemed unjust, there is a mode prescribed in
> the instrument itself by which it may be amended; but while it

[5] Arthur Goldberg, *Equal Justice: The Warren Era of the Supreme Court*
(Evanston, Ill.: Northwestern University Press, 1971), p. 37.

*remains unaltered, it must be construed now as it was understood
at the time of its adoption. It is not only the same in words, but the
same in meaning, and delegates the same powers to the government, and reserves and secures the same rights and privileges to the
citizen; and as long as it continues to exist in its present form, it
speaks not only in the same words, but with the same meaning and
intent with which it spoke when it came from the hands of its
framers, and was voted on and adopted by the people of the United
States. Any other rule of construction would abrogate the judicial
character of this court, and make it the mere reflex of the popular
opinion or passion of the day. . . .*

Differing concepts of judicial restraint often separated Frankfurter and Black as they have historically separated many members of the Court on many issues. Deference to the judgment
of legislatures was a cornerstone of Justice Frankfurter's judicial faith. But a deference to the judgment of legislatures must
not be carried over into an abdication of judicial responsibility.
Justice Black's idea of judicial restraint centered in a deference
to the literal commands of the Constitution—another instance
of *his* "strict constructionism." The Court's first function, as he
saw it, was to restrain legislative or executive excesses—and
especially when they impinged upon the political process or
upon individual liberties guaranteed by the Constitution. "The
essential protection of the liberty of our people," he declared,
"should not be denied them by invocation of a doctrine of so-
called judicial restraint." If these approaches are in conflict,
they are manifestly also complementary and must be reconciled.

Judicial judging is not encompassed by general expressions
of principle and theory. Intuition, personal experience, surges
of human sympathy are also influences upon decision. And, in
the end, judges, like other human beings, are certain to be
swayed by what they think, and feel, is *right*. The Supreme
Court may be a court of law, but it is a court of justice, too.
For justice must be the end of law. And law is but a reflection
of ethical values.

The judicial decisions recounted in this book—the dissents

that won the vindication of acceptance by the Court and the country—are not the final word on the difficult issues they seem to settle. Already, as this is written, there have been significant modifications of the rulings reported here. Decisions regarding the busing of school children have had marked effects on desegregation of the public schools, and have taken the Court far beyond its simple decision in *Brown* v. *Board of Education*. The Burger Court has significantly relaxed, although it has by no means abandoned, the one-man, one-vote principle laid down by the Warren Court in its districting and apportionment decisions. New developments in electronic eavesdropping techniques are likely to require new strictures by the Court if privacy is to have any protection against official surveillance. There appears to be a strong disposition in the 1970s to undo some of the liberal and libertarian rulings of the 1960s with regard to the rights of criminal defendants. Perhaps there will be reversals of the reversals. But justices, regardless of their personal philosophies when they go on the bench and regardless of the expectations of the president who put them there, are likely to be mindful of their responsibility to the Court as an institution with roots in all that has gone before. It is an institution that tends to ennoble its members.

There will continue to be conflict in the Court, of course. Conflict is its generative force. Its best assurance of wisdom will come, as it has in the past, from the clashes within it among strong men committed to their own perceptions of the law. Like the nation it created, the Constitution is imbued with life—and therefore with a capability for growth. A constitution that looked no farther into the future than the horizon of its authors would be not a charter, but a chain. At the same time, a constitution that did not fix firm boundaries for the reach of governmental power would be but an invitation to the most blighting of all tyrannies—the tyranny of majorities seeking to impose conformity and subdue idiosyncrasy.

Construing a constitution in the light of changing needs and conditions is a creative task. The Court will need for that task not only knowledge and understanding but the gift of prophecy as well. For "it is not the words of the law, but the internal sense of it that makes the law; the letter of the law is the body of the law; the sense and reason of the law is the soul."[6] Discovery of the soul is the special function of prophets—and of Supreme Court justices, too.

[6] Plowden (reporter), *Commentaries on Reports*, Vol II, *Eyston* v. *Studd* (1574), p. 465.

APPENDICES

APPENDIX A

Plessy v. Ferguson, 163 U.S. 537
Mr. Justice Harlan, dissenting.

By the Louisiana statute, the validity of which is here involved, all railway companies (other than street railway companies) carrying passengers in that state are required to have separate but equal accommodations for white and colored persons, "by providing two or more passenger coaches for each passenger train, *or* by dividing the passenger coaches by *partition* so as to secure separate accommodations." Under this statute, no colored person is permitted to occupy a seat in a coach assigned to white persons; nor any white person to occupy a seat in the coach assigned to colored persons. The managers of the railroad are not allowed to exercise any discretion in the premises, but are required to assign each passenger to some coach or compartment set apart for the exclusive use of his race. If a passenger insists upon going into a coach or compartment not set apart for persons of his race, he is subject to be fined, or to be imprisoned in the parish jail. Penalties are prescribed for the refusal or neglect of the officers, directors, conductors, and employees of railroad companies to comply with the provisions of the act.

Only "nurses attending children of the other race" are excepted from the operation of the statute. No exception is made of colored attendants traveling with adults. A white man is not permitted to have his colored servant with him in the same coach, even if his condition of health requires the constant personal assistance of such servant. If a colored maid insists upon riding in the same coach with a white woman whom she has been employed to serve, and who may need her personal attention while traveling, she is subject to be fined or imprisoned for such an exhibition of zeal in the discharge of duty.

While there may be in Louisiana persons of different races who are not citizens of the United States, the words in the act, "white and colored races" necessarily include all citizens of the United States of both races residing in that state. So that we have before us a state enactment that compels, under penalties, the separation of the two races in railroad passenger coaches, and makes it a crime for a citizen of either race to enter a coach that has been assigned to citizens of the other race.

Thus the state regulates the use of a public highway by citizens of the United States solely upon the basis of race.

However apparent the injustice of such legislation may be, we have only to consider whether it is consistent with the Constitution of the United States.

That a railroad is a public highway, and that the corporation which owns or operates it is in the exercise of public functions, is not, at this day, to be disputed. Mr. Justice Nelson, speaking for this court in *New Jersey Steam Co.* v. *Merchants' Bank,* 47 U. S. 6 How. 344, 382 [12: 465, 482], said that a common carrier was in the exercise "of a sort of public office, and has public duties to perform, from which he should not be permitted to exonerate himself without the assent of the parties concerned." Mr. Justice Strong, delivering the judgment of this court in *Olcott* v. *Fond du Lac County Supers.* 83 U. S. 16 Wall. 678, 694 [21:382, 388], said: "That railroads, though constructed by private corporations and owned by them, are public highways, has been the doctrine of nearly all the courts ever since such conveyances for passage and transportation have had any existence. Very early the question arose whether a state's right of eminent domain could be exercised by a private corporation created for the purpose of constructing a railroad. Clearly it could not, unless taking land for such a purpose by such an agency is taking land for public use. The right of eminent domain nowhere justifies taking property for a private use. Yet it is a doctrine universally accepted that the state legislature may authorize a private corporation to take land for the construction of such a road, making compensation to the owner. What else does this doctrine mean if not that building a railroad, though it be built by a private corporation, is an act done for a public use?" So, in *Pine Grove Twp.* v. *Talcott,* 86 U. S. 19 Wall. 666, 676 [22:227, 233]: "Though the corporation [a railroad company] was private, its work was public, as much so as if it were to be constructed by the state." So, in *Worcester* v. *Western R. Corp.* 4 Met. 564: "The establishment of that great thoroughfare is regarded as a public work, established by public authority, intended for the public use and benefit, the use of which is secured to the whole community, and constitutes therefore, like a canal, turnpike, or highway, a public easement. . . . It is true that the real and personal property necessary to the establishment and management of the railroad is vested in the corporation; but it is in trust for the public."

In respect of civil rights, common to all citizens, the Constitution of the United States does not, I think, permit any public authority to know the race of those entitled to be protected in the enjoyment of such rights. Every true man has pride of race, and under appropriate circumstances, when the rights of others, his equals before the law, are not to be affected, it is his privilege to express such pride and to take such action based upon it as to him seems proper. But I deny that any legislative body or judicial tribunal may have regard to the race of citizens when the civil rights of those citizens are involved. Indeed such legislation as that here in question is inconsistent, not only with that equality of rights which pertains to citizenship, national and state, but with the personal liberty enjoyed by every one within the United States.

The 13th Amendment does not permit the withholding or the deprivation of any right necessarily inhering in freedom. It not only struck down the institution of slavery as previously existing in the United States, but it prevents the imposition of any burdens or disabilities that constitute badges of slavery or servitude. It decreed universal civil freedom in this country. This court has so adjudged. But that amendment having been found inadequate to the protection of the rights of those who had been in slavery, it was followed by the 14th Amendment, which added greatly to the dignity and glory of American citizenship, and to the security of personal liberty, by declaring that "all persons born or naturalized in the United States, and subject to the jurisdiction thereof, are citizens of the United States and of the state wherein they reside," and that "no state shall make or enforce any law which shall abridge the privileges or immunities of citizens of the United States; nor shall any state deprive any person of life, liberty, or property without due process of law, nor deny to any person within its jurisdiction the equal protection of the laws." These two amendments, if enforced according to their true intent and meaning, will protect all the civil rights that pertain to freedom and citizenship. Finally, and to the end that no citizen should be denied, on account of his race, the privilege of participating in the political control of his country, it was declared by the 15th Amendment that "the right of citizens of the United States to vote shall not be denied or abridged by the United States or by any state on account of race, color, or previous condition of servitude."

These notable additions to the fundamental law were welcomed by the friends of liberty throughout the world. They removed the race line from our governmental systems. They had, as this court has said, a common purpose, namely, to secure "to a race recently emancipated, a race that through many generations have been held in slavery, all the civil rights that the superior race enjoy." They declared, in legal effect, this court has further said, "that the law in the states shall be the same for the black as for the white; that all persons, whether colored or white, shall stand equal before the laws of the states, and, in regard to the colored race, for whose protection the amendment was primarily designed, that no discrimination shall be made against them by law because of their color." We also said: "The words of the amendment, it is true, are prohibitory, but they contain a necessary implication of a positive immunity, or right, most valuable to the colored race— the right to exemption from unfriendly legislation against them distinctively as colored—exemption from legal discriminations, implying inferiority in civil society, lessening the security of their enjoyment of the rights which others enjoy, and discriminations which are steps towards reducing them to the condition of a subject race." It was consequently adjudged that a state law that excluded citizens of the colored race from juries because of their race and however well qualified in other respects to discharge the duties of jurymen was repugnant to the 14th Amendment. *Strauder* v. *West Virginia*, 100 U. S. 303, 306, 307 [25:664, 665]: *Exparte Virginia* ("*Virginia* v. *Rives*"), 100 U. S. 313 [25:667]; *Ex parte Virginia*, 100 U. S. 339 [25: 676]; *Neal* v. *Delaware*, 103 U. S. 370, 386 [26:567, 570]: *Bush* v. *Kentucky*, 107 U. S. 110, 116 [27:354, 356]. At the present term, referring to the previous adjudications, this court declared that "underlying all of those decisions is the principle that the Constitution of the United States, in its present form, forbids, so far as civil and political rights are concerned, discrimination by the general government or the states against any citizen because of his race. All citizens are equal before the law." *Gibson* v. *Mississippi*, 162 U. S. 565 [40: 1075].

The decisions referred to show the scope of the recent amendments of the Constitution. They also show that it is not within the power of a state to prohibit colored citizens, because of their race, from participating as jurors in the administration of justice.

It was said in argument that the statute of Louisiana does not discriminate against either race, but prescribes a rule applicable alike to white and colored citizens. But this argument does not meet the difficulty. Everyone knows that the statute in question had its origin in the purpose, not so much to exclude white persons from railroad cars occupied by blacks, as to exclude colored people from coaches occupied by or assigned to white persons. Railroad corporations of Louisiana did not make discrimination among whites in the matter of accommodation for travelers. The thing to accomplish was, under the guise of giving equal accommodation for whites and blacks to compel the latter to keep to themselves while traveling in railroad passenger coaches. No one would be so wanting in candor as to assert the contrary. The fundamental objection, therefore, to the statute, is that it interferes with the personal freedom of citizens. "Personal liberty," it has been well said, "consists in the power of locomotion, of changing situation, or removing one's person to whatsoever places one's own inclination may direct, without imprisonment or restraint, unless by due course of law." 1 Bl. Com. °134. If a white man and a black man choose to occupy the same public conveyance on a public highway, it is their right to do so, and no government, proceeding alone on grounds of race, can prevent it without infringing the personal liberty of each.

It is one thing for railroad carriers to furnish, or to be required by law to furnish, equal accommodations for all whom they are under a legal duty to carry. It is quite another thing for government to forbid citizens of the white and black races from traveling in the same public conveyance, and to punish officers of railroad companies for permitting persons of the two races to occupy the same passenger coach. If a state can prescribe as a rule of civil conduct, that whites and blacks shall not travel as passengers in the same railroad coach, why may it not so regulate the use of the streets of its cities and towns as to compel white citizens to keep on one side of the street and black citizens to keep on the other? Why may it not, upon like grounds, punish whites and blacks who ride together in street cars or in open vehicles on a public road or street? Why may it not require sheriffs to assign whites to one side of a court-room and blacks to the other? And why may it not also prohibit the commingling of the two races in the galleries of legislative halls or in public assemblages convened for the political questions of the day? Further, if this statute of Louisiana is consistent with the personal liberty of citizens, why may not the state require the separation in railroad coaches of native and naturalized citizens of the United States, or of Protestants and Roman Catholics?

The answer given at the argument to these questions was that regulations of the kind they suggest would be unreasonable, and could not, therefore, stand before the law. Is it meant that the determination of questions of legislative power depends upon the inquiry whether the statute whose validity is questioned is, in the judgment of the courts, a reasonable one, taking all the circumstances into consideration? A statute may be unreasonable merely because a sound public policy forbade its enactment. But I do not understand that the courts have anything to do with the policy or expediency of legislation. A statute may be valid, and yet upon grounds of public policy may well be characterized as unreasonable. Mr. Sedgwick correctly states the rule when he says that the legislative intention being clearly ascertained, "the courts have no other duty to perform than to execute the legislative will, without any regard to their views as to the wisdom or justice of the particular enactment." Sedgw. Stat. & Const.L. 324. There is a dangerous tendency in these latter days to enlarge the functions of the courts, by means of judicial interference with the will of the people as expressed by the legislature. Our institutions have the distinguishing characteristic that the three departments of government are co-ordinate and separate. Each must keep within the limits defined by the Constitution. And the courts best discharge their duty by executing the will of the lawmaking power, constitutionally expressed, leaving the results of legislation to be dealt with by the people through their representatives. Statutes must always have a reasonable construction. Sometimes they are to be construed strictly; sometimes literally, in order to carry out the legislative will. But however construed, the intent of the legislature is to be respected, if the particular statute in question is valid, although the courts, looking at the public interests, may conceive the statute to be both unreasonable and impolitic. If the power exists to enact a statute, that ends the matters so far as the courts are concerned. The adjudged cases in which statutes have been held to be void, because unreasonable, are those in which the means employed by the legislature were not at all germane to the end to which the legislature was competent.

The white race deems itself to be the dominant race in this country. And so it is, in prestige, in achievements, in education, in wealth, and in power. So, I doubt not that it will continue to be for all time, if it remains true to its great heritage and holds fast to the principles of constitutional liberty. But in view of the Constitution, in the eye of the law, there is in this country no superior, dominant, ruling class of citizens. There is no caste here. Our Constitution is color-blind, and neither knows nor tolerates classes among citizens. In respect of civil rights, all citizens are equal before the law. The humblest is the peer of the most powerful. The law regards man as man, and takes no account of his surroundings or of his color when his civil rights as guaranteed by the supreme law of the land are involved. It is therefore to be regretted that this high tribunal, the final expositor of the fundamental laws of the land, has reached the conclusion that it is competent for a state to regulate the enjoyment by citizens of their civil rights solely upon the basis of race.

In my opinion, the judgment this day rendered will, in time, prove to be quite as pernicious as the decision made by this tribunal in the *Dred Scott Case*. It was adjudged in that case that the descendants of Africans who were imported into this country and sold as slaves were not included nor intended to be included under the word "citizens" in the Constitution, and could not claim any of the rights and privileges which that instrument provided for and secured to citizens of the United States; that at the time of the adoption of the Constitution they were "considered as a subordinate and inferior class of beings, who had been subjugated by the dominant race, and, whether emancipated or not, yet remained subject to their authority, and had no rights or privileges but such as those who held the power and the government might choose to grant them." 60 U. S. 19 How. 393, 404 [15: 691, 700]. The recent amendments of the Constitution, it was supposed, had eradicated these principles from our institutions. But it seems that we have yet, in some of the states, a dominant race, a superior class of citizens, which assumes to regulate the enjoyment of civil rights, common to all citizens, upon the basis of race. The present decision, it may well be apprehended, will not [only] stimulate aggressions, more or less brutal and irritating, upon the admitted rights of colored citizens, but will encourage the belief that it is possible, by means of state enactments, to defeat the beneficent purposes which the people of the United States had in view when they adopted the recent amendments of the Constitution, by one of which the blacks of this country were made citizens of the United States and of the states in which they respectively reside, and whose privileges and immunities, as citizens, the states are forbidden to abridge. Sixty millions of whites are in no danger from the presence here of eight millions of blacks. The destinies of the two races in this country are indissolubly linked together, and the interests of both require that the common government of all shall not permit the seeds of race hate to be planted under the sanction of law. What can more certainly arouse race hate, what more certainly create and perpetuate a feeling of distrust between these races, than state enactments which in fact proceed on the ground that colored citizens are so inferior and degraded that they cannot be allowed to sit in public coaches occupied by white citizens? That, as all will admit, is the real meaning of such legislation as was enacted in Louisiana.

The sure guaranty of the peace and security of each race is the clear, distinct, unconditional recognition by our governments, national and state, of every right that inheres in civil freedom, and of the equality before the law of all citizens of the United States without regard to race. State enactments, regulating the enjoyment of civil rights, upon the basis of race, and cunningly devised to defeat legitimate results of the war, under the pretense of recognizing equality of rights, can have no other result than to render permanent peace impossible and to keep alive a conflict of races, the continuance of which must do harm to all concerned. This question is not met by the suggestion that social equality cannot exist between the white and black races in this country. That argument, if it can be properly regarded as one, is scarcely worthy of consideration, for social equality no more exists between two races when traveling in a passenger coach or a public highway than when members of the same races sit by each other in a street car or in the jury box, or stand or sit with each other in a political assembly, or when they use in common the streets of a city or town, or when they are in the same room for the purpose of having their names placed on the registry of voters, or when they approach the ballot-box in order to exercise the high privilege of voting.

There is a race so different from our own that we do not permit those belonging to it to become citizens of the United States. Persons belonging to it are, with few exceptions, absolutely excluded from our country. I allude to the Chinese race. But by the statute in question a Chinaman can ride in the same passenger coach with white citizens of the United States, while citizens of the black race in Louisiana, many of whom, perhaps, risked their lives for the preservation of the Union, who are entitled by law to participate in the political control of the state and nation, who are not excluded, by law or by reason of their race, from public stations of any kind, and who have all the legal rights that belong to white citizens, are yet declared to be criminals, liable to imprisonment, if they ride in a public coach occupied by citizens of the white race. It is scarcely just to say that a colored citizen should not object to occupying a public coach assigned to his own race. He does not object, nor, perhaps, would he object to separate coaches for his race, if his rights under the law were recognized. But he does object, and he ought never to cease objecting, that citizens of the white and black races can be adjudged criminals because they sit, or claim the right to sit, in the same public coach on a public highway.

The arbitrary separation of citizens, on the basis of race, while they are on a public highway, is a badge of servitude wholly inconsistent with the civil freedom and the equality before the law established by the Constitution. It cannot be justified upon any legal grounds.

If evils will result from the commingling of the two races upon public highways established for the benefit of all, they will be infinitely less than those that will surely come from state legislation regulating the enjoyment of civil rights upon the basis of race. We boast of the freedom enjoyed by our people above all other peoples. But it is difficult to reconcile that boast with a state of the law which, practically, puts the brand of servitude and degradation upon a large class of our fellow citizens, our equals before the law. The thin disguise of "equal" accommodations for passengers in railroad coaches will not mislead anyone, or atone for the wrong this day done.

The result of the whole matter is that while this court has frequently adjudged, and at the present term has recognized the doctrine, that a state cannot, consistently with the Constitution of the United States, prevent white and black citizens, having the required qualifications for jury service, from sitting in the same jury box, it is now solemnly held that a state may prohibit white and black citizens from sitting in the same passenger coach on a public highway, or may require that they be separated by a "partition," when in the same passenger coach. May it not now be reasonably expected that astute men of the dominant race, who affect to be disturbed at the possibility that the integrity of the white race may be corrupted, or that its supremacy will be imperiled, by contact on public highways with black people, will endeavor to procure statutes requiring white and black jurors to be separated in the jury box by a "partition," and that, upon retiring from the court room to consult as to their verdict, such partition, if it be a movable one, shall be taken to their consultation room, and set up in such way as to prevent black jurors from coming too close to their brother jurors of the white race. If the "partition" used in the court room happens to be stationary, provision could be made for screens with openings through which jurors of the two races could confer as to their verdict without coming into personal contact with each other. I cannot see but that, according to the principles this day announced, such state legislation, although conceived in hostility to, and enacted for the purpose of humiliating, citizens of the United States of a particular race, would be held to be consistent with the Constitution.

I do not deem it necessary to review the decisions of state courts to which reference was made in argument. Some, and the most important, of them are wholly inapplicable, because rendered prior to the adoption of the last amendment of the Constitution, when colored people had very few rights which the dominant race felt obliged to respect. Others were made at a time when public opinion, in many localities, was dominated by the institution of slavery; when it would not have been safe to do justice to the black man: and when, so far as the rights of blacks were concerned, race prejudice was, practically, the supreme law of the land. Those decisions cannot be guides in the era introduced by the recent amendments of the supreme law, which established universal civil freedom, gave citizenship to all born or naturalized in the United States and residing here, obliterated the race line from our systems of governments, national and state, and placed our free institutions upon the broad and sure foundation of the equality of all men before the law.

I am of opinion that the statute of Louisiana is inconsistent with the personal liberty of citizens, white and black, in that state, and hostile to both the spirit and letter of the Constitution of the United States. If laws of like character should be enacted in the several states of the Union, the effect would be in the highest degree mischievous. Slavery as an institution tolerated by law would, it is true, have disappeared from our country, but there would remain a power in the states, by sinister legislation, to interfere with the full enjoyment of the blessings of freedom; to regulate civil rights, common to all citizens, upon the basis of race; and to place in a condition of legal inferiority a large body of American citizens, now constituting a part of the political community, called the people of the United States, for whom and by whom, through representatives, our government is administered. Such a system is inconsistent with the guarantee given by the Constitution to each state of a republican form of government, and may be stricken down by congressional action, or by the courts in the discharge of their solemn duty to maintain the supreme law of the land, anything in the Constitution or laws of any state to the contrary notwithstanding.

For the reasons stated, I am constrained to withhold my assent from the opinion and judgment of the majority.

APPENDIX B

Olmstead v. U.S., 277 U.S. 438
Mr. Justice Brandeis, dissenting.

The defendants were convicted of conspiring to violate the National Prohibition Act. Before any of the persons now charged had been arrested or indicted, the telephones by means of which they habitually communicated with one another and with others had been tapped by federal officers. To this end, a lineman of long experience in wire-tapping was employed, on behalf of the Government and at its expense. He tapped eight telephones, some in the homes of the persons charged, some in their offices. Acting on behalf of the Government and in their official capacity, at least six other prohibition agents listened over the tapped wires and reported the messages taken. Their operations extended over a period of nearly five months. The typewritten record of the notes of conversations overheard occupies 775 typewritten pages. By objections seasonably made and persistently renewed, the defendants objected to the admission of the evidence obtained by wire-tapping, on the ground that the Government's wire-tapping constituted an unreasonable search and seizure, in violation of the Fourth Amendment; and that the use as evidence of the conversations overheard compelled the defendants to be witnesses against themselves, in violation of the Fifth Amendment.

The Government makes no attempt to defend the methods employed by its officers. Indeed, it concedes that if wire-tapping can be deemed a search and seizure within the Fourth Amendment, such wire-tapping as was practiced in the case at bar was an unreasonable search and seizure, and that the evidence thus obtained was inadmissible. But it relies on the language of the Amendment; and it claims that the protection given thereby cannot properly be held to include a telephone conversation.

"We must never forget," said Mr. Chief Justice Marshall in *Mc-*

Culloch v. *Maryland,* 4 Wheat. 316, 407, "that it is a constitution we are expounding." Since then, this Court has repeatedly sustained the exercise of power by Congress, under various clauses of that instrument, over objects of which the Fathers could not have dreamed. See *Pensacola Telegraph Co.* v. *Western Union Telegraph Co.,* 96 U.S. 1, 9; *Northern Pacific Ry. Co.* v. *North Dakota,* 250 U.S. 135; *Dakota Central Telephone Co.* v. *South Dakota,* 250 U.S. 163; *Brooks* v. *United States,* 267 U.S. 432. We have likewise held that general limitations on the powers of Government, like those embodied in the due process clauses of the Fifth and Fourteenth Amendments, do not forbid the United States or the States from meeting modern conditions by regulations which "a century ago, or even half a century ago, probably would have been rejected as arbitrary and oppressive." *Village of Euclid* v. *Ambler Realty Co.,* 272 U.S. 365, 387; *Buck* v. *Bell,* 274 U.S. 200. Clauses guaranteeing to the individual protection against specific abuses of power, must have a similar capacity of adaptation to a changing world. It was with reference to such a clause that this Court said in *Weems* v. *United States,* 217 U.S. 349, 373: "Legislation, both statutory and constitutional, is enacted, it is true, from an experience of evils, but its general language should not, therefore, be necessarily confined to the form that evil had theretofore taken. Time works changes, brings into existence new conditions and purposes. Therefore a principle to be vital must be capable of wider application than the mischief which gave it birth. This is peculiarly true of constitutions. They are not ephemeral enactments, designed to meet passing occasions. They are, to use the words of Chief Justice Marshall 'designed to approach immortality as nearly as human institutions can approach it.' The future is their care and provision for events of good and bad tendencies of which no prophecy can be made. In the application of a constitution, therefore, our contemplation cannot be only of what has been but of what may be. Under any other rule a constitution would indeed be as easy of application as it would be deficient in efficacy and power. Its general principles would have little value and be converted by precedent into impotent and lifeless formulas. Rights declared in words might be lost in reality."

When the Fourth and Fifth Amendments were adopted, "the form that evil had theretofore taken," had been necessarily simple. Force and violence were then the only means known to man by which a Government could directly effect self-incrimination. It could compel the individual to testify—a compulsion effected, if need be, by torture. It could secure possession of his papers and other articles incident to his private life—a seizure effected, if need be, by breaking and entry. Protection against such invasion of "the sanctities of a man's home and the privacies of life" was provided in the Fourth and Fifth Amendments by specific language. *Boyd* v. *United States,* 116 U.S. 616, 630. But "time works changes, brings into existence new conditions and purposes." Subtler and more far-reaching means of invading privacy have become available to the government. Discovery and invention have made it possible for the Government, by means far more effective than stretching upon the rack, to obtain disclosure in court of what is whispered in the closet.

Moreover, "in the application of a constitution, our contemplation cannot be only of what has been but of what may be." The progress of science in furnishing the Government with means of espionage is not likely to stop with wire-tapping. Ways may some day be developed by which the Government, without removing papers from secret drawers, can reproduce them in court, and by which it will be enabled to expose to a jury the most intimate occurrences of the home. Advances in the psychic and related sciences may bring means of exploring unexpressed beliefs, thoughts and emotions. "That places the liberty of every man in the hands of every petty officer" was said by James Otis of much lesser intrusions than these.[1] To Lord Camden, a far slighter intrusion seemed "subversive of all the comforts of society."[2] Can it be that the Constitution affords no protection against such invasions of individual security?

A sufficient answer is found in *Boyd* v. *United States,* 116 U.S. 616, 627–630, a case that will be remembered as long as civil liberty lives in the United States. This Court there reviewed the history that lay behind the Fourth and Fifth Amendments. We said with reference to Lord Camden's judgment in *Entick* v. *Carrington,* 19 Howell's State Trials, 1030: "The principles laid down in this opinion affect the very essence of constitutional liberty and security. They reach farther than the concrete form of the case there before the court, with its adventitious circumstances; they apply to all invasions on the part of the Government and its employés of the sanctities of a man's home and the privacies of life. It is not the breaking of his doors, and the rummaging of his drawers, that constitutes the essence of the offence; but it is the invasion of his indefeasible right of personal security, personal liberty and private property, where that right has never been forfeited by his conviction of some public offence,—it is the invasion of this sacred right which underlies and constitutes the essence of Lord Camden's judgment. Breaking into a house and opening boxes and drawers are circumstances of aggravation; but any forcible and compulsory extortion of a man's own testimony or of his private papers to be used as evidence of a crime or to forfeit his goods, is within the condemnation of that judgment. In

---

[1] Otis' Argument against Writs of Assistance. See Tudor, James Otis, p. 66; John Adams, Works, Vol. II, p. 524; Minot, Continuation of the History of Massachusetts Bay, Vol. II, p. 95.

[2] *Entick* v. *Carrington,* 19 Howell's State Trials, 1030, 1066.

this regard the Fourth and Fifth Amendments run almost into each other."[3]

In *Ex parte Jackson,* 96 U.S. 727, it was held that a sealed letter entrusted to the mail is protected by the Amendments. The mail is a public service furnished by the Government. The telephone is a public service furnished by its authority. There is, in essence, no difference between the sealed letter and the private telephone message. As Judge Rudkin said below: "True the one is visible, the other invisible; the one is tangible, the other intangible; the one is sealed and the other unsealed, but these are distinctions without a difference." The evil incident to invasion of the privacy of the telephone is far greater than that involved in tampering with the mails. Whenever a telephone line is tapped, the privacy of the persons at both ends of the line is invaded and all conversations between them upon any subject, and although proper, confidential and privileged, may be overheard. Moreover, the tapping of one man's telephone line involves the tapping of the telephone of every other person whom he may call or who may call him. As a means of espionage, writs of assistance and general warrants are but puny instruments of tyranny and oppression when compared with wire-tapping.

Time and again, this Court in giving effect to the principle underlying the Fourth Amendment, has refused to place an unduly literal construction upon it. This was notably illustrated in the *Boyd* case itself. Taking language in its ordinary meaning, there is no "search" or "seizure" when a defendant is required to produce a document in the orderly process of a court's procedure. "The right of the people to be secure in their persons, houses, papers, and effects, against unreasonable searches and seizures," would not be violated, under any ordinary construction of language, by compelling obedience to a subpoena. But this Court holds the evidence inadmissible simply because the information leading to the issue of the subpoena has been unlawfully secured. *Silverthorne Lumber Co.* v. *United States,* 251 U.S. 385. Literally, there is no "search" or "seizure" when a friendly visitor abstracts papers from an office; yet we held in *Gouled* v. *United States,* 255 U.S. 298, that evidence so obtained could not be used. No court which looked at the words of the

---

[3] In *Interstate Commerce* v. *Brimson,* 154 U.S. 447, 479, the statement made in the *Boyd* case was repeated; and the Court quoted the statement of Mr. Justice Field in *In re Pacific Railway Commission,* 32 Fed. 241, 250: "Of all the rights of the citizen, few are of greater importance or more essential to his peace and happiness than the right of personal security, and that involves, not merely protection of his person from assault, but exemption of his private affairs, books, and papers, from the inspection and scrutiny of others. Without the enjoyment of this right, all others would lose half their value." The *Boyd* case has been recently reaffirmed in *Silverthorne Lumber Co.* v. *United States,* 251 U.S. 385, in *Gouled* v. *United States,* 255 U.S. 298, and in *Byars* v. *United States,* 273 U.S. 28.

Amendment rather than at its underlying purpose would hold, as this Court did in *Ex parte Jackson,* 96 U.S. 727, 733, that its protection extended to letters in the mails. The provision against self-incrimination in the Fifth Amendment has been given an equally broad construction. The language is: "No person . . . shall be compelled in any criminal case to be a witness against himself." Yet we have held, not only that the protection of the Amendment extends to a witness before a grand jury, although he has not been charged with crime, *Counselman* v. *Hitchcock,* 142 U.S. 547, 562, 586, but that: "It applies alike to civil and criminal proceedings, wherever the answer might tend to subject to criminal responsibility him who gives it. The privilege protects a mere witness as fully as it does one who is also a party defendant." *McCarthy* v. *Arndstein,* 266 U.S. 34, 40. The narrow language of the Amendment has been consistently construed in the light of its object, "to insure that a person should not be compelled, when acting as a witness in any investigation, to give testimony which might tend to show that he himself had committed a crime. The privilege is limited to criminal matters, but it is as broad as the mischief against which it seeks to guard." *Counselman* v. *Hitchcock, supra,* p. 562.

Decisions of this Court applying the principle of the *Boyd* case have settled these things. Unjustified search and seizure violates the Fourth Amendment, whatever the character of the paper;[4] whether the paper when taken by the federal officers was in the home,[5] in an office[6] or elsewhere;[7] whether the taking was effected by force,[8] by fraud,[9] or in the orderly process of a court's procedure.[10] From these decisions, it follows necessarily that the Amendment is violated by the officer's reading the paper without a physical seizure, without his even touching it; and that use, in any criminal proceeding, of the contents of the paper so examined—as where they are testified to by a federal officer who

[4] *Gouled* v. *United States,* 255 U.S. 298.

[5] *Weeks* v. *United States,* 232 U.S. 383; *Amos* v. *United States,* 255 U.S. 313; *Agnello* v. *United States,* 269 U.S. 20; *Byars* v. *United States,* 273 U.S. 28.

[6] *Boyd* v. *United States,* 116 U.S. 616; *Hale* v. *Henkel,* 201 U.S. 43, 70; *Silverthorne Lumber Co.* v. *United States,* 251 U.S. 385; *Gouled* v. *United States,* 255 U.S. 298; *Marron* v. *United States,* 275 U.S. 192.

[7] *Ex parte Jackson,* 96 U.S. 727, 733; *Carroll* v. *United States,* 267 U.S. 132, 156; *Gambino* v. *United States,* 275, U.S. 310.

[8] *Weeks* v. *United States,* 232 U.S. 383; *Silverthorne Lumber Co.* v. *United States,* 251 U.S. 385; *Amos* v. *United States,* 255 U.S. 313; *Carroll* v. *United States,* 267 U.S. 132, 156; *Agnello* v. *United States,* 269, U.S. 20; *Gambino* v. *United States,* 275 U.S. 310.

[9] *Gouled* v. *United States,* 255 U.S. 298.

[10] *Boyd* v. *United States,* 116 U.S. 616; *Hale* v. *Henkel,* 201 U.S. 43, 70. See *Gouled* v. *United States,* 255 U.S. 298; *Byars* v. *United States,* 273 U.S. 28; *Marron* v. *United States,* 275 U.S. 192.

thus saw the document or where, through knowledge so obtained, a copy has been procured elsewhere[11]—any such use constitutes a violation of the Fifth Amendment.

The protection guaranteed by the Amendments is much broader in scope. The makers of our Constitution undertook to secure conditions favorable to the pursuit of happiness. They recognized the significance of man's spiritual nature, of his feelings and of his intellect. They knew that only a part of the pain, pleasure and satisfactions of life are to be found in material things. They sought to protect Americans in their beliefs, their thoughts, their emotions and their sensations. They conferred, as against the Government, the right to be let alone—the most comprehensive of rights and the right most valued by civilized men. To protect that right every unjustifiable intrusion by the Government upon the privacy of the individual, whatever the means employed, must be deemed a violation of the Fourth Amendment. And the use, as evidence in a criminal proceeding, of facts ascertained by such intrusion must be deemed a violation of the Fifth.

Applying to the Fourth and Fifth Amendments the established rule of construction, the defendants' objections to the evidence obtained by wiretapping must, in my opinion, be sustained. It is, of course, immaterial where the physical connection with the telephone wires leading into the defendants' premises was made. And it is also immaterial that the intrusion was in aid of law enforcement. Experience should teach us to be most on our guard to protect liberty when the Government's purposes are beneficent. Men born to freedom are naturally alert to repel invasion of their liberty by evil-minded rulers. The greatest dangers to liberty lurk in insidious encroachment by men of zeal, well-meaning but without understanding.[12]

Independently of the constitutional question, I am of opinion that the judgment should be reversed. By the laws of Washington, wire-tapping

---

[11] *Silverthorne Lumber Co.* v. *United States,* 251 U.S. 385. Compare *Gouled* v. *United States,* 255 U.S. 298, 307. In *Stroud* v. *United States,* 251 U.S. 15, and *Hester* v. *United States,* 265 U.S. 57, the letter and articles admitted were not obtained by unlawful search and seizure. They were voluntary disclosures by the defendant. Compare *Smith* v. *United States,* 2 F. (2nd) 715; *United States* v. *Lee,* 274, U.S. 559.

[12] The point is thus stated by counsel for the telephone companies, who have filed a brief as *amici curiae*: "Criminals will not escape detection and conviction merely because evidence obtained by tapping wires of a public telephone system is inadmissible, if it should be so held; but, in any event, it is better that a few criminals escape than that the privacies of life of all the people be exposed to the agents of the government, who will act at their own discretion, the honest and dishonest, unauthorized and unrestrained by the courts. Legislation making wire tapping a crime will not suffice if the courts nevertheless hold the evidence to be lawful."

is a crime.[13] Pierce's Code, 1921, § 8976(18). To prove its case, the Government was obliged to lay bare the crimes committed by its officers on its behalf. A federal court should not permit such a prosecution to continue. Compare *Harkin* v. *Brundage*, 276 U.S. 36, *id.* 604.

[13] In the following states it is a criminal offense to intercept a message sent by telegraph and/or telephone: Alabama, Code, 1923, § 5256; Arizona, Revised Statutes, 1913, Penal Code, § 692; Arkansas, Crawford & Moses Digest, 1921, § 10246; California, Deering's Penal Code, 1927, § 640; Colorado, Compiled Laws, 1921, § 6969; Connecticut, General Statutes, 1918, § 6292; Idaho, Compiled Statutes, 1919, §§ 8574, 8586; Illinois, Revised Statutes, 1927, c. 134, § 21; Iowa, Code 1927, § 13121; Kansas, Revised Statutes, 1923, c. 17, § 1908; Michigan, Compiled Laws, 1915, § 15403; Montana, Penal Code, 1921, § 11518; Nebraska, Compiled Statutes, 1922, § 7115; Nevada, Revised Laws, 1912, §§ 4608, 6572(18); New York, Consolidated Laws, c. 40, § 1423(6); North Dakota, Compiled Laws, 1913, § 10231; Ohio, Page's General Code, 1926, § 13402; Oklahoma, Session Laws, 1923, c. 46; Oregon, Olson's Laws, 1920, § 2265; South Dakota, Revised Code, 1919, § 4312; Tennessee, Shannon's Code, 1919, §§ 1839, 1840; Utah, Compiled Laws, 1917, § 8433; Virginia Code, 1924, § 4477(2), (3); Washington, Pierce's Code, 1921, § 8976(18); Wisconsin, Statutes, 1927, § 348.37; Wyoming, Compiled Statutes, 1920, § 7148. Compare *State* v. *Behringer*, 19 Ariz. 502; *State* v. *Nordskog*, 76 Wash. 472.

In the following states it is a criminal offense for a company engaged in the transmission of messages by telegraph and/or telephone, or its employees, or, in many instances, persons conniving with them, to disclose or to assist in the disclosure of any message: Alabama, Code, 1923, §§5543, 5545; Arizona, Revised Statutes, 1913, Penal Code, §§ 621, 623, 691; Arkansas, Crawford & Moses Digest, 1921, § 10250; California, Deering's Penal Code, 1927, §§619, 621, 639, 641; Colorado, Compiled Laws, 1921, §§ 6966, 6968, 6970; Connecticut, General Statutes, 1918, § 6292; Florida, Revised General Statutes, 1920, §§ 5754, 5755; Idaho, Compiled Statutes, 1919, §§ 8568, 8570; Illinois, Revised Statutes, 1927, c. 134, §§ 7, 7a; Indiana, Burns' Revised Statutes, 1926, § 2802; Iowa, Code, 1924, § 8305, Louisiana, Acts, 1918, o. 134, p. 228; Maine, Revised Statutes, 1916, c. 60, § 24; Maryland, Bagby's Code, 1926, § 489; Michigan, Compiled Statutes, 1915, § 15104; Minnesota, General Statutes, 1923, §§ 10423, 10424; Mississippi, Hemingway's Code, 1927, § 1174; Missouri, Revised Statutes, 1919, § 3605; Montana, Penal Code, 1921, § 11494; Nebraska, Compiled Statutes, 1922, § 7088; Nevada, Revised Laws, 1912, §§ 4603, 4605, 4609, 4631; New Jersey, Compiled Statutes, 1910, p. 5319; New York, Consolidated Laws, c. 40, §§ 552, 553; North Carolina, Consolidated Statutes, 1919, §§ 4497, 4498, 4499; North Dakota, Compiled Laws, 1913, § 10078; Ohio, Page's General Code, 1926, §§ 13388, 13419; Oklahoma, Session Laws, 1923, c. 46; Oregon, Olson's Laws, 1920, §§ 2260, 2262, 2266; Pennsylvania, Statutes, 1920, §§ 6306, 6308, 6309; Rhode Island, General Laws, 1923, § 6104; South Dakota, Revised Code, 1919, §§ 4346, 9801; Tennessee, Shannon's Code, 1919, §§ 1837, 1838; Utah, Compiled Laws, 1917, §§ 8403, 8405, 8434; Washington, Pierce's Code, 1921, §§ 8982, 8983, Wisconsin, Statutes, 1927, § 348.36.

The Alaskan Penal Code, Act of March 3, 1899, c. 429, 30 Stat. 1253, 1278, provides that "if any officer, agent, operator, clerk, or employee of any telegraph company, or any other person, shall wilfully divulge to any other person than the party from whom the same was received, or to whom the same was

The situation in the case at bar differs widely from that presented in *Burdeau* v. *McDowell*, 256 U.S. 465. There, only a single lot of papers was involved. They had been obtained by a private detective while acting on behalf of a private party; without the knowledge of any federal official; long before anyone had thought of instituting a federal prosecution. Here, the evidence obtained by crime was obtained at the Government's expense, by its officers, while acting on its behalf; the officers who committed these crimes are the same officers who were charged with the enforcement of the Prohibition Act; the crimes of these officers were committed for the purpose of securing evidence with which to obtain an indictment and to secure a conviction. The evidence so obtained constitutes the warp and woof of the Government's case. The aggregate of the Government evidence occupies 306 pages of the printed record. More than 210 of them are filled by recitals of the details of the wire-tapping and of facts ascertained thereby.[14] There is literally no other evidence of guilt on the part of some of the defendants except that illegally obtained by these officers. As to nearly all the defendants (except those who admitted guilt), the evidence relied upon to secure a conviction consisted mainly of that which these officers had so obtained by violating the state law.

As Judge Rudkin said below: "Here we are concerned with neither eavesdroppers nor thieves. Nor are we concerned with the acts of private

---

addressed, or his agent or attorney, any message received or sent, or intended to be sent, over any telegraph line, or the contents, substance, purport, effect, or meaning of such message, or any part thereof, . . . the person so offending shall be deemed guilty of a misdemeanor, and shall be punished by a fine not to exceed one thousand dollars or imprisonment not to exceed one year, or by both such fine and imprisonment, in the discretion of the court."

The Act of October 29, 1918, c. 197, 40 Stat. 1017, provided: "That whoever during the period of governmental operation of the telephone and telegraph systems of the United States . . . shall, without authority and without the knowledge and consent of the other users thereof, except as may be necessary for operation of the service, tap any telegraph or telephone line, or wilfully interfere with the operation of such telephone and telegraph systems or with the transmission of any telephone or telegraph message, or with the delivery of any such message, or whoever being employed in any such telephone or telegraph service shall divulge the contents of any such telephone or telegraph message to any person not duly authorized to receive the same, shall be fined not exceeding $1,000 or imprisoned for not more than one year, or both."

The Radio Act, February 23, 1927, c. 169, § 27, 44 Stat. 1162, 1172, provides that "no person not being authorized by the sender shall intercept any message and divulge or publish the contents, substance, purport, effect, or meaning of such intercepted message to any person."

[14] The above figures relate to Case No. 493. In Nos. 532–533, the Government evidence fills 278 pages, of which 140 are recitals of the evidence obtained by wire-tapping.

individuals. . . . We are concerned only with the acts of federal agents whose powers are limited and controlled by the Constitution of the United States." The Eighteenth Amendment has not in terms empowered Congress to authorize anyone to violate the criminal laws of a State. And Congress has never purported to do so. Compare *Maryland* v. *Soper,* 270 U.S. 9. The terms of appointment of federal prohibition agents do not purport to confer upon them authority to violate any criminal law. Their superior officer, the Secretary of the Treasury, has not instructed them to commit crime on behalf of the United States. It may be assumed that the Attorney General of the United States did not give any such instruction.[15]

When these unlawful acts were committed, they were crimes only of the officers individually. The Government was innocent, in legal contemplation; for no federal official is authorized to commit a crime on its behalf. When the Government, having full knowledge, sought, through the Department of Justice, to avail itself of the fruits of these acts in order to accomplish its own ends, it assumed moral responsibility for the officers' crimes. Compare *The Paquete Habana,* 189 U.S. 453, 465; *O'Reilly deCamara* v. *Brooke,* 209 U.S. 45, 52; *Dodge* v. *United States,* 272 U.S. 530, 532; *Gambino* v. *United States,* 275 U.S. 310. And if this Court should permit the Government, by means of its officers' crimes, to effect its purpose of punishing the defendants, there would seem to be present all the elements of a ratification. If so, the Government itself would become a lawbreaker.

Will this Court by sustaining the judgment below sanction such conduct on the part of the Executive? The governing principle has long been settled. It is that a court will not redress a wrong when he who invokes its aid has unclean hands.[16] The maxim of unclean hands comes

---

[15] According to the Government's brief, p. 41, "The Prohibition Unit of the Treasury disclaims it [wire-tapping] and the Department of Justice has frowned on it." See also "Prohibition Enforcement," 69th Congress, ad Session, Senate Doc. No. 198, pp. iv, v. 13, 15, referred to Committee, January 13, 1927, also Same, Part 2.

[16] See *Hannay* v. *Eve,* 3 Cranch, 242, 247; *Bank of the United States* v. *Owens,* 2 Pet. 527, 538; *Bartle* v. *Coleman,* 4 Pet. 184, 188; *Kennett* v. *Chambers,* 14 How. 38, 52; *Marshall* v. *Baltimore & Ohio R. R. Co.,* 16 How. 314, 334; *Tool Co.* v. *Norris,* 2 Wall 45, 54; *The Ouachita Cotton,* 6 Wall. 521, 532; *Coppell* v. *Hall,* 7 Wall. 542; *Forsyth* v. *Woods,* 11 Wall. 484, 486; *Hanauer* v. *Doane,* 12 Wall. 342, 349; *Trist* v. *Child,* 21 Wall. 441, 448; *Meguire* v. *Corwine,* 101 U.S. 108, 111; *Oscanyan* v. *Arms Co.,* 103 U.S. 261; *Irwin* v. *Williar,* 110 U.S. 499, 510; *Woodstock Iron Co.* v. *Richmond & Danville Extension Co.,* 129 U.S. 643; *Gibbs* v. *Consolidated Gas Co.,* 130 U.S. 369, 411; *Embrey* v. *Jemison,* 131 U.S. 336, 348; *West* v. *Camden,* 135 U.S. 507, 521; *McMullen* v. *Hoffman,* 174 U.S. 639, 654; *Hazelton* v. *Sheckells,* 202 U.S. 71; *Crocker* v. *United States,* 240 U.S. 74, 78. Compare *Holman* v. *Johnson,* 1. Cowp., 341.

from courts of equity.[17] But the principle prevails also in courts of law. Its common application is in civil actions between private parties. Where the Government is the actor, the reasons for applying it are even more persuasive. Where the remedies invoked are those of the criminal law, the reasons are compelling.[18]

The door of a court is not barred because the plaintiff has committed a crime. The confirmed criminal is as much entitled to redress as his most virtuous fellow citizen; no record of crime, however long, makes one an outlaw. The court's aid is denied only when he who seeks it has violated the law in connection with the very transaction as to which he seeks legal redress.[19] Then aid is denied despite the defendant's wrong. It is denied in order to maintain respect for law; in order to promote confidence in the administration of justice; in order to preserve the judicial process from contamination. The rule is one, not of action, but of inaction. It is sometimes spoken of as a rule of substantive law. But it extends to matters of procedure as well.[20] A defense may be waived. It is waived when not pleaded. But the objection that the plaintiff comes with unclean hands will be taken by the court itself.[21] It will be taken despite the wish to the contrary of all the parties to the litigation. The court protects itself.

Decency, security and liberty alike demand that government officials shall be subjected to the same rules of conduct that are commands to the citizen. In a government of laws, existence of the government will be imperilled if it fails to observe the law scrupulously. Our Government is

[17] See *Creath's Administrator* v. *Sims*, 5 How. 192, 204; *Kennett* v. *Chambers*, 14 How. 38, 49; *Randall* v. *Howard*, 2 Black, 585, 586; *Wheeler* v. *Sage*, 1 Wall. 518, 530; *Dent* v. *Ferguson*, 132 U.S. 50, 64; *Pope Manufacturing Co.* v. *Gormully*, 144 U.S. 224, 236; *Miller* v. *Ammon*, 145 U.S. 421, 425; *Hazelton* v. *Sheckells*, 202 U.S. 71, 79. Compare *International News Service* v. *Associated Press*, 248 U.S. 215, 245.

[18] Compare *State* v. *Simmons*, 39 Kan. 262, 264–265; *State* v. *Miller*, 44 Mo. App. 159, 163–164; *In re Robinson*, 29 Neb. 135; *Harris* v. *State*, 15 Tex. App. 629, 634–635, 639.

[19] See *Armstrong* v. *Toler*, 11 Wheat. 258; *Brooks* v. *Martin*, 2 Wall. 70; *Planters' Bank* v. *Union Bank*, 16 Wall. 483, 499–500; *Houston & Texas Central R. R. Co.* v. *Texas*, 177 U.S. 66, 99; *Bothwell* v. *Buckbee, Mears Co.*, 275 U.S. 274.

[20] See *Lutton* v. *Benin*, 11 Mod. 50; *Barlow* v. *Hall*, 2 Anst. 461; *Wells* v. *Gurney*, 8 Barn. & Cress. 769; *Ilsley* v. *Nichols*, 12 Pick. 270; *Carpenter* v. *Spooner*, 2 Sandf. 717; *Metcalf* v. *Clark*, 41 Barb. 45; *Williams* ads. *Reed*, 29 N. J. L. 385; *Hill* v. *Goodrich*, 32 Conn. 588; *Townsend* v. *Smith*, 47 Wis. 623; *Blandin* v. *Ostrander*, 239 Fed. 700; *Harkin* v. *Brundage*, 276 U. S. 36, *id.*, 604.

[21] *Coppell* v. *Hall*, 7 Wall. 542, 558; *Oscanyan* v. *Arms Co.*, 103 U.S. 261, 267; *Higgins* v. *McCrea*, 116 U.S. 671, 685. Compare *Evans* v. *Richardson*, 3 Mer. 469; *Norman* v. *Cole*, 3 Esp. 253; *Northwestern Salt Co.* v. *Electrolytic Alkali Co.*, [1913] 3 K.B. 422.

the potent, the omnipresent teacher. For good or for ill, it teaches the whole people by its example. Crime is contagious. If the Government becomes a lawbreaker, it breeds contempt for law; it invites every man to become a law unto himself; it invites anarchy. To declare that in the administration of the criminal law the end justifies the means—to declare that the Government may commit crimes in order to secure the conviction of a private criminal—would bring terrible retribution. Against that pernicious doctrine this Court should resolutely set its face.

APPENDIX C

Betts v. Brady, 316 U.S. 455
Mr. Justice Black, dissenting, with whom
Mr. Justice Douglas and Mr. Justice Murphy concur.

To hold that the petitioner had a constitutional right to counsel in this case does not require us to say that "no trial for any offense, or in any court, can be fairly conducted and justice accorded a defendant who is not represented by counsel." This case can be determined by a resolution of a narrower question: whether in view of the nature of the offense and the circumstances of his trial and conviction, this petitioner was denied the procedural protection which is his right under the Federal Constitution. I think he was.

The petitioner, a farm hand, out of a job and on relief, was indicted in a Maryland state court on a charge of robbery. He was too poor to hire a lawyer. He so informed the court and requested that counsel be appointed to defend him. His request was denied. Put to trial without a lawyer, he conducted his own defense, was found guilty, and was sentenced to eight years' imprisonment. The court below found that the petitioner had "at least an ordinary amount of intelligence." It is clear from his examination of witnesses that he was a man of little education.

If this case had come to us from a federal court, it is clear we should have to reverse it, because the Sixth Amendment makes the right to counsel in criminal cases inviolable by the Federal Government. I believe that the Fourteenth Amendment made the Sixth applicable to the states.[1] But this view, although often urged in dissents, has never been accepted by a majority of this Court and is not accepted today. A state-

---

[1] Discussion of the Fourteenth Amendment by its sponsors in the Senate and House shows their purpose to make secure against invasion by the states the fundamental liberties and safeguards set out in the Bill of Rights. The legislative history and subsequent course of the amendment to its final adoption have been discussed in Flack, "The Adoption of the Fourteenth

ment of the grounds supporting it is, therefore, unnecessary at this time. I believe, however, that, under the prevailing view of due process, as reflected in the opinion just announced, a view which gives this Court such vast supervisory powers that I am not prepared to accept it without grave doubts, the judgment below should be reversed.

This Court has just declared that due process of law is denied if a trial is conducted in such manner that it is "shocking to the universal sense of justice" or "offensive to the common and fundamental ideas of fairness and right." On another occasion, this Court has recognized that whatever is "implicit in the concept of ordered liberty" and "essential to the substance of a hearing" is within the procedural protection afforded by the constitutional guaranty of due process. *Palko* v. *Connecticut*, 302 U.S. 319, 325, 327.

The right to counsel in a criminal proceeding is "fundamental." *Powell* v. *Alabama*, 287 U. S. 45, 70; *Grosjean* v. *American Press Co.*, 297 U. S. 233, 243–244. It is guarded from invasion by the Sixth Amendment, adopted to raise an effective barrier against arbitrary or unjust deprivation of liberty by the Federal Government. *Johnson* v. *Zerbst*, 304 U. S. 458, 462.

An historical evaluation of the right to a full hearing in criminal cases, and the dangers of denying it, were set out in the *Powell* case, where this Court said: "What . . . does a hearing include? Historically and in practice, in our own country at least, it has always included the right to the aid of counsel when desired and provided by the person asserting the right . . . Even the intelligent and educated layman . . . lacks both the skill and knowledge adequately to prepare his defense, even though he have a perfect one. He requires the guiding hand of counsel in every step in the proceedings against him. Without it, though he be not guilty, he faces the danger of conviction because he does not know how to establish his innocence." *Powell* v. *Alabama*, *supra*, 68–69. Cf. *Johnson* v. *Zerbst*, *supra*, 462–463.

A practice cannot be reconciled with "common and fundamental ideas of fairness and right," which subjects innocent men to increased dangers of conviction merely because of their poverty. Whether a man is innocent cannot be determined from a trial in which, as here, denial of counsel has made it impossible to conclude, with any satisfactory degree of certainty, that the defendant's case was adequately presented.

Amendment." Flack cites the Congressional debates, committee reports, and other data on the subject. Whether the amendment accomplished the purpose its sponsors intended has been considered by this Court in the following decisions, among others: *O'Neil* v. *Vermont*, 144 U.S. 323, dissent, 337; *Maxwell* v. *Dow*, 176 U.S. 581, dissent, 605; *Twining* v. *New Jersey*, 211 U.S. 78, 98–99, dissent, 114.

No one questions that due process requires a hearing before conviction and sentence for the serious crime of robbery. As the Supreme Court of Wisconsin said, in 1859, ". . . would it not be a little like mockery to secure to a pauper these solemn constitutional guaranties for a fair and full trial of the matters with which he was charged, and yet say to him when on trial, that he must employ his own counsel, who could alone render these guaranties of any real permanent value to him. . . . Why this great solicitude to secure him a fair trial if he cannot have the benefit of counsel?" *Carpenter* v. *Dane County,* 9 Wis. 274,276–277.

Denial to the poor of the request for counsel in proceedings based on charges of serious crime has long been regarded as shocking to the "universal sense of justice" throughout this country. In 1854, for example, the Supreme Court of Indiana said: "It is not to be thought of, in a civilized community, for a moment, that any citizen put in jeopardy of life or liberty, should be debarred of counsel because he was too poor to employ such aid. No Court could be respected, or respect itself, to sit and hear such a trial. The defence of the poor, in such cases, is a duty resting somewhere, which will be at once conceded as essential to the accused, to the Court, and to the public." *Webb* v. *Baird,* 6 Ind. 13, 18. And most of the other States have shown their agreement by constitutional provisions, statutes, or established practice judicially approved, which assure that no man shall be deprived of counsel merely because of his poverty.[2] Any other practice seems to me to defeat the promise of our democratic society to provide equal justice under the law.

Appendix

I. States which require that indigent defendants in non-capital as well as capital criminal cases be provided with counsel on request:

A. *By Statute.* ARIZONA: Revised Statutes of Arizona Territory, 1901, Penal Code, Pt. II, Title VII, § 858; Arizona Code Ann. 1939, Vol. III,

[2] In thirty-five states, there is some clear legal requirement or an established practice that indigent defendants in serious non-capital as well as capital criminal cases (*e.g.,* where the crime charged is a felony, a "penitentiary offense," an offense punishable by imprisonment for several years) be provided with counsel on request. In nine states, there are no clearly controlling statutory or constitutional provisions and no decisive reported cases on the subject. In two states, there are dicta in judicial decisions indicating a probability that the holding of the court below in this case would be followed under similar circumstances. In only two states (including the one in which this case arose) has the practice here upheld by this Court been affirmatively sustained. Appended to this opinion is a list of the several states divided into these four categories.

§ 44–904. ARKANSAS: Compiled Laws, Arkansas Territory, 1835, Crimes and Misdemeanors, § 37; Pope's Digest, 1937, Vol. I, c. 43, § 3877. CALIFORNIA: California Penal Code of 1872, § 987; Deering's Penal Code, 1937, § 987. IDAHO: Territorial Criminal Practice Act, 1864, § 267; Idaho Code, 1932 §§ 19–1412, 19–1413. ILLINOIS: Rev: Stat. 1874, Criminal Code, § 422; Jones's Ill. Stat. Ann. 1936, § 37.707. *Cf.* Laws, 1933, 430–431. See also, *Vise* v. *County of Hamilton*, 19 Ill. 78, 79 (1857) IOWA: Territorial Laws, 1839, Courts, § 64; Iowa Code, 1939, § 13773. KANSAS: See Compilation published in 1856 as S. Doc. No. 23, 34th Cong., 1st Sess., 520 (c. 129, Art. V, § 4). Laws, 1941, c. 291. LOUISIANA: Act of May 4, 1805, of the Territory of Orleans, § 35; Dart's Louisiana Code of Criminal Procedure, 1932, Title XIII, Art. 143. MINNESOTA: Minnesota General Laws, 1869, c. LXXII, § 1; Mason's Minnesota Statutes, 1927, §§ 9957, 10667. MISSOURI: Digest of Laws of Missouri Territory, 1818, Crimes and Misdemeanours, § 35; Rev. Stat. 1939, § 4003. MONTANA: Montana Territory Criminal Practice Act of 1872, § 196 (Laws of Montana, Codified Stat. 1871–1872, 220); Revised Code, 1935, § 11886. NEBRASKA: General Statutes, 1873, c. 58, § 437; Compiled Stat. 1929, § 29–1803. NEVADA: Act of November 26, 1861 (Compiled Laws, 1861–1873, Vol. I, 477, 493); Compiled Laws, 1929, Vol. 5, § 10883. NEW HAMPSHIRE: Laws, 1907, c. 136; Laws, 1937, c. 22. NEW JERSEY: Act of March 6, 1795, § 2; New Jersey Stat. § 2.190–3. NEW YORK: Code of Criminal Procedure, § 308 (enacted in 1881, still in force). See *People* v. *Supervisors of Albany County*, 28 How. Pr. 22, 24 (1864). NORTH DAKOTA: Dakota Territory Code of Procedure, 1863, § 249 (Rev. Codes, 1877, Criminal Procedure, 875); Compiled Laws, 1913, Vol. II, §§ 8965, 10721. OHIO: Act of February 26, 1816, § 14 (Chase, Statutes of Ohio, 1788 1833, Vol. II, 982); Throckmorton's Ohio Code Ann. 1940, Vol. II, § 13439–2. OKLAHOMA: Oklahoma Territorial Stat. 1890, c. 70, §10; Stat. Ann. 1941 Supp., Title 22, § 464. OREGON: Act of October 19, 1864 (General Laws, 1845–1864, c. 37, § 381; Laws 1937, c. 406 (Compiled Laws Ann., Vol III, § 26–804) SOUTH DAKOTA: Dakota Territory Code of Procedure, 1863, § 249 (Rev. Codes, 1877, Criminal Procedure 875); Code of 1939, Vol. II, § 34.1901. TENNESSEE: Code of 1857–1858, §§ 5205, 5206; Code of 1938, §§ 11733, 11734. UTAH: Laws of Territory of Utah, 1878, Criminal Procedure, § 181; Rev. Stat. 1933, 105–22–12. WASHINGTON: Statutes of Territory of Washington, 1854, Criminal Practice Act, § 89; Remington's Revised Statutes, 1932, Vol. IV, §§ 2095, 2305. WYOMING: Laws of Wyoming Territory, 1869, Criminal Procedure, § 98; Rev. Stat. 1931, § 33–501.

B. *By judicial decision or established practice judicially approved.* CONNECTICUT: For an account of early practice in Connecticut, see Zephaniah Swift "A System of the Laws of the State of Connecticut,"

Vol. II, 392: "The chief justice then, before the prisoner is called upon to plead, asks the prisoner if he desires counsel, which if requested, is always granted, as a matter of course. On his naming counsel, the court will appoint or assign them. If from any cause, the prisoner decline to request or name counsel, and a trial is had, especially in the case of minors, the court will assign proper counsel. When counsel are assigned, the court will enquire of them, whether they have advised with the prisoner, so that he is ready to plead, and if not, will allow them proper time for that purpose. But it is usually the case that the prisoner has previously employed and consulted counsel, and of course is prepared to plead." See *Powell* v. *Alabama,* 287 U.S. 45, footnote, 63–64. See also, Connecticut General Statutes, Revision of 1930, §§ 2267, 6476. FLORIDA: *Cutts* v. *State,* 54 Fla. 21, 23, 45 So. 491 (1907). See Compiled General Laws, 1927, § 8375 (capital crimes). INDIANA: *Webb* v. *Baird,* 6 Ind. 13, 18 (1854). See also *Knox County Council* v. *State ex rel. McCormick,* 217 Ind. 493, 497–498, 29 N.E. 2d 405 (1940); *State* v. *Hilgemann,* 218 Ind. 572, 34 N.E. 2d 129, 131 (1941). MICHIGAN: *People* v. *Crandell,* 270 Mich. 124, 127, 258 N. W. 224 (1935). PENNSYLVANIA: *Commonwealth* v. *Richards,* 111 Pa. Super. 124, 169 A. 464 (1933). See *Commonwealth ex rel. McGlinn* v. *Smith,* 344 Pa. 41, 49, 59, 24 A. 2d 1. VIRGINIA: *Watkins* v. *Commonwealth,* 174 Va. 518, 521–525, 6 S. E. 2d 670 (1940). WEST VIRGINIA: *State* v. *Kellison,* 56 W. Va. 690, 692–693, 47 S. E. 166 (1904). WISCONSIN: *Carpenter* v. *Dane County,* 9 Wis. 274 (1859). See Stat. 1941, § 357.26.

C. *By constitutional provision.* GEORGIA: Constitution of 1865, Art. 1, Par. 8. See *Martin* v. *Georgia,* 51 Ga. 567, 568 (1874). KENTUCKY: Kentucky Constitution, § 11. See *Fugate* v. *Commonwealth,* 254 Ky. 663, 665, 72 S .W. 2d 47 (1934).

II. States which are without constitutional provision, statutes, or judicial decisions clearly establishing this requirement:

COLORADO: General Laws, 1877, §§ 913–916; Colorado Stat. Ann. 1935, Vol. 2, c. 48, §§ 502, 505, as amended by Laws of 1937, 498, § 1. See *Abshier* v. *People,* 87 Colo. 507, 517, 289 P. 1081. DELAWARE: See 6 Laws of Delaware 741; 7 *id.* 410; Rev. Code, 1935, §§ 4306, 4310. MAINE: See Rev. Stat. 1857, 713; Rev. Stat. 1930, c. 146, § 14. MASSACHUSETTS: See *McDonald* v. *Commonwealth,* 173 Mass. 322, 327, 53 N. E. 874 (1899). NEW MEXICO. NORTH CAROLINA. RHODE ISLAND: See *State* v. *Hudson,* 55 R. I. 141, 179, A. 130 (1935); General Laws, 1938, c. 625, § 62. SOUTH CAROLINA: See *State* v. *Jones,* 172 S. C. 129, 130, 173 S. E. 77 (1934); Code 1932, Vol. I, § 980. VERMONT.

III. States in which dicta of judicial opinions are in harmony with the decision by the court below in this case:

ALABAMA: *Gilchrist* v. *State,* 234 Ala. 73, 74, 173 So. 651. MISSISSIPPI: *Reed* v. *State,* 143 Miss. 686, 689, 109 So. 715.

IV. States in which the requirement of counsel for indigent defendants in non-capital cases has been affirmatively rejected:

MARYLAND: See, however, *Coates* v. *State*, 180 Md. 502, 25 A. 2d 676. TEXAS: *Gilley* v. *State*, 114 Tex. Cr. 548, 26 S. W. 2d 1070. But *cf. Brady* v. *State*, 122 Tex. Cr. 275, 278, 54 S. W. 2d 513.

APPENDIX D

Minersville School District v. Gobitis, 310 U.S. 586
Mr. Justice Stone, dissenting.

I think the judgment below should be affirmed.

Two youths, now fifteen and sixteen years of age, are by the judgment of this Court held liable to expulsion from the public schools and to denial of all publicly supported educational privileges because of their refusal to yield to the compulsion of a law which commands their participation in a school ceremony contrary to their religious convictions. They and their father are citizens and have not exhibited by any action or statement of opinion, any disloyalty to the Government of the United States. They are ready and willing to obey all its laws which do not conflict with what they sincerely believe to be the higher commandments of God. It is not doubted that these convictions are religious, that they are genuine, or that the refusal to yield to the compulsion of the law is in good faith and with all sincerity. It would be a denial of their faith as well as the teachings of most religions to say that children of their age could not have religious convictions.

The law which is thus sustained is unique in the history of Anglo-American legislation. It does more than suppress freedom of speech and more than prohibit the free exercise of religion, which concededly are forbidden by the First Amendment and are violations of the liberty guaranteed by the Fourteenth. For by this law the state seeks to coerce these children to express a sentiment which, as they interpret it, they do not entertain, and which violates their deepest religious convictions. It is not denied that such compulsion is a prohibited infringement of personal liberty, freedom of speech and religion, guaranteed by the Bill of Rights, except in so far as it may be justified and supported as a proper exercise of the state's power over public education. Since the state, in competition with parents, may through teaching in the public schools indoctrinate the minds of the young, it is said that in aid of its undertaking to

inspire loyalty and devotion to constitutional authority and the flag
which symbolizes it, it may coerce the pupil to make affirmation contrary to his belief and in violation of his religious faith. And, finally, it is
said that since the Minersville School Board and others are of the opinion that the country will be better served by conformity than by the observance of religious liberty which the Constitution prescribes, the
courts are not free to pass judgment on the Board's choice.

Concededly the constitutional guaranties of personal liberty are not
always absolutes. Government has a right to survive and powers con-
fered upon it are not necessarily set at naught by the express prohibi-
tions of the Bill of Rights. It may make war and raise armies. To that
end it may compel citizens to give military service, *Selective Draft Law
Cases*, 245 U.S. 366, and subject them to military training despite
their religious objections. *Hamilton* v. *Regents,* 293 U. S. 245. It may
suppress religious practices dangerous to morals, and presumably those
also which are inimical to public safety, health and good order. *Davis* v.
Beason, 133 U. S. 333. But it is a long step, and one which I am unable
to take, to the position that government may, as a supposed educational
measure and as a means of disciplining the young, compel public affir-
mations which violate their religious conscience.

The very fact that we have constitutional guaranties of civil liberties
and the specificity of their command where freedom of speech and of
religion are concerned require some accommodation of the powers which
government normally exercises, when no question of civil liberty is involved, to the constitutional demand that those liberties be protected
against the action of government itself. The state concededly has power
to require and control the education of its citizens, but it cannot by a
general law compelling attendance at public schools preclude attendance
at a private school adequate in its instruction, where the parent seeks to
secure for the child the benefits of religious instruction not provided by
the public school. *Pierce* v. *Society of Sisters,* 268 U. S. 510. And only
recently we have held that the state's authority to control its public
streets by generally applicable regulations is not an absolute to which
free speech must yield, and cannot be made the medium of its suppression, *Hague* v. *Committee for Industrial Organization,* 307 U. S. 496,
514, *et seq.,* any more than can its authority to penalize littering of the
streets by a general law be used to suppress the distribution of hand-
bills as a means of communicating ideas to their recipients. *Schneider* v.
State, 308 U. S. 147.

In these cases it was pointed out that where there are competing demands of the interests of government and of liberty under the Constitution, and where the performance of governmental functions is brought
into conflict with specific constitutional restrictions, there must, when
that is possible, be reasonable accommodation between them so as to

preserve the essentials of both and that it is the function of courts to determine whether such accommodation is reasonably possible. In the cases just mentioned the Court was of opinion that there were ways enough to secure the legitimate state end without infringing the asserted immunity, or that the inconvenience caused by the inability to secure that end satisfactorily through other means, did not outweigh freedom of speech or religion. So here, even if we believe that such compulsions will contribute to national unity, there are other ways to teach loyalty and patriotism which are the sources of national unity, than by compelling the pupil to affirm that which he does not believe and by commanding a form of affirmance which violates his religious convictions. Without recourse to such compulsion the state is free to compel attendance at school and require teaching by instruction and study of all in our history and in the structure and organization of our government, including the guaranties of civil liberty which tend to inspire patriotism and love of country. I cannot say that government here is deprived of any interest or function which it is entitled to maintain at the expense of the protection of civil liberties by requiring it to resort to the alternatives which do not coerce an affirmation of belief.

The guaranties of civil liberty are but guaranties of freedom of the human mind and spirit and of reasonable freedom and opportunity to express them. They presuppose the right of the individual to hold such opinions as he will and to give them reasonably free expression, and his freedom, and that of the state as well, to teach and persuade others by the communication of ideas. The very essence of the liberty which they guaranty is the freedom of the individual from compulsion as to what he shall think and what he shall say, at least where the compulsion is to bear false witness to his religion. If these guaranties are to have any meaning they must, I think, be deemed to withhold from the state any authority to compel belief or the expression of it where that expression violates religious convictions, whatever may be the legislative view of the desirability of such compulsion.

History teaches us that there have been but few infringements of personal liberty by the state which have not been justified, as they are here, in the name of righteousness and the public good, and few which have not been directed, as they are now, at politically helpless minorities. The framers were not unaware that under the system which they created most governmental curtailments of personal liberty would have the support of a legislative judgment that the public interest would be better served by its curtailment than by its constitutional protection. I cannot conceive that in prescribing, as limitations upon the powers of government, the freedom of the mind and spirit secured by the explicit guaranties of freedom of speech and religion, they intended or rightly could have left any latitude for a legislative judgment that the compulsory expression of belief which violates religious convictions would better serve the public interest than their protection. The Constitution may well elicit expressions of loyalty to it and to the government which it created, but it does not command such expressions or otherwise give any indication that compulsory expressions of loyalty play any such part in our scheme of government as to override the constitutional protection of freedom of speech and religion. And while such expressions of loyalty, when voluntarily given, may promote national unity, it is quite another matter to say that their compulsory expression by children in violation of their own and their parents' religious convictions can be regarded as playing so important a part in our national unity as to leave school boards free to exact it despite the constitutional guarantee of freedom of religion. The very terms of the Bill of Rights preclude, it seems to me, any reconciliation of such compulsions with the constitutional guaranties by a legislative declaration that they are more important to the public welfare than the Bill of Rights

But even if this view be rejected and it is considered that there is some scope for the determination by legislatures whether the citizen shall be compelled to give public expression of such sentiments contrary to his religion, I am not persuaded that we should refrain from passing upon the legislative judgment "as long as the remedial channels of the democratic process remain open and unobstructed." This seems to me no less than the surrender of the constitutional protection of the liberty of small minorities to the popular will. We have previously pointed to the importance of a searching judicial inquiry into the legislative judgment in situations where prejudice against discrete and insular minorities may tend to curtail the operation of those political processes ordinarily to be relied on to protect minorities. See *United States* v. *Carolene Products Co.*, 304 U. S. 144, 152, note 4. And until now we have not hesitated similarly to scrutinize legislation restricting the civil liberty of racial and religious minorities although no political process was affected. *Meyer* v. *Nebraska*, 262 U. S. 390; *Pierce* v. *Society of Sisters, supra; Farington* v. *Tokushige*, 273 U. S. 284. Here we have such a small minority entertaining in good faith a religious belief, which is such a departure from the usual course of human conduct, that most persons are disposed to regard it with little toleration or concern. In such circumstances careful scrutiny of legislative efforts to secure conformity of belief and opinion by a compulsory affirmation of the desired belief, is especially needful if civil rights are to receive any protection. Tested by this standard, I am not prepared to say that the right of this small and helpless minority, including children having a strong religious conviction, whether they understand its nature or not, to refrain from an expression obnoxious to their religion, is to be overborne by the interest of the state in maintaining discipline in the schools.

The Constitution expresses more than the conviction of the people that democratic processes must be preserved at all costs. It is also an expression of faith and a command that freedom of mind and spirit must be preserved, which government must obey, if it is to adhere to that justice and moderation without which no free government can exist. For this reason it would seem that legislation which operates to repress the religious freedom of small minorities, which is admittedly within the scope of the protection of the Bill of Rights, must at least be subject to the same judicial scrutiny as legislation which we have recently held to infringe the constitutional liberty of religious and racial minorities.

With such scrutiny I cannot say that the inconveniences which may attend some sensible adjustment of school discipline in order that the religious convictions of these children may be spared, presents a problem so momentous or pressing as to outweigh the freedom from compulsory violation of religious faith which has been thought worthy of constitutional protection.

APPENDIX E

Colegrove v. Green, 328 U.S. 549
Mr. Justice Black, dissenting.

The complaint alleges the following facts essential to the position I take: Appellants, citizens and voters of Illinois, live in congressional election districts, the respective populations of which range from 612,-000 to 914,000. Twenty other congressional election districts have populations that range from 112,116 to 385,207. In seven of these districts the population is below 200,000. The Illinois Legislature established these districts in 1901 on the basis of the Census of 1900. The Federal Census of 1910, of 1920, of 1930, and of 1940, each showed a growth of population in Illinois and a substantial shift in the distribution of population among the districts established in 1901. But up to date, attempts to have the State Legislature reapportion congressional election districts so as more nearly to equalize their population have been unsuccessful. A contributing cause of this situation, according to appellants, is the fact that the State Legislature is chosen on the basis of state election districts inequitably apportioned in a way similar to that of the 1901 congressional election districts. The implication is that the issues of state and congressional apportionment are thus so interdependent that it is to the interest of state legislators to perpetuate the inequitable apportionment of both state and congressional election districts. Prior to this proceeding a series of suits had been brought in the state courts challenging the State's local and federal apportionment system. In all these cases the Supreme Court of the State had denied effective relief.[1]

[1] *People* v. *Thompson,* 155 Ill. 451, 40 N.E. 307; *Fergus* v. *Marks,* 321 Ill. 510, 152 N.E. 557; *Fergus* v. *Kinney,* 333 Ill. 437, 164 N.E. 665; *People* v. *Clardy,* 334 Ill. 160, N.E. 638; *People* v. *Blackwell,* 342 Ill. 223, 173 N.E. 750; *Daly* v. *Madison County,* 378 Ill. 357, 38 N.E. 2d 160. Cf. *Moran* v. *Bowley,* 347 Ill. 148, 179 N.E. 526.

In the present suit the complaint attacked the 1901 State Apportionment Act on the ground that it among other things violates Article I and
the Fourteenth Amendment of the Constitution. Appellants claim that
since they live in the heavily populated districts their vote is much less
effective than the vote of those living in a district which under the 1901
Act is also allowed to choose one Congressman, though its population is
sometimes only one-ninth that of the heavily populated districts. Appellants contend that this reduction of the effectiveness of their vote is
the result of a wilful legislative discrimination against them and thus
amounts to a denial of the equal protection of the laws guaranteed by
the Fourteenth Amendment. They further assert that this reduction of
the effectiveness of their vote also violates the privileges and immunities
clause of the Fourteenth Amendment in abridging their privilege as
citizens of the United States to vote for Congressmen, a privilege guaranteed by Article I of the Constitution. They further contend that the
State Apportionment Act directly violates Article I which guarantees
that each citizen eligible to vote has a right to vote for Congressmen
and to have his vote counted. The assertion here is that the right to
have their vote counted is abridged unless that vote is given approximately equal weight to that of other citizens. It is my judgment that the
District Court had jurisdiction;[2] that the complaint presented a justiciable case and controversy;[3] and that appellants had standing to sue,
since the facts alleged show that they have been injured as individuals.[4]
Unless previous decisions of this Court are to be overruled, the suit is
not one against the State but against state officials as individuals.[5] The
complaint attacked the 1901 Apportionment Act as unconstitutional and
alleged facts indicating that the Act denied appellants the full right to
vote and the equal protection of the laws. These allegations have not
been denied. Under these circumstances, and since there is no adequate
legal remedy for depriving a citizen of his right to vote, equity can and
should grant relief.

It is difficult for me to see why the 1901 State Apportionment Act
does not deny appellants equal protection of the laws. The failure of
the Legislature to reapportion the congressional election districts for
forty years, despite census figures indicating great changes in the distribution of the population, has resulted in election districts the populations of which range from 112,000 to 900,000. One of the appellants

---

[2] 28 U.S.C. 41 (14); Bell v. Hood, 327 U.S. 678.
[3] Smiley v. Holm, 285 U.S. 355; Koenig v. Flynn, 285 U.S. 375; Carroll v.
Becker, 285 U.S. 380; Wood v. Broom, 287 U.S. 1; Nixon v. Herndon, 273 U.S.
536; 540; McPherson v. Blacker, 146 U.S. 1, 23–24; see also cases collected in
2 A.L.R. note, 1337 et seq.
[4] Coleman v. Miller, 307 U.S. 433, 438, 467.
[5] Ex parte Young, 209 U.S. 123; Sterling v. Constantin, 287 U.S. 378, 393.

lives in a district of more than 900,000 people. His vote is consequently much less effective than that of each of the citizens living in the district of 112,000. And such a gross inequality in the voting power of citizens irrefutably demonstrates a complete lack of effort to make an equitable apportionment. The 1901 State Apportionment Act if applied to the next election would thus result in a wholly indefensible discrimination against appellants and all other voters in heavily populated districts. The equal protection clause of the Fourteenth Amendment forbids such discrimination. It does not permit the States to pick out certain qualified citizens or groups of citizens and deny them the right to vote at all. See *Nixon v. Herndon,* 273 U. S. 536, 541; *Nixon v. Condon,* 286 U. S. 73. No one would deny that the equal protection clause would also prohibit a law that would expressly give certain citizens a half-vote and others a full vote. The probable effect of the 1901 State Apportionment Act in the coming election will be that certain citizens, and among them the appellants, will in some instances have votes only one-ninth as effective in choosing representatives to Congress as the votes of other citizens. Such discriminatory legislation seems to me exactly the kind that the equal protection clause was intended to prohibit.

The 1901 State Apportionment Act in reducing the effectiveness of appellants' votes abridges their privilege as citizens to vote for Congressmen and violates Article I of the Constitution. Article I provides that Congressmen "shall be . . . chosen . . . by the People of the several States . . ." It thus gives those qualified a right to vote and a right to have their vote counted. *Ex parte Yarbrough,* 110 U. S. 651; *United States v. Mosley,* 238 U. S. 383. This Court in order to prevent "an interference with the effective choice of the voters" has held that this right extends to primaries. *United States v. Classic,* 313 U. S. 299, 314. While the Constitution contains no express provision requiring that congressional election districts established by the States must contain approximately equal populations, the constitutionally guaranteed right to vote and the right to have one's vote counted clearly imply the policy that state election systems, no matter what their form, should be designed to give approximately equal weight to each vote cast. To some extent this implication of Article I is expressly stated by § 2 of the Fourteenth Amendment which provides that "Representatives shall be apportioned among the several States according to their respective numbers . . ." The purpose of this requirement is obvious: It is to make the votes of the citizens of the several States equally effective in the selection of members of Congress. It was intended to make illegal a nationwide "rotten borough" system as between the States. The policy behind it is broader than that. It prohibits as well congressional "rotten boroughs" within the States, such as the ones here involved. The policy is that which is laid down by all the constitutional provisions regulating the election of members of the House of Representatives, including Article I which guarantees the right to vote and to have that vote effectively counted: All groups, classes, and individuals shall to the extent that it is practically feasible be given equal representation in the House of Representatives, which, in conjunction with the Senate, writes the laws affecting the life, liberty, and property of all the people.

It is true that the States are authorized by § 2 of Article I of the Constitution to legislate on the subject of congressional elections to the extent that Congress has not done so. Thus the power granted to the State Legislature on this subject is primarily derived from the Federal and not from the State Constitution. But this federally-granted power with respect to elections of Congressmen is not to formulate policy but rather to implement the policy laid down in the Constitution, that, so far as feasible, votes be given equally effective weight. Thus, a state legislature cannot deny eligible voters the right to vote for Congressmen and the right to have their vote counted. It can no more destroy the effectiveness of their vote in part and no more accomplish this in the name of "apportionment" than under any other name. For legislation which must inevitably bring about glaringly unequal representation in the Congress in favor of special classes and groups should be invalidated, "whether accomplished ingeniously or ingenuously." *Smith* v. *Texas*, 311 U. S. 128, 132. See also *Lane* v. *Wilson*, 307 U. S. 268, 272.

Had Illinois passed an Act requiring that all of its twenty-six Congressmen be elected by the citizens of one county, it would clearly have amounted to a denial to the citizens of the other counties of their constitutionally guaranteed right to vote. And I cannot imagine that an Act that would have apportioned twenty-five Congressmen to the State's smallest county and one Congressman to all the others, would have been sustained by any court. Such an Act would clearly have violated the constitutional policy of equal representation. The 1901 Apportionment Act here involved violates that policy in the same way. The policy with respect to federal elections laid down by the Constitution, while it does not mean that the courts can or should prescribe the precise methods to be followed by state legislatures and the invalidation of all Acts that do not embody those precise methods, does mean that state legislatures must make real efforts to bring about approximately equal representation of citizens in Congress. Here the Legislature of Illinois has not done so. Whether that was due to negligence or was a wilful effort to deprive some citizens of an effective vote, the admitted result is that the constitutional policy of equality of representation has been defeated. Under these circumstances it is the Court's duty to invalidate the state law.

It is contended, however, that a court of equity does not have the power, or even if it has the power, that it should not exercise it in this case. To do so, it is argued, would mean that the Court is entering the area of "political questions." I cannot agree with that argument. There have been cases, such as *Coleman* v. *Miller, supra,* pp. 454, 457, where this Court declined to decide a question because it was political. In the *Miller* case, however, the question involved was ratification of a constitutional amendment, a matter over which the Court believed Congress had been given final authority. To have decided that question would have amounted to a trespass upon the constitutional power of Congress. Here we have before us a state law which abridges the constitutional rights of citizens to cast votes in such way as to obtain the kind of congressional representation the Constitution guarantees to them.

It is true that voting is a part of elections and that elections are "political." But as this Court said in *Nixon* v. *Herndon, supra,* it is a mere "play upon words" to refer to a controversy such as this as "political" in the sense that courts have nothing to do with protecting and vindicating the right of a voter to cast an effective ballot. The *Classic* case, among myriads of others, refutes the contention that courts are impotent in connection with evasions of all "political" rights. *Wood* v. *Broom,* 287 U. S. 1, does not preclude the granting of equitable relief in this case. There this Court simply held that the State Apportionment Act did not violate the Congressional Reapportionment Act of 1929, 46 Stat. 21, 26, 27, since that Act did not require election districts of equal population. The Court expressly reserved the question of "the right of complainant to relief in equity." *Giles* v. *Harris,* 189 U. S. 475, also did not hold that a court of equity could not, or should not, exercise its power in a case like this. As we said with reference to that decision in *Lane* v. *Wilson,* 307 U. S. 268, 272–273, it stands for the principle that courts will not attempt to "supervise" elections. Furthermore, the author of the *Giles* v. *Harris* opinion also wrote the opinion in *Nixon* v. *Herndon,* in which a voter's right to cast a ballot was held to give rise to a justiciable controversy.

In this case, no supervision over elections is asked for. What is asked is that this Court do exactly what it did in *Smiley* v. *Holm, supra.* It is asked to declare a state apportionment bill invalid and to enjoin state officials from enforcing it. The only difference between this case and the *Smiley* case is that there the case originated in the state courts while here the proceeding originated in the Federal District Court. The only type of case in which this Court has held that a federal district court should in its discretion stay its hand any more than a state court is where the question is one which state courts or administrative agencies have special competence to decide. This is not that type of question. What is involved here is the right to vote guaranteed by the Federal Constitution. It has always been the rule that where a federally protected right has been invaded the federal courts will provide the remedy to rectify the wrong done. Federal courts have not hesitated to exercise their equity power in cases involving deprivation of property and liberty. *Ex parte Young, supra; Hague* v. *C. I. O.* 307 U.S. 496. There is no reason why they should do so where the case involves the right to choose representatives that make laws affecting liberty and property.

Nor is there any more difficulty in enforcing a decree in this case than there was in the *Smiley* case. It is true that declaration of invalidity of the State Act and the enjoining of state officials would result in prohibiting the State from electing Congressmen under the system of the old congressional districts. But it would leave the State free to elect them from the State at large, which, as we held in the *Smiley* case, is a manner authorized by the Constitution. It is said that it would be inconvenient for the State to conduct the election in this manner. But it has an element of virtue that the more convenient method does not have —namely, it does not discriminate against some groups to favor others, it gives all the people an equally effective voice in electing their representatives as is essential under a free government, and it is constitutional.

MR. JUSTICE DOUGLAS and MR. JUSTICE MURPHY join in this dissent.

APPENDIX F

Dennis v. U.S., 341 U.S. 494
Mr. Justice Douglas, dissenting.

If this were a case where those who claimed protection under the First Amendment were teaching the techniques of sabotage, the assassination of the President, the filching of documents from public files, the planting of bombs, the art of street warfare, and the like, I would have no doubts. The freedom to speak is not absolute; the teaching of methods of terror and other seditious conduct should be beyond the pale along with obscenity and immorality. This case was argued as if those were the facts. The argument imported much seditious conduct into the record. That is easy and it has popular appeal, for the activities of Communists in plotting and scheming against the free world are common knowledge. But the fact is that no such evidence was introduced at the trial. There is a statute which makes a seditious conspiracy unlawful.[1] Petitioners, however, were not charged with a "conspiracy to overthrow" the Government. They were charged with a conspiracy to form a party and groups and assemblies of people who teach and advocate the overthrow of our Government by force or violence and with a conspiracy to advocate and teach its overthrow by force and violence.[2] It may well be that indoctrination in the techniques of terror to destroy the Government would be indictable under either statute.

[1] 18 U. S. C. § 2384 provides: "If two or more persons in any State or Territory, or in any place subject to the jurisdiction of the United States, conspire to overthrow, put down, or to destroy by force the Government of the United States, or to levy war against them, or to oppose by force the authority thereof, or by force to prevent, hinder, or delay the execution of any law of the United States, or by force to seize, take, or possess any property of the United States contrary to the authority thereof, they shall each be fined not more than $5,000 or imprisoned not more than six years, or both."

[2] 54 Stat. 671 18 U. S. C. §§ 10, 11.

But the teaching which is condemned here is of a different character.

So far as the present record is concerned, what petitioners did was to organize people to teach and themselves teach the Marxist-Leninist doctrine contained chiefly in four books:[3] Stalin, Foundations of Leninism (1924); Marx and Engels, Manifesto of the Communist Party (1848); Lenin, The State and Revolution (1917); History of the Communist Party of the Soviet Union (B.) (1939).

Those books are to Soviet Communism what Mein Kampf was to Nazism. If they are understood, the ugliness of Communism is revealed, its deceit and cunning are exposed, the nature of its activities becomes apparent, and the chances of its success less likely. That is not, of course, the reason why petitioners chose these books for their classrooms. They are fervent Communists to whom these volumes are gospel. They preached the creed with the hope that some day it would be acted upon.

The opinion of the Court does not outlaw these texts nor condemn them to the fire, as the Communists do literature offensive to their creed. But if the books themselves are not outlawed, if they can lawfully remain on library shelves, by what reasoning does their use in a classroom become a crime? It would not be a crime under the Act to introduce these books to a class, though that would be teaching what the creed of violent overthrow of the Government is. The Act, as construed, requires the element of intent—that those who teach the creed believe in it. The crime then depends not on what is taught but on who the teacher is. That is to make freedom of speech turn not on *what is said*, but on the *intent* with which it is said. Once we start down that road we enter territory dangerous to the liberties of every citizen.

There was a time in England when the concept of constructive treason flourished. Men were punished not for raising a hand against the king but for thinking murderous thoughts about him. The Framers of the Constitution were alive to that abuse and took steps to see that the practice would not flourish here. Treason was defined to require overt acts—the evolution of a plot against the country into an actual project. The present case is not one of treason. But the analogy is close when the illegality is made to turn on intent, not on the nature of the act. We then start probing men's minds for motive and purpose; they become entangled in the law not for what they did but *for what they thought*; they get convicted not for what they said but for the purpose with which they said it.

[3] Other books taught were Stalin, Problems of Leninism, Strategy and Tactics of World Communism (H. R. Doc. No. 619, 80th Cong., 2nd Sess.), and Program of the Communist International.

Intent, of course, often makes the difference in the law. An act otherwise excusable or carrying minor penalties may grow to an abhorrent thing if the evil intent is present. We deal here, however, not with ordinary acts but with speech, to which the Constitution has given a special sanction.

The vice of treating speech as the equivalent of overt acts of a treasonable or seditious character is emphasized by a concurring opinion, which by invoking the law of conspiracy makes speech do service for deeds which are dangerous to society. The doctrine of conspiracy has served divers and oppressive purposes and in its broad reach can be made to do great evil. But never until today has anyone seriously thought that the ancient law of conspiracy could constitutionally be used to turn speech into seditious conduct. Yet that is precisely what is suggested. I repeat that we deal here with speech alone, not with speech *plus* acts of sabotage or unlawful conduct. Not a single seditious act is charged in the indictment. To make a lawful speech unlawful because two men conceive it is to raise the law of conspiracy to appalling proportions. That course is to make a radical break with the past and to violate one of the cardinal principles of our constitutional scheme.

Free speech has occupied an exalted position because of the high service it has given our society. Its protection is essential to the very existence of a democracy. The airing of ideas releases pressures which otherwise might become destructive. When ideas compete in the market for acceptance, full and free discussion exposes the false and they gain few adherents. Full and free discussion even of ideas we hate encourages the testing of our own prejudices and preconceptions. Full and free discussion keeps a society from becoming stagnant and unprepared for the stresses and strains that work to tear all civilizations apart.

Full and free discussion has indeed been the first article of our faith. We have founded our political system on it. It has been the safeguard of every religious, political, philosophical, economic, and racial group amongst us. We have counted on it to keep us from embracing what is cheap and false; we have trusted the common sense of our people to choose the doctrine true to our genius and to reject the rest. This has been the one single outstanding tenet that has made our institutions the symbol of freedom and equality. We have deemed it more costly to liberty to suppress a despised minority than to let them vent their spleen. We have above all else feared the political censor. We have wanted a land where our people can be exposed to all the diverse creeds and cultures of the world.

There comes a time when even speech loses its constitutional immunity. Speech innocuous one year may at another time fan such destructive flames that it must be halted in the interests of the safety of the Republic. That is the meaning of the clear and present danger test.

When conditions are so critical that there will be no time to avoid the evil that the speech threatens, it is time to call a halt. Otherwise, free speech which is the strength of the Nation will be the cause of its destruction.

Yet free speech is the rule, not the exception. The restraint to be constitutional must be based on more than fear, on more than passionate opposition against the speech, on more than a revolted dislike for its contents. There must be some immediate injury to society that is likely if speech is allowed. The classic statement of these conditions was made by Mr. Justice Brandeis in his concurring opinion in *Whitney* v. *California*, 274 U. S. 357, 376–377,

"Fear of serious injury cannot alone justify suppression of free speech and assembly. Men feared witches and burnt women. It is the function of speech to free men from the bondage of irrational fears. To justify suppression of free speech there must be reasonable ground to fear that serious evil will result if free speech is practiced. There must be reasonable ground to believe that the danger apprehended is imminent. There must be reasonable ground to believe that the evil to be prevented is a serious one. Every denunciation of existing law tends in some measure to increase the probability that there will be violation of it. Condonation of a breach enhances the probability. Expressions of approval add to the probability. Propagation of the criminal state of mind by teaching syndicalism increases it. Advocacy of law-breaking heightens it still further. But even advocacy of violation, however reprehensible morally, is not a justification for denying free speech where the advocacy falls short of incitement and there is nothing to indicate that the advocacy would be immediately acted on. The wide difference between advocacy and incitement, between preparation and attempt, between assembling and conspiracy, must be borne in mind. In order to support a finding of clear and present danger it must be shown either that immediate serious violence was to be expected or was advocated. or that the past conduct furnished reason to believe that such advocacy was then contemplated.

"Those who won our independence by revolution were not cowards. They did not fear political change. They did not exalt order at the cost of liberty. To courageous, self-reliant men, with confidence in the power of free and fearless reasoning applied through the processes of popular government, no danger flowing from speech can be deemed clear and present, unless the incidence of the evil apprehended is so imminent that it may befall before there is opportunity for full discussion. *If there be time to expose through discussion the falsehood and fallacies, to avert the evil by the processes of education, the remedy to be applied is more speech, not enforced silence."* (Italics added.)

I had assumed that the question of the clear and present danger, being so critical an issue in the case, would be a matter for submission to the jury. It was squarely held in *Pierce* v. *United States*, 252 U. S. 239, 244, to be a jury question. Mr. Justice Pitney, speaking for the Court, said, "Whether the statement contained in the pamphlet had a natural tendency to produce the forbidden consequences, as alleged, was a question to be determined not upon demurrer but by the jury at the trial." That is the only time the Court has passed on the issue. None of our other decisions is contrary. Nothing said in any of the nonjury cases has detracted from that ruling.[4] The statement in *Pierce* v. *United States*, *supra*, states the law as it has been and as it should be. The Court, I think, errs when it treats the question as one of law.

Yet, whether the question is one for the Court or the jury, there should be evidence of record on the issue. This record, however, contains no evidence whatsoever showing that the acts charged, *viz.*, the teaching of the Soviet theory of revolution with the hope that it will be realized, have created any clear and present danger to the Nation. The Court, however, rules to the contrary. It says, "The formation by petitioners of such a highly organized conspiracy, with rigidly disciplined members subject to call when the leaders, these petitioners, felt that the time had come for action, coupled with the inflammable nature of world conditions, similar uprisings in other countries, and the touch-and-go nature of our relations with countries with whom petitioners were in the very least ideologically attuned, convince us that their convictions were justified on this score."

That ruling is in my view not responsive to the issue in the case. We might as well say that the speech of petitioners is outlawed because Soviet Russia and her Red Army are a threat to world peace.

The nature of Communism as a force on the world scene would, of course, be relevant to the issue of clear and present danger of petitioners' advocacy within the United States. But the primary consideration is the strength and tactical position of petitioners and their converts in this country. On that there is no evidence in the record. If we are to take judicial notice of the threat of Communists within the nation, it should not be difficult to conclude that *as a political party* they are of little consequence. Communists in this country have never made a respectable or serious showing in any election. I would doubt that there is a village, let alone a city or county or state, which the Communists

---

[4] The cases which reached the Court are analyzed in the Appendix attached to this opinion, *post*, p. 591.

could carry. Communism in the world scene is no bogeyman; but Communism as a political faction or party in this country plainly is. Communism has been so thoroughly exposed in this country that it has been crippled as a political force. Free speech has destroyed it as an effective political party. It is inconceivable that those who went up and down this country preaching the doctrine of revolution which petitioners espouse would have any success. In days of trouble and confusion, when bread lines were long, when the unemployed walked the streets, when people were starving, the advocates of a short-cut by revolution might have a chance to gain adherents. But today there are no such conditions. The country is not in despair; the people know Soviet Communism; the doctrine of Soviet revolution is exposed in all of its ugliness and the American people want none of it.

How it can be said that there is a clear and present danger that this advocacy will succeed is, therefore, a mystery. Some nations less resilient than the United States, where illiteracy is high and where democratic traditions are only budding, might have to take drastic steps and jail these men for merely speaking their creed. But in America they are miserable merchants of unwanted ideas; their wares remain unsold. The fact that their ideas are abhorrent does not make them powerful.

The political impotence of the Communists in this country does not, of course, dispose of the problem. Their numbers; their positions in industry and government; the extent to which they have in fact infiltrated the police, the armed services, transportation, stevedoring, power plants, munitions works, and other critical places—these facts all bear on the likelihood that their advocacy of the Soviet theory of revolution will endanger the Republic. But the record is silent on these facts. If we are to proceed on the basis of judicial notice, it is impossible for me to say that the Communists in this country are so potent or so strategically deployed that they must be suppressed for their speech. I could not so hold unless I were willing to conclude that the activities in recent years of committees of Congress, of the Attorney General, of labor unions, of state legislatures, and of Loyalty Boards were so futile as to leave the country on the edge of grave peril. To believe that petitioners and their following are placed in such critical positions as to endanger the Nation is to believe the incredible. It is safe to say that the followers of the creed of Soviet Communism are known to the F. B. I.; that in case of war with Russia they will be picked up overnight as were all prospective saboteurs at the commencement of World War II; that the invisible army of petitioners is the best known, the most beset, and the least thriving of any fifth column in history. Only those held by fear and panic could think otherwise.

This is my view if we are to act on the basis of judicial notice. But the mere statement of the opposing views indicates how important it is that we know the facts before we act. Neither prejudice nor hate nor senseless fear should be the basis of this solemn act. Free speech—the glory of our system of government—should not be sacrificed on anything less than plain and objective proof of danger that the evil advocated is imminent. On this record no one can say that petitioners and their converts are in such a strategic position as to have even the slightest chance of achieving their aims.

The First Amendment provides that "Congress shall make no law . . . abridging the freedom of speech." The Constitution provides no exception. This does not mean, however, that the Nation need hold its hand until it is in such weakened condition that there is no time to protect itself from incitement to revolution. Seditious conduct can always be punished. But the command of the First Amendment is so clear that we should not allow Congress to call a halt to free speech except in the extreme case of peril from the speech itself. The First Amendment makes confidence in the common sense of our people and in their maturity of judgment the great postulate of our democracy. Its philosophy is that violence is rarely, if ever, stopped by denying civil liberties to those advocating resort to force. The First Amendment reflects the philosophy of Jefferson "that it is time enough for the rightful purposes of civil government, for its officers to interfere when principles break out into overt acts against peace and good order."[5] The political censor has no place in our public debates. Unless and until extreme and necessitous circumstances are shown, our aim should be to keep speech unfettered and to allow the processes of law to be invoked only when the provocateurs among us move from speech to action.

Vishinsky wrote in 1938 in The Law of the Soviet State, "In our state, naturally, there is and can be no place for feedom of speech, press, and so on for the foes of socialism."

Our concern should be that we accept no such standard for the United States. Our faith should be that our people will never give support to those advocates of revolution, so long as we remain loyal to the purposes for which our Nation was founded.

[5] 12 Hening's Stat. (Virginia 1823), c. 34, p. 84. Whipple, Our Ancient Liberties (1927), p. 95, states: "This idea that the limit on freedom of speech or press should be set only by an actual overt act was not new. It had been asserted by a long line of distinguished thinkers including John Locke, Montesquieu in his The Spirit of the Laws ('Words do not constitute an overt act'), the Rev. Phillip Furneaux, James Madison, and Thomas Jefferson."

Appendix to Opinion of Mr. Justice Douglas.

There have been numerous First Amendment cases before the Court raising the issue of clear and present danger since Mr. Justice Holmes first formulated the test in *Schenck* v. *United States,* 249 U. S. 47, 52. Most of them, however, have not involved jury trials.

The cases which may be deemed at all relevant to our problem can be classified as follows:

CONVICTIONS FOR CONTEMPT OF COURT (NON-JURY): *Near* v. *Minnesota,* 283 U. S. 697; *Bridges* v. *California,* 314 U. S. 252; *Thomas* v. *Collins,* 323 U. S. 516; *Pennekamp* v. *Florida,* 328 U. S. 331; *Craig* v. *Harney,* 331 U. S. 367.

CONVICTIONS BY STATE COURTS SITTING WITHOUT JURIES, GENERALLY FOR VIOLATIONS OF LOCAL ORDINANCE: *Lovell* v. *Griffin,* 303 U. S. 444; *Schneider* v. *State,* 308 U. S. 147; *Cantwell* v. *Connecticut,* 310 U. S. 296; *Marsh* v. *Alabama,* 326 U. S. 501; *Tucker* v. *Texas,* 326 U. S. 517; *Winters* v. *New York,* 333 U. S. 507; *Saia* v. *New York,* 334 U. S. 558; *Kovacs* v. *Cooper,* 336 U. S. 77; *Kunz* v. *New York,* 340 U. S. 290; *Feiner* v. *New York,* 340 U. S. 315.

INJUNCTIONS AGAINST ENFORCEMENT OF STATE OR LOCAL LAWS (NON-JURY): *Grosjean* v. *American Press Co.,* 297 U. S. 233; *Hague* v. *C. I. O.,* 307 U. S. 496; *Minersville School District* v. *Gobitis,* 310 U. S. 586; *West Virginia Board of Education* v. *Barnette,* 319 U. S. 624.

ADMINISTRATION PROCEEDINGS (NON-JURY): *Bridges* v. *Wixon,* 326 U. S. 135; *Schneiderman* v. *United States,* 320 U. S. 118; *American Communications Association* v. *Douds,* 339 U. S. 382.

CASES TRIED BEFORE JURIES FOR VIOLATIONS OF STATE LAWS DIRECTED AGAINST ADVOCACY OF ANARCHY, CRIMINAL SYNDICALISM, ETC.: *Gilbert* v. *Minnesota,* 254 U. S. 325; *Gitlow* v. *New York,* 268 U. S. 652; *Whitney* v. *California,* 274 U. S. 357; *Fiske* v. *Kansas,* 274 U. S. 380; *Stromberg* v. *California,* 283 U. S. 359; *De Jonge* v. *Oregon,* 299 U. S. 353; *Herndon* v. *Lowry,* 301 U. S. 242; *Taylor* v. *Mississippi,* 319 U. S. 583; or for minor local offenses: *Cox* v. *New Hampshire,* 312 U. S. 569; *Chaplinsky* v. *New Hampshire,* 315 U. S. 568; *Terminiello* v. *Chicago,* 337 U. S. 1; *Niemotko* v. *Maryland,* 340 U. S. 268.

FEDERAL PROSECUTIONS BEFORE JURIES UNDER THE ESPIONAGE ACT OF 1917 FOLLOWING WORLD WAR I: *Schenck* v. *United States,* 249 U.S. 47; *Frohwerk* v. *United States,* 249 U. S. 204; *Debs* v. *United States,* 249 U. S. 211; *Abrams* v. *United States,* 250 U. S. 616; *Schaefer* v. *United States,* 251 U. S. 466; *Pierce* v. *United States,* 252 U. S. 239.

Pierce v. *United States* ruled that the question of clear and present danger was for the jury. In the other cases in this group the question whether the issue was for the court or the jury was not raised or passed upon.

FEDERAL PROSECUTION BEFORE A JURY UNDER THE ESPIONAGE ACT OF 1917 FOLLOWING WORLD WAR II: *Hartzel* v. *United States*, 322 *U.S.* 680. The jury was instructed on clear and present danger in terms drawn from the language of Mr. Justice Holmes in *Schenck* v. *United States, supra,* p. 52. The Court reversed the conviction on the ground that there had not been sufficient evidence for submission of the case to the jury.

APPENDIX G

Abrams v. U.S., 250 U.S. 616
Mr. Justice Holmes, dissenting.

This indictment is founded wholly upon the publication of two leaflets which I shall describe in a moment. The first count charges a conspiracy pending the war with Germany to publish abusive language about the form of government of the United States, laying the preparation and publishing of the first leaflet as overt acts. The second count charges a conspiracy pending the war to publish language intended to bring the form of government into contempt, laying the preparation and publishing of the two leaflets as overt acts. The third count alleges a conspiracy to encourage resistance to the United States in the same war and to attempt to effectuate the purpose by publishing the same leaflets. The fourth count lays a conspiracy to incite curtailment of production of things necessary to the prosecution of the war and to attempt to accomplish it by publishing the second leaflets to which I have referred.

The first of these leaflets says that the President's cowardly silence about the intervention in Russia reveals the hypocrisy of the plutocratic gang in Washington. It intimates that "German militarism combined with allied capitalism to crush the Russian revolution"—goes on that the tyrants of the world fight each other until they see a common enemy—working class enlightenment, when they combine to crush it; and that now militarism and capitalism combined, though not openly, to crush the Russian revolution. It says that there is only one enemy of the workers of the world and that is capitalism; that it is a crime for workers of America, &c., to fight the workers' republic of Russia, and ends "Awake! Awake, you Workers of the World! Revolutionists." A note adds "It is absurd to call us pro-German. We hate and despise German militarism more than do you hypocritical tyrants. We have more reasons for denouncing German militarism than has the coward of the White House."

The other leaflet, headed "Workers—Wake Up," with abusive language says that America together with the Allies will march for Russia to help the Czecho-Slovaks in their struggle against the Bolsheviki, and that this time the hypocrites shall not fool the Russian emigrants and friends of Russia in America. It tells the Russian emigrants that they now must spit in the face of the false military propaganda by which their sympathy and help to the prosecution of the war have been called forth and says that with the money they have lent or are going to lend "they will make bullets not only for the Germans but also for the Workers Soviets of Russia," and further, "Workers in the ammunition factories, you are producing bullets, bayonets, cannon, to murder not only the Germans, but also your dearest, best, who are in Russia and are fighting for freedom." It then appeals to the same Russian emigrants at some length not to consent to the "inquisitionary expedition to Russia," and says that the destruction of the Russian revolution is "the politics of the march to Russia " The leaflet winds up by saying "Workers, our reply to this barbaric intervention has to be a general strike!," and after a few words on the spirit of revolution, exhortations not to be afraid, and some usual tall talk, ends "Woe unto those who will be in the way of progress. Let solidarity live! The Rebels."

No argument seems to me necessary to show that these pronunciamentos in no way attack the form of government of the United States, or that they do not support either of the first two counts. What little I have to say about the third count may be postponed until I have considered the fourth. With regard to that it seems too plain to be denied that the suggestion to workers in the ammunition factories that they are producing bullets to murder their dearest, and the further advocacy of a general strike, both in the second leaflet, do urge curtailment of production of things necessary to the prosecution of the war within the meaning of the Act of May 16, 1918, c. 75, 40 Stat. 553, amending § 3 of the earlier Act of 1917. But to make the conduct criminal that statute requires that it should be "with intent by such curtailment to cripple or hinder the United States in the prosecution of the war." It seems to me that no such intent is proved.

I am aware of course that the word intent as vaguely used in ordinary legal discussion means no more than knowledge at the time of the act that the consequences said to be intended will ensue. Even less than that will satisfy the general principle of civil and criminal liability. A man may have to pay damages, may be sent to prison, at common law might be hanged if at the time of his act he knew facts from which common experience showed that the consequences would follow, whether he individually could foresee them or not. But, when words are used exactly, a deed is not done with intent to produce a consequence unless that consequence is the aim of the deed. It may be obvious, and obvious to the actor, that the consequence will follow, and he may be liable for it even if he regrets it, but he does not do the act with intent to produce it unless the aim to produce it is the proximate motive of the specific act, although there may be some deeper motive behind.

It seems to me that this statute must be taken to use its words in a strict and accurate sense. They would be absurd in any other. A patriot might think that we were wasting money or aeroplanes, or making more cannon of a certain kind than we needed, and might advocate curtailment with success, yet even if it turned out that the curtailment hindered and was thought by other minds to have been obviously likely to hinder the United States in the prosecution of the war, no one would hold such conduct a crime. I admit that my illustration does not answer all that might be said but it is enough to show what I think and to let me pass to a more important aspect of the case. I refer to the First Amendment to the Constitution that Congress shall make no law abridging the freedom of speech.

I never have seen any reason to doubt that the questions of law that alone were before this Court in the cases of *Schenck, Frohwerk* and *Debs*, 249 U. S. 47, 204, 211, were rightly decided. I do not doubt for a moment that by the same reasoning that would justify punishing persuasion to murder, the United States constitutionally may punish speech that produces or is intended to produce a clear and imminent danger that it will bring about forthwith certain substantive evils that the United States constitutionally may seek to prevent. The power undoubtedly is greater in time of war than in time of peace because war opens dangers that do not exist at other times.

But as against dangers peculiar to war, as against others, the principle of the right to free speech is always the same. It is only the present danger of immediate evil or an intent to bring it about that warrants Congress in setting a limit to the expression of opinion where private rights are not concerned. Congress certainly cannot forbid all effort to change the mind of the country. Now nobody can suppose that the surreptitious publishing of a silly leaflet by an unknown man, without more, would present any immediate danger that its opinions would hinder the success of the government arms or have any appreciable tendency to do so. Publishing those opinions for the very purpose of obstructing however, might indicate a greater danger and at any rate would have the quality of an attempt. So I assume that the second leaflet if published for the purposes alleged in the fourth count might be punishable. But it seems pretty clear to me that nothing less than that would bring these papers within the scope of this law. An actual intent in the sense that I have explained is necessary to constitute an attempt, where a further act of the same individual is required to complete the substantive crime, for reasons given in *Swift & Co.* v. *United States*, 196 U. S.

375, 396. It is necessary where the success of the attempt depends upon others because if that intent is not present the actor's aim may be accomplished without bringing about the evils sought to be checked. An intent to prevent interference with the revolution in Russia might have been satisfied without any hindrance to carrying on the war in which we were engaged.

I do not see how anyone can find the intent required by the statute in any of the defendants' words. The second leaflet is the only one that affords even a foundation for the charge, and there, without invoking the hatred of German militarism expressed in the former one, it is evident from the beginning to the end that the only object of the paper is to help Russia and stop American intervention there against the popular government—not to impede the United States in the war that it was carrying on. To say that two phrases taken literally might import a suggestion to conduct that would have interference with the war as an indirect and probably undesired effect seems to me by no means to show an attempt to produce that effect.

I return for a moment to the third count. That charges an intent to provoke resistance to the United States in its war with Germany. Taking the clause in the statute that deals with that in connection with the other elaborate provisions of the act, I think that resistance to the United States means some forcible act of opposition to some proceeding of the United States in pursuance of the war. I think the intent must be the specific intent that I have described and for the reasons that I have given I think that no such intent was proved or existed in fact. I also think that there is no hint at resistance to the United States as I construe the phrase.

In this case sentences of twenty years imprisonment have been imposed for the publishing of two leaflets that I believe the defendants had as much right to publish as the Government has to publish the Constitution of the United States now vainly invoked by them. Even if I am technically wrong and enough can be squeezed from these poor and puny anonymities to turn the color of legal litmus paper; I will add, even if what I think the necessary intent were shown; the most nominal punishment seems to me all that possibly could be inflicted, unless the defendants are to be made to suffer not for what the indictment alleges but for the creed that they avow—a creed that I believe to be the creed of ignorance and immaturity when honestly held, as I see no reason to doubt that it was held here, but which, although made the subject of examination at the trial, no one has a right even to consider in dealing with the charges before the Court.

Persecution for the expression of opinions seems to me perfectly logical. If you have no doubt of your premises or your power and want a certain result with all your heart you naturally express your wishes in

law and sweep away all opposition. To allow opposition by speech
seems to indicate that you think the speech impotent, as when a man
says that he has squared the circle, or that you do not care wholeheartedly for the result, or that you doubt either your power or your
premises. But when men have realized that time has upset many fighting faiths, they may come to believe even more than they believe the
very foundations of their own conduct that the ultimate good desired is
better reached by free trade in ideas—that the best test of truth is the
power of the thought to get itself accepted in the competition of the
market, and that truth is the only ground upon which their wishes
safely can be carried out. That at any rate is the theory of our Constitution. It is an experiment, as all life is an experiment. Every year if
not every day we have to wager our salvation upon some prophecy
based upon imperfect knowledge. While that experiment is part of our
system I think that we should be eternally vigilant against attempts to
check the expression of opinions that we loathe and believe to be
fraught with death, unless they so imminently threaten immediate interference with the lawful and pressing purposes of the law that an immediate
check is required to save the country. I wholly disagree with the argument of the Government that the First Amendment left the common
law as to seditious libel in force. History seems to me against the notion.
I had conceived that the United States through many years had shown
its repentance for the Sedition Act of 1798, by repaying fines that it
imposed. Only the emergency that makes it immediately dangerous to
leave the correction of evil counsels to time warrants making any exception to the sweeping command, "Congress shall make no law . . . abridging the freedom of speech." Of course I am speaking only of expressions
of opinion and exhortations, which were all that were uttered here,
but I regret that I cannot put into more impressive words my belief
that in their conviction upon this indictment the defendants were
deprived of their rights under the Constitution of the United States.

MR. JUSTICE BRANDEIS concurs with the foregoing opinion.

APPENDIX H

Whitney v. California, 274 U.S. 357
Mr. Justice Brandeis, concurring.

Miss Whitney was convicted of the felony of assisting in organizing, in the year 1919, the Communist Labor Party of California, of being a member of it, and of assembling with it. These acts are held to constitute a crime, because the party was formed to teach criminal syndicalism. The statute which made these acts a crime restricted the right of free speech and of assembly theretofore existing. The claim is that the statute, as applied, denied to Miss Whitney the liberty guaranteed by the Fourteenth Amendment.

The felony which the statute created is a crime very unlike the old felony of conspiracy or the old misdemeanor of unlawful assembly. The mere act of assisting in forming a society for teaching syndicalism, of becoming a member of it, or of assembling with others for that purpose is given the dynamic quality of crime. There is guilt although the society may not contemplate immediate promulgation of the doctrine. Thus the accused is to be punished, not for contempt, incitement or conspiracy, but for a step in preparation, which, if it threatens the public order at all, does so only remotely. The novelty in the prohibition introduced is that the statute aims, not at the practice of criminal syndicalism, nor even directly at the preaching of it, but at association with those who propose to preach it.

Despite arguments to the contrary which had seemed to me persuasive, it is settled that the due process clause of the Fourteenth Amendment applies to matters of substantive law as well as to matters of procedure. Thus all fundamental rights comprised within the term liberty are protected by the Federal Constitution from invasion by the States. The right of free speech, the right to teach and the right of assembly are, of course, fundamental rights. See *Meyer v. Nebraska*, 262 U.S. 390; *Pierce v. Society of Sisters*, 268 U.S. 510; *Gitlow v. New York*, 268

U.S. 652, 666; *Farrington* v. *Tokushige,* 273 U.S. 284. These may not be denied or abridged. But, although the rights of free speech and assembly are fundamental, they are not in their nature absolute. Their exercise is subject to restriction, if the particular restriction proposed is required in order to protect the State from destruction or from serious injury, political, economic or moral. That the necessity which is essential to a valid restriction does not exist unless speech would produce, or is intended to produce, a clear and imminent danger of some substantive evil which the State constitutionally may seek to prevent has been settled. See *Schenck* v. *United States,* 249 U.S. 47, 52.

It is said to be the function of the legislature to determine whether at a particular time and under the particular circumstances the formation of, or assembly with, a society organized to advocate criminal syndicalism constitutes a clear and present danger of substantive evil; and that by enacting the law here in question the legislature of California determined that question in the affirmative. Compare *Gitlow* v. *New York,* 268 U.S. 652, 668–671. The legislature must obviously decide, in the first instance, whether a danger exists which calls for a particular protective measure. But where a statute is valid only in case certain conditions exist, the enactment of the statute cannot alone establish the facts which are essential to its validity. Prohibitory legislation has repeatedly been held invalid, because unnecessary, where the denial of liberty involved was that of engaging in a particular business.[1] The power of the courts to strike down an offending law is no less when the interests involved are not property rights, but the fundamental personal rights of free speech and assembly.

This Court has not yet fixed the standard by which to determine when a danger shall be deemed clear; how remote the danger may be and yet be deemed present; and what degree of evil shall be deemed sufficiently substantial to justify resort to abridgement of free speech and assembly as the means of protection. To reach sound conclusions on these matters, we must bear in mind why a State is, ordinarily, denied the power to prohibit dissemination of social, economic and political doctrine which a vast majority of its citizens believes to be false and fraught with evil consequence.

Those who won our independence believed that the final end of the State was to make men free to develop their faculties; and that in its government the deliberative forces should prevail over the arbitrary. They valued liberty both as an end and as a means. They believed

---

[1] Compare *Frost* v. *R. R. Comm. of California,* 271 U.S. 583; *Weaver* v. *Palmer Bros. Co.,* 270 U.S. 402; *Jay Burns Baking Co.* v. *Bryan,* 264 U.S. 504; *Pennsylvania Coal Co.* v. *Mahon,* 260 U.S. 393; *Adams* v. *Tanner,* 244 U.S. 590.

liberty to be the secret of happiness. They believed that freedom to think as you will and to speak as you think are means indispensable to the discovery and spread of political truth; that without free speech and assembly discussion would be futile; that with them, discussion affords ordinarily adequate protection against the dissemination of noxious doctrine; that the greatest menace to freedom is an inert people; that public discussion is a political duty; and that this should be a fundamental principle of the American government.[2] They recognized the risks to which all human institutions are subject. But they knew that order cannot be secured merely through fear of punishment for its infraction; that it is hazardous to discourage thought, hope and imagination; that fear breeds repression; that repression breeds hate; that hate menaces stable government; that the path of safety lies in the opportunity to discuss freely supposed grievances and proposed remedies; and that the fitting remedy for evil counsels is good ones. Believing in the power of reason as applied through public discussion, they eschewed silence coerced by law—the argument of force in its worst form. Recognizing the occasional tyrannies of governing majorities, they amended the Constitution so that free speech and assembly should be guaranteed.

Fear of serious injury cannot alone justify suppression of free speech and assembly. Men feared witches and burnt women. It is the function of speech to free men from the bondage of irrational fears. To justify suppression of free speech there must be reasonable ground to fear that serious evil will result if free speech is practiced. There must be reasonable ground to believe that the danger apprehended is imminent. There must be reasonable ground to believe that the evil to be prevented is a serious one. Every denunciation of existing law tends in some measure to increase the probability that there will be violation of it.[3] Condonation of a breach enhances the probability. Propagation of the criminal state of mind by teaching syndicalism increases it. Advocacy of lawbreaking heightens it still further. But even advocacy of violation, however reprehensible morally, is not a justification for denying free speech where the advocacy falls short of incitement and there is nothing to

[2] Compare Thomas Jefferson: "We have nothing to fear from the demoralizing reasonings of some, if others are left free to demonstrate their errors and especially when the law stands ready to punish the first criminal act produced by the false reasonings; these are safer corrections than the conscience of the judge." Quoted by Charles A. Beard, *The Nation*, July 7, 1926, vol. 123, p. 8. Also in first Inaugural Address: "If there be any among us who would wish to dissolve this union or change its republican form, let them stand undisturbed as monuments of the safety with which error of opinion may be tolerated where reason is left free to combat it."

[3] Compare Judge Learned Hand in *Masses Publishing Co.* v. *Patten*, 244 Fed. 535, 540; Judge Amidon in *United States* v. *Fontana*, Bull. Dept. of Justice No. 148, pp. 4–5; Chafee, "Freedom of Speech," pp. 46–56, 174.

indicate that the advocacy would be immediately acted on. The wide difference between advocacy and incitement, between preparation and attempt, between assembling and conspiracy, must be borne in mind. In order to support a finding of clear and present danger it must be shown either that immediate serious violence was to be expected or was advocated, or that the past conduct furnished reason to believe that such advocacy was then contemplated.

Those who won our independence by revolution were not cowards. They did not fear political change. They did not exalt order at the cost of liberty. To courageous, self-reliant men, with confidence in the power of free and fearless reasoning applied through the processes of popular government, no danger flowing from speech can be deemed clear and present, unless the incidence of the evil apprehended is so imminent that it may befall before there is opportunity for full discussion. If there be time to expose through discussion the falsehood and fallacies, to avert the evil by the processes of education, the remedy to be applied is more speech, not enforced silence. Only an emergency can justify repression. Such must be the rule if authority is to be reconciled with freedom.[4] Such, in my opinion, is the command of the Constitution. It is therefore always open to Americans to challenge a law abridging free speech and assembly by showing that there was no emergency justifying it.

Moreover, even imminent danger cannot justify resort to prohibition of these functions essential to effective democracy, unless the evil apprehended is relatively serious. Prohibition of free speech and assembly is a measure so stringent that it would be inappropriate as the means for averting a relatively trivial harm to society. A police measure may be unconstitutional merely because the remedy, although effective as means of protection, is unduly harsh or oppressive. Thus, a State might, in the exercise of its police power, make any trespass upon the land of another a crime, regardless of the results or of the intent or purpose of the trespasser. It might, also, punish an attempt, a conspiracy, or an incitement to commit the trespass. But it is hardly conceivable that this Court would hold constitutional a statute which punished as a felony the mere voluntary assembly with a society formed to teach that pedestrians had the moral right to cross unenclosed, unposted, waste lands and to advocate their doing so, even if there was imminent danger that advocacy would lead to a trespass. The fact that speech is likely to result in some

---

[4] Compare Z. Chafee, Jr., "Freedom of Speech", pp. 24–39, 207–221, 228, 262–265; H. J. Laski, "Grammar of Politics", pp. 120, 121; Lord Justice Scrutton in *Rex* v. *Secretary of Home Affairs, Ex parte O'Brien,* [1923] 2 K.B. 361, 382: "You really believe in freedom of speech, if you are willing to allow it to men whose opinions seem to you wrong and even dangerous; . . ." Compare Warren, "The New Liberty Under the Fourteenth Amendment," 39 *Harvard Law Review,* 431, 461.

violence or in destruction of property is not enough to justify its suppression. There must be the probability of serious injury to the State.
Among free men, the deterrents ordinarily to be applied to prevent crime
are education and punishment for violations of the law, not abridgement
of the rights of free speech and assembly.

The California Syndicalism Act recites in § 4:

"Inasmuch as this act concerns and is necessary to the immediate
preservation of the public peace and safety, for the reason that at the
present time large numbers of persons are going from place to place
in this state advocating, teaching and practicing criminal syndicalism,
this act shall take effect upon approval by the Governor."

This legislative declaration satisfies the requirement of the constitution of the State concerning emergency legislation. *In re McDermott*,
180 Cal. 783. But it does not preclude enquiry into the question whether,
at the time and under the circumstances, the conditions existed which
are essential to validity under the Federal Constitution. As a statute,
even if not void on its face, may be challenged because invalid as
applied, *Dahnke-Walker Milling Co.* v. *Bondurant*, 257 U.S. 282, the
result of such an enquiry may depend upon the specific facts of the
particular case. Whenever the fundamental rights of free speech and
assembly are alleged to have been invaded, it must remain open to a
defendant to present the issue whether there actually did exist at the time
a clear danger; whether the danger, if any, was imminent; and whether
the evil apprehended was one so substantial as to justify the stringent
restriction interposed by the legislature. The legislative declaration, like
the fact that the statute was passed and was sustained by the highest
court of the State, creates merely a rebuttable presumption that these
conditions have been satisfied.

Whether in 1919, when Miss Whitney did the things complained of,
there was in California such clear and present danger of serious evil,
might have been made the important issue in the case. She might have
required that the issue be determined either by the court or the jury.
She claimed below that the statute as applied to her violated the Federal Constitution; but she did not claim that it was void because there
was no clear and present danger of serious evil, nor did she request that
the existence of these conditions of a valid measure thus restricting the
rights of free speech and assembly be passed upon by the court or a
jury. On the other hand, there was evidence on which the court or jury
might have found that such danger existed. I am unable to assent to
the suggestion in the opinion of the Court that assembling with a political party, formed to advocate the desirability of a proletarian revolution by mass action at some date necessarily far in the future, is not a
right within the protection of the Fourteenth Amendment. In the present
case, however, there was other testimony which tended to establish the

existence of a conspiracy, on the part of members of the International Workers of the World, to commit present serious crimes; and likewise to show that such a conspiracy would be furthered by the activity of the society of which Miss Whitney was a member. Under these circumstances the judgment of the state court cannot be disturbed.

Our power of review in this case is limited not only to the question whether a right guaranteed by the Federal Constitution was denied, *Murdock* v. *City of Memphis*, 20 Wall. 590; *Haire* v. *Rice*, 204 U.S. 291, 301; but to the particular claims duly made below, and denied. *Seaboard Air Line Ry.* v. *Duvall*, 225 U.S. 477, 485–488. We lack here the power occasionally exercised on review of judgments of lower federal courts to correct in criminal cases vital errors, although the objection was not taken in the trial court. *Wiborg* v. *United States*, 163 U.S. 632, 658–660; *Clyatt* v. *United States*, 197 U.S. 207, 221–222. This is a writ of error to a state court. Because we may not enquire into the errors now alleged, I concur in affirming the judgment of the state court.

MR. JUSTICE HOLMES joins in this opinion.

Index

A Note About the Author

Alan Barth served as an editorial writer with the
Washington *Post* from 1943 to 1973. Born in
New York City, he took his bachelor's degree at
Yale College in 1929 and was a Nieman Fellow
at Harvard in 1949. He is the author of *The
Loyalty of Free Men* (for which he won the
Sidney Hillman Award in 1952), *Government by
Investigation* (1955), *The Price of Liberty*
(1961), and *The Heritage of Liberty* (1965).
His articles have been published in *Harper's,
The New Republic, The New York Times Maga-
zine, The Nation,* and other periodicals. In addi-
tion to the Sidney Hillman Award, he has received
the Sigma Delta Chi Award for Distinguished
Service to American Journalism, in 1947, the
Oliver Wendell Holmes Bill of Rights Award, in
1964, and the Florina Lasker Civil Liberties
Award, in 1967. Mr. Barth and his wife live in
Washington, D.C., and have two children.